BARCELONA

Do You Feel Like …

… fantastic views, impressive museums, atmospheric locations, beaches and the seafront, or shows and performances to touch the heart?

**Quick and easy: out and about
with a Segway**

TOURS

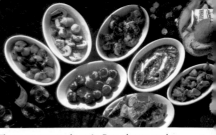

There are many bars In Barcelona serving delicious tapas

SIGHTS FROM A TO Z

PRICE CLASSES
Restaurants
(main course without drinks)
€€€€ = more than €30
€€€ = €25 – €35
€€ = €15 – €25
€ = up to €15
Hotels (double room)
€€€€ = more than €250
€€€ = €140 – €250
€€ = €80 – €140
€ = up to €80

Note
Billable service telephone numbers are marked with an asterisk: *0180....

PRACTICAL INFORMATION

**Modernisme supreme:
Casa Amatller and Casa Batlló**

BACKGROUND

Barcelona impressed the world with its staging of the 1992 Olympic Games. Since then it has constantly reinvented itself, and more surprises to be expected.

Facts

Population · Politics · Economy

Barcelonans like to be in the limelight. They boast of being considerate but also passionate, and they appreciate their city becoming more and more wealthy, including from tourism.

POPULATION

The population of the urban centre, hemmed in between the sea and the mountains, is about 1.6 million (Greater Barcelona 4.5 million). This makes Barcelona **the most densely populated area in Spain after Madrid**. The population of Barcelona is only about 60 % Catalan. The remaining 40 % are **Spanish immigrants** from other (mostly less developed) provinces, such as Andalusia and Murcia, as well as foreigners who mainly come from Northern Africa, Latin America, India and Pakistan. Foreigners make up around 17% of the population of Barcelona Province, 5% more than the national average.

The relationship between the Catalans and the immigrants from Southern Spain is not entirely without tension. The Catalan language ("Art and Culture, Language), in particular, poses a great problem for immigrants, for it has become increasingly more difficult to find work without any knowledge of Catalan. One problem for many Barcelonans (not only for the often economically deprived southern Spanish) is the **high rental costs** in the city. Barcelona competes with Madrid and the Basque city of San Sebastián for the unofficial title of the nation's most expensive city to live in.

Like all Spanish people, Barcelonans prefer being outside rather than cooped up at home. Friends and acquaintances meet on the street or

MARCO ⊕ POLO INSIGHT

? *Catalan invention?*

When strolling down Barcelona's streets in search of a pub, from the numerous tapas bars you would think they were a Barcelonan or Catalan invention. Not at all! The delicious tapas snacks were invented in Andalusia. Only a few years back, there was not a single bar in Barcelona that served food in the familiar dishes or small bowls. Today, many bars compete to create ever-newer tapas variations. When asked about these snacks, Barcelona's tourist office once even spun a tale about it being »possibly the only cultural revolution the city has experienced in the last 100 years«.

Musical entertainment provided by dulcimer players in front of the cathedral in the Gothic Quarter

Facts and Figures

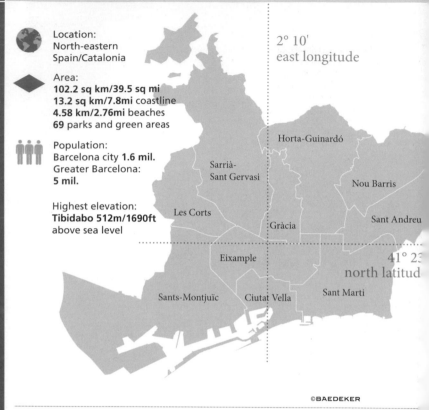

Location:
North-eastern
Spain/Catalonia

Area:
102.2 sq km/39.5 sq mi
13.2 sq km/7.8mi coastline
4.58 km/2.76mi beaches
69 parks and green areas

Population:
Barcelona city **1.6 mil.**
Greater Barcelona:
5 mil.

Highest elevation:
Tibidabo 512m/1690ft
above sea level

2° 10'
east longitude

Horta-Guinardó

Sarrià-
Sant Gervasi

Nou Barris

Les Corts

Sant Andreu

Gràcia

Eixample

41° 23
north latitud

Sants-Montjuïc

Ciutat Vella

Sant Marti

©BAEDEKER

▶ Economy

Next to Madrid the country's most important economic location

Spain's publishing capital

Spain's major port city
(trading centre, passenger ships and ferries)

2.6 mil. passengers annually

Barcelona airport (most important
airport after Madrid))

35 mil. passengers annually (2013)

Most important employers:
Administration
Industry
Port
Service sector
Tourism
(14 % of GDP; 60,000 hotel beds)

about 13 mil. guest-nights annual

▶ Climate

The Mediterranean climate gives the capital of Catalonia mild winters. The Collserola mountain range protects it from cold winds, so that daily temperatures are mostly between 11° and 14° C (51° and 57° F). Summers begin early and reach their highest temperatures in July and August, an average 27° C (80° F).

▶ Languages

Catalan, Spanich

▶ Administration

Capital of the Spanish Autonomous Region of Catalonia

Head of administration:
mayor

University city:
234,000 students

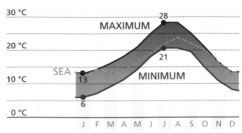

Average temperatures

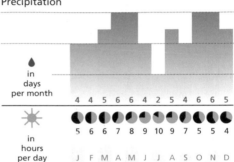

Precipitation

	J	F	M	A	M	J	J	A	S	O	N	D
in days per month	4	4	5	6	6	4	2	5	4	6	6	5
in hours per day	5	6	6	7	8	9	10	9	7	5	5	4

▶ The highest buildings in the region

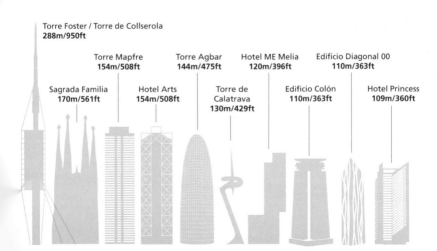

Torre Foster / Torre de Collserola
288m/950ft

Torre Mapfre
154m/508ft

Torre Agbar
144m/475ft

Hotel ME Melia
120m/396ft

Edificio Diagonal 00
110m/363ft

Sagrada Familia
170m/561ft

Hotel Arts
154m/508ft

Torre de Calatrava
130m/429ft

Edificio Colón
110m/363ft

Hotel Princess
109m/360ft

Looking down to the harbour from Montjuïc

in a pub, while invitations to someone's house are the exception. Here, going out means moving from place to place on a pub crawl – **ir de copas** – and a night out often lasts until the next day. It is surprising how many Barcelonans manage to go to work after a whole night's drinking and appear as if the nightly escapades had never happened. The diligent, disciplined, efficiently organized and rather business-oriented Catalans describe this ability as **seny i rauxa**: reason and sensual pleasure; head and stomach. »Seny« stands for tough intellect, prudence and stealth, as well as for caution and trust in the success of work well done. »Rauxa« stands for a boisterous joie de vivre and wild passion, a character trait which is also responsible for artistic and business creativity as well as inexhaustible resourcefulness..

POLITICS

When it was reintroduced in 1980, the Catalan parliamentary election was won by Jordi Pujol's **Conservative Party »Convergéncia i Unió«** (Convergence and Union, CiU); the Socialists (under Pasqual Maragall from 1982) governed at Barcelona's Town Hall. In the ensuing one-and-a-half decades there was never a particularly neighbourly relationship between the two government buildings at Plaça Sant Jaume, in the Barri Gòtic district, i. e. between the Palau de la Generalitat (the office of Catalan prime minister Pujol), and the Casa de la Ciutat (residence of Mayor Maragall) opposite.

During the regional elections in November 2003, the victory of **a new left-wing coalition**, consisting of the Socialist Party of Catalonia (PSC, a branch of the Spanish PSOE), the Republican Left of

Catalonia (Esquerra Republicana, ERC) and the Green Party (ICV), marked the end of Jordi Pujol's era in Catalonia after 23 years. The leader of the Catalan Socialists, **Pasqual Maragall**, was elected new Catalan regional president. He was succeeded by his party colleague his party colleague **José Montilla** in 2006.

After the restoration of democracy in Spain the Partido Socialista de Catalunya (PSC) was the most elected party in Catalonia. That changed for the first time in 2011, with the electoral victory of the CiU. Since then the Mayor of Barcelona has been **Xavier Trias**. Even in the region of Catalonia, CiU has been the strongest party since 2010. It provides the Prime Minister, **Artur Mas**.

ECONOMY

Barcelona is the most prominent **industrial city** in Catalonia and, alongside the capital of Madrid, also the most significant in all of Spain. With a main focus on the metal industry, other sectors include the textile industry, mechanical engineering and vehicle construction, civil engineering and road construction, as well as paper manufacturing and the printing industry. The majority of companies are either small or mid-sized. Far more extensive than the industrial branch are wholesale (textiles and leather goods, food, technical devices and transport machinery, furniture and household appliances) and retail trading (food, textiles and shoes, chemical and pharmaceutical products, furniture, office supplies, and printing products). The service industry has become an enormously significant economic branch, with a special focus on publishing: Barcelona is **Spain's publishing capital**. The tourism industry also greatly contributes to the wealth of the city, which is currently experiencing the **most rapid tourism growth** of all European city destinations, having the fourth-largest number of tourists after London, Paris and Rome. Barcelona's visitor numbers shot up from 3 million visitors annually in 1995 to 7.4 million in 2012, making it the European city with the most tourists after London, Paris and Rome. Over the same period of time the number of cruise ship passengers visiting the city multiplied by a factor of ten. Of the almost 35,000 companies based in Barcelona, more than a third are involved in the booming hotel and restaurant trade. They are followed by transport, repair and maintenance services. Credit institutions and insurance companies are another large sector. Barcelona is also an important port city, home to the second-biggest port in Spain. Together with the outer harbour, the Port France de Barcelona comprises an area of approx. 300ha/740 acres. Also significant is the ferry service to the Balearics (primarily for tourism) and the terminal for cruise ships arriving from all over the world.

Welcome to Everyday Life!

Experience Barcelona up-close with local experts. Some of them might even come from the UK.

ON SOMEONE ELSE'S SOFA

It's exciting for both the guest and the host, who know each other only from a photo and a profile on the internet. Couchsurfing.org is a hospitality network through which members from many countries around the world offer each other free a couch (or a bed) for one night. They often eat together and the guests are shown interesting places. Meanwhile, there have been numerous imitators, but the original remains the non-profit website:

www.couchsurfing.org

GETTING AROUND BY SEGWAY

The Segway is a two-wheeled, battery-powered electric vehicle for one, ideal, for example, for getting from the Barri Gòtic via Port Vell and Barceloneta to the Port Olímpic and back again via Parc de la Ciutadella! SegwayCAT operates such tours, which last from 2 to 2.5 hours and can have up to eight participants (€50 per person). And during the tours guides will tell you some interesting things about their city.

www.segwaytours.cat

JOGGING BARCELONA

The German Arnd Krüger is a sports scientist and experienced marathon runner. In 2005 he founded Sightjogging-Barcelona. Since then he has been leading early morning runs of between 10–14km through his adopted city. And there is enough time to learn not just more about the sights of Barcelona but also about life in the Catalan metropolis.

www.sightjogging-barcelona.com

MORNING AT THE MARKET

Early risers can see how the city slowly wakes up. Like at the Boqueria market, for example. The unloading of the produce and setting up of the stalls begins at 6am. The 70-year-old Carlos gets up at 4am so that his fish delivery is ready when the first customers arrive. »Barcelona has changed a lot«, he explains, »but the work of a market trader has stayed more or less the same.« After a walk around the market you can head for one of the simple cafés where suppliers, traders and other locals call in for a fortifying coffee.

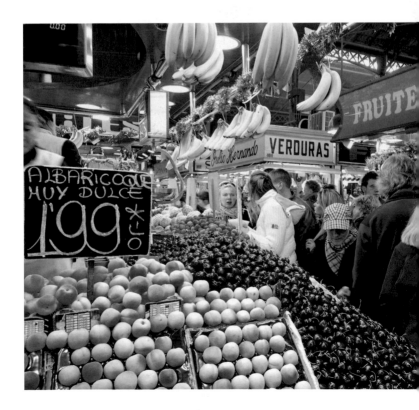

Highs and Lows

Barcelona was a major power in the Middle Ages. At the beginning of modern times, however, the city lost its autonomy to the Crown of Castile and was often brutally oppressed, right up to the end of the Franco era. Nevertheless, Barcelona has experienced several economic heydays.

COLONY OF ROME

15 BC.	Founding oft he Roman colony of Barcino
late 3rd century AD	First Christian community
409 AD	End of Roman rule
415 AD	Visigoths conquer Barcelona.

The history of Barcelona starts with the Romans. About 4,000 years ago, Celtiberians lived here on the slopes of Montjuïc. Yet it is unknown whether they also established a fixed settlement. After their victory over the Carthaginians in the Second Punic War (218–201 BC) the Romans gradually conquered nearly the entire Iberian Peninsula.

Foundation and Pax Romana

In 15 BC, during the reign of the emperor Augustus, they founded a Roman colony named **Colonia Julia Augusta Faventia Paterna Barcino**. This colony was probably a garrison situated on a hill called Mons Taber, which today is the highest point of the Barri Gòtic. The enclosed layout was rectangular in shape; two central arterial roads led from north to south and from east to west, with a temple and a forum positioned at the crossroads. Under the Romans, the small settlement Barcino enjoyed 400 years of peace in the shadow of Tarraco (Tarragona), situated further to the southwest, which was the capital of the Roman province Hispania Citerio, also called Tarraconensis. That period, however, was overshadowed by the gruesome persecution of Christians, when Barcino developed a first Christian community towards the end of the 3rd century AD. Its most prominent martyr was said to have been the young virgin

? MARCO ⊕ POLO INSIGHT *Did St Eulàlia really exist?*

There is some doubt as to whether St Eulàlia really lived. Barcelona probably would have preferred to have a male patron saint. But the only choice they had was St Cucuphas (Cugat), who was a Phoenician from Carthage in North Africa.

In the past, the castle o top of Montjuïc was often perceived as a threat by Barcelona's citizens

Eulàlia, today's patron saint of the city. Her relics are said to rest in the Gothic cathedral.

Time of the Migration of Peoples
The end of Roman rule on the Iberian Peninsula began with the invasion of Germanic tribes in 409. In 415, the Christianized **Visigoths** conquered Barcelona and temporarily used it as their capital.

COUNTY OF BARCELONA

716	Moors occupy the city.
778	Barcelona is the capital of the Spanish March.
878	Establishment of the County of Barcelona

Moors and Franks
From 711, the Moors took over nearly the entire Iberian Peninsula, including Barcelona. They captured the city in 716 and named it **Bardschaluna**. The city remained under Arab rule for almost 100 years, until Louis the Pious invaded Barcelona in 801 and made it capital of Charlemagne's **Spanish March**, which was founded in 778 as a buffer state between the Arabs in the south and Frankish and Christian Europe in the north.

Plaça del Rei, Catalonia's political centre in the Middle Ages

Frankish power gradually diminished in the Spanish March, which allowed Count **Guifré el Pelós** (Wilfred the Hairy) to found the dynasty of the County of Barcelona in 878. Guifré died in 897 in a battle against the Moors, but the dynasty of the Counts of Barcelona continued for another 500 years. In 985, Barcelona was conquered by Almanzor, Grand Vizier of Caliph Hisham II, also titled »the Victorious«. Only three years later, however, the city was liberated from the Moors without any support from the Franks. In 988 **Count Borell II** proclaimed the independence of the County of Catalonia. In the following period, Catalan counts fought against the Moors, expanded their dominion to south of Tarragona and, through marriage, even as far as Provence in France.

Catalan independence

MAJOR MARITIME POWER

1137	Union with Aragón
1359	Constitution of the Generalitat
1391	Jewish pogrom

Another important step toward the city's developement was made in 1137 when the County of Barcelona, which covered nearly the same area of what is now Catalonia, merged with **Aragón** in the marriage of Ramón Berenguer IV and the Infanta Petronila of Aragón. Catalonia and Aragón were thus joined by a dynastic union until the 15th century. Although each country always kept its own administration, the union allowed the more populated and wealthy Catalonia to further expand its trading empire – Catalonia entered its first Golden Age.

Union with Aragón

With Barcelona as royal residence, maritime trade was intensified and new sea routes were established to extend the city's power and its economic competition with the Italian trading centres of Venice and Genoa. Mallorca was taken in 1229, Valencia in 1238, Sicily in 1282, Menorca in 1287 and Sardinia in 1323. The world's largest surviving medieval shipyard (les drassanes), the Gothic cathedral, the church of Santa Maria del Mar, the Palau de la Generalitat, the Palau del Rei and the stock exchange La Llotja originate from this period, when Barcelona was the **most important city in Spain** and dominated the Western Mediterranean. The population grew, new businesses were founded, and trade and banking flourished – as did the arts at the royal court, in particular Catalan literature. In 1395, Barcelona held its first annual poetry competition, the Jocs Florals. Almost revolutionary by the standards of the day, the Catalan Parliament, the **Corts Catalanes** was established in 1289, to represent the nobility, the church and the citizens. The Generalitat was first constituted in 1359,

Golden Age

and is still used as provincial government to this day. Also founded was the **Consell de Cent** (Council of the Hundred), which resided in the Town Hall on what is now Plaça Sant Jaume. In the second half of the 14th century Barcelona hit rock bottom when the Plague broke out several times and the entire Jewish Quarter El Call was demolished during a pogrom in 1391 (▶MARCO POLO Insight, p.160)

PART OF THE CASTILIAN EMPIRE

1469	Marriage of Ferdinand and Isabella
1714	Catalonia loses sovereignty
ab 1859	Creation of the Eixample district

Downfall

DownfallAt the dawn of the 15th century, Barcelona's political power gradually diminished. The death of King Martí the Humane in 1410 also marks the end of the House of Barcelona in the Kingdom of Catalonia and Aragón, which consequently led to the dominance of the Aragonese House of Trastámara, making Catalan interests secondary. In 1469 the marriage of King Ferdinand of Aragón and Isabella of Castile **united the two rival kingdoms**. When Christopher Columbus reached the shores of the Americas in 1492, sea trade shifted from the Mediterranean to Seville and Cádiz on the Atlantic. While Castile rapidly rose to world power, Aragón-Catalonia, excluded from the conquest of the New World and related overseas trade, experienced an economic and political collapse.

Wars with Castil

In the 17th century, Catalonia's economy was on the mend so the House of Habsburg, then the ruling power in Castile since 1516, soon asked Catalonia to help fund its politics. During the Thirty Years' War (1618–48), when Spain fought against France, the Spanish King Philip IV forced Catalan troops to fight against the hostile neighbours in the north and imposed great tax burdens on the Catalans. This eventually led to Catalonia's uprising against the central power in Madrid with support from the French. The **Guerra dels Segadors**, »Reapers' War«, to which the national anthem »Els Segadors« harks back, was won by the superior Castilian army.

In the **War of the Spanish Succession** (1701–14) Catalonia faced yet another confrontation with Madrid. Following the death of Charles II, the last Habsburg king of Spain, in 1700, the two most powerful European dynasties fought over the Spanish Crown: the French House of Bourbon and the Austrian Habsburgs. Although the Catalans first supported the Bourbon Philippe of Anjou, they later sympathised with the Habsburg Archduke Charles of Austria, for he seemed the more promising candidate for restoring their national independence. However, he lost the war and the winner, Philippe of

Anjou, now King Philip V of Spain, occupied Barcelona until it finally surrendered on **11 September 1714** (11 September is now a National Holiday in Catalonia). A fortified citadel by the harbour was erected to suppress the rebellious Barcelona population. In addition, Philip V abolished the fundamental Catalan laws (usatges), had all regional political institutions closed and prohibited the use of Catalan. With this act of revenge from the Bourbon king, Catalonia entirely lost its sovereignty to the Spanish Crown. Nevertheless, it soon experienced a new economic revival. .

While Spain lived from the tax revenues of its colonies, Catalonia, now merely a Spanish province, was only permitted to trade with America from 1778. Within the course of a century, however, it advanced to the richest and most industrialised region of the Iberian Peninsula – a precursor of the industrial revolution in Spain. **Barcelona became Spain's first industrial centre** and the first textile factory in the Catalan capital was founded in 1741.

Catalan Renaissance

This economic recovery ended temporarily when **Napoleon Bonaparte** invaded Spain with his troops in 1808, in the attempt to bring the country under his control. The occupied city of Barcelona capitulated the same year. Yet Napoleon ultimately failed against the deter-

Original plan for »Eixample«, Ildefons Cerdà's urban extension for Barcelona

mined resistance of the Spaniards when in 1813, with help from the British, they successfully drove their enemy out of the country. During the course of the 19th century Catalonia experienced another economic boom. During the interim years the Catalan version of Art Nouveau, **Modernisme**, celebrated its heyday. **The first Spanish railway line was inaugurated in 1848**, connecting Barcelona with the Northern city of Mataró. 1859 was the start of the extension of Barcelona according to the design of civil engineer Ildefons Cerdà. The **Eixample**, an expansive district north of the old town, is distinctly shaped by the Modernisme style. In 1888 the city publicly displayed its acquired wealth for the first time, in a large exhibition in the Parc de la Ciutadella. In 1929, the second World Exhibition was held on Montjuïc. Due to the economic upswing, national identity in Catalonia regained its strength. The autonomy movement and industrial wealth resulted in the Renaixença, a return to the country's own history and culture. The medieval poetry competition Jocs Florals was reintroduced in 1859. In 1906 Barcelona was host of the first congress held in Catalan, one of its main goals being the standardisation of the language. During the 17th and 18th centuries Catalan had practically only existed as a spoken language. Eventually, the foundation of the Institut d'Estudis Catalans (Institute for Catalan Studies) in 1907 was an indication for the growing importance of the Catalan language, which was increasingly accepted by officials.

20TH CENTURY

1909	Setmana Tràgica
1936–1939	Spanish Civil War
1979	Statute of Autonomy
1992	Olympic Games

Colonial war, military regime, second republic
In the early 20th century, social, economic and political problems in Spain increased dramatically. Catalonia, too, experienced a political and economic crisis. After France and Spain agreed on their individual spheres of influence in North Africa (1904), the Spanish Crown undertook several military campaigns against Morocco. In Barcelona – the European stronghold for unions (sindicatos) and socialist and anarchist workers' movements - the forced recruitments in 1909 led to massive protests among workers, which were rigorously struck down by the state. More than 100 people were killed in riots during the **Setmana Tràgica** (Tragic Week). In 1914 Catalonia established the Mancomunitat, a regional government, which was meant to be a first step towards autonomy. Primo de Rivera's military regime (1923 – 1930), tolerated by King Alfonso XIII, quickly abolished the country's self-governance. In 1931, Alfonso XIII lost his

crown after the Republican victory at the municipal elections and the proclamation of the Second Spanish Republic. The liberal and progressive constitution became effective in 1932 and included **regional autonomy for Catalonia**. The Catalan language was permitted in offices and schools. More and more printed material was published in Catalan. For the Spanish nation, however, the Republican era was not a peaceful time. The political spectrum became increasingly more radical and the gap between left-wing and right-wing groups became ever wider. In February of 1936, when the left-wing Popular Front (Frente Popular) won a re-election to the Spanish parliament by a close vote, it was just a question of time before the powder keg would blow.

19 July 1936 was meant to be the first day of the **People's Olympics**   Civil War
in Barcelona – a protest event against the Berlin Olympics hosted by the Nazi regime at the same time. The games never took place. On 18 July 1936, the right-wing military, including General Francisco Franco, who later became commander-in-chief of the rebelling troops, led a coup against the rightfully elected government in Madrid. This event caused the three-year Spanish Civil War, which was fought bitterly on both sides. This war was not merely a conflict between the Republican left wing and Franco's right wing troops, but an ideological war between communism and national socialism / fascism (So-

Soldiers of the International Brigade during a demonstration before their mission against Franco's troops

Civil War in Barcelona

Franco's revolt leading to the Spanish Civil War (1936–39) was never going to be successful in Barcelona, but anarchy and civil war raged in the Catalan metropolis nevertheless, and the city was damaged by severe air raids. Churchill expressed his respect towards Barcelona's stalwart population.

Sunday, 19 July 1936 was supposed to be the first day of the **Alternative Olympics in Barcelona**. These Games in the capital of Catalonia were the European left-wing parties' response to the Olympic Games that had just taken place in Berlin which, in the view of many young liberals and Socialists, Hitler and his German Nazi regime merely exploited as a means for propaganda. Hundreds of athletes from all over the world came to Barcelona to engage in a sports competition in the spirit of freedom.

The Coup Fails

But then on 18 July 1936, one day before the opening of the Barcelona Olympics, civil war broke out in Spain. The majority of the Spanish army sympathized with General Franco and overthrew the legitimately elected Popular Front government in Madrid. Rebels seized control in many parts of the Spanish Republic. In some cities, such as Madrid and Bilbao, however, the military units were powerless against the population's will to defend itself.

In Barcelona too – Spain's second-biggest city – Franco's coup was quickly nipped in the bud. During the night of 18–19 July, 12,000 soldiers moved concentrically towards to the city centre. The officers had lied to their men claiming they were fighting to protect the republic. But **Barcelona was a stronghold for Anarchists and their CNT union**, and they had more than 350,000 members in the Catalan capital alone. So they did not wait for the government's call to arms. Instead, when the news of a military coup spread, union members opened their secret arsenal and erected the barricades. After hours of fighting, the rebels were finally forced to surrender on the evening of 19 July. The officers responsible for the military plot were later found guilty by court martial and sentenced to death by firing squad in the Castell de Montjuïc.

A Civil War within a Civil War

Now Anarchists seized power in the city. From the very first day, they tried to realize their utopia of a classless society. The once so casual trading metropolis now came under the grim rule of the proletariat: armed militia in workers' outfits patrolled the streets. Restaurants, luxury hotels and theatres were closed, their owners driven out or shot. The government of the largely autonomous Catalan region warned the population not to wear bourgeois clothing, espe-

Newspaper stands inform Barcelonians about the outbreak of the Civil War

cially hats. The church, however, was terrorised the most, as the Anarchists considered it to be the worst opponent of social justice. Priests were murdered and churches were plundered or burnt. Only one cathedral in Barcelona was spared.

Red vs. Reds

At that time in Spain, there was not only the Civil War between the legitimate Republic and Franco's rebellious army. There was also another civil war raging within the Republican camp: Reds vs. Reds – a fight between the Moscow-ruled Communists and an assortment Anarchists, Trotskyites and various left-wing revolutionaries.

This civil war broke out in Barcelona in May 1937, when the Catalan regional government sent out a police command to occupy the city's main telecommunications office, which had been controlled by Anarchists unashamedly tapping the phones of government officials. The policemen were greeted by machine gun fire. The battles between Anarchists against units of Communists, Socialists, civil republicans and central and regional government forces were more violent than those in July 1936 against Franco's army. After four days, the Anarchists were forced to surrender. Their defeat also meant the end of their political power. Meanwhile, the Communists increasingly prevailed in Republican Spain. Already in 1937, all suspected enemies of the Comintern, the Communist International, were persecuted. Even in Barcelona, thousands disappeared in the torture cells of the Soviet secret police organisation **NKVD**. Even members of the International Brigades fighting for the Republic on the battlefields became victims of the witchhunt. To the outside world, however, the Spanish Republic had restored its respectable image of power. In November 1937 the **government of the Republic** moved to Barcelona.

Militiaman preparing for battle

Danger from the Air

The battlefront remained far away from Barcelona until the end of the war. Yet the Catalan capital suffered greatly from the terrors of war. For two years, the Republican trading metropolis was subjected to heavy aerial bombardment during raids conducted by Franco's allies, Hitler and Mussolini. In March 1938, especially, as well as in the autumn of the same year, **large parts of the city were completely destroyed**, most notably the workers' and Anarchist district of El Raval. By the end of 1938, Franco embarked on a major offensive against Catalonia, which was still governed by the Republicans. The Republican front collapsed. Defending Barcelona was no longer

an option. On 15 November 1938 the remaining fighters of the International Brigades were officially bid farewell on the Diagonal. Those who stayed in Barcelona and were still willing to fight now gave up hope; thousands fled the city and went to France. On 26 January 1939, Franco's troops moved into the Catalan capital without a struggle. On 21 February, the future dictator held a triumphal parade.

After the fall of Barcelona, there were no more organized revolts. On 1 April, Franco won the Spanish Civil War.

Barcelona the Brave

When the English Prime Minister **Winston Churchill** buoyed up the citizens of London after German air raids in 1940, he reminded them of the »brave people of Barcelona« who had resisted aerial bombardment for two years.

viet ruler Stalin actively supported the Republicans; the International Brigades including socialists, communists, anarchists, writers and intellectuals helped in fighting for the Republic, while Franco's troops depended on soldier contingents from Hitler's Germany and Mussolini's Italy). A no less brutal **conflict between Communists and Anarchists** raged among the Republicans. Barcelona, in particular, saw major battles in 1937 (▶ MARCO POLO Insight, p.28). The conflict between Communists and Aanarchists was finally won by the Communists with assistance from the Soviet intelligence service. Catalonia remained loyally Republican until the end of the civil war. **Between 1937 and 1939, the Popular Front government was based in Barcelona**. Before General Franco's victorious troops marched into the city on 26 January 1939, thousands of Catalans fled north to find refuge in France.

After defeating the Republicans, General **Franco established an authoritarian** regime that lasted for 36 years. All forms of regionalism were brutally struck down: Catalan autonomy was deferred, and the dictator suppressed Catalan language and culture. However, the Catalans never gave in to dictatorship. By the end of the 1950s, some Barcelona intellectuals and artists began reactivating Catalonia's national identity, which culminated in a **Catalan protest movement** against the Franco regime. The opponents did not form a secret society but protested silently in everyday life. Official forms were filled out in Catalan; Catalan songs were hummed in the presence of members of the Madrid government; policemen were asked for directions in Catalan. Repression by the state, such as the censorship of Catalan lyrics attacking the regime, was to no avail. Moreover, the black market for resistance songs flourished. Eventually, lower clerics and influential branches of the economy also sympathised with the Catalans' claim for more autonomy.

Following the death of the old dictator Francisco Franco, the country finally became a federal democracy in 1975. In 1979, after millions of Catalans had gone on the streets to reclaim their old rights, Catalonia and the Basque Country were granted **autonomous status** allowing a limited form of self-governance. Since then, Català has been reintroduced as the official and working language, and the federal state government, the Generalitat, represents the interests of Catalan citizens.

The **first elections for a Catalan regional parliament** in 1980 were won by the conservative Convergencia i Unio (CiU) party, led by Jordi Pujol, who remained president of the Generalitat de Catalunya up until the beginning of the 21st century. Barcelona's first mayor under a democracy, however, became Narcís Serra, a left-wing politician, followed by Socialist Pasqual Maragall in 1982, who became

Under Franco

Democracy

president of the Generalitat in 2003. Xavier Trias from the Ciu has been mayor since 2011.

Urban restructuring In the same year of his election Pasqual Maragall gave the order: »**Posa't guapa**«, Barcelona, make yourself pretty! And Barcelona did make itself pretty, especially after winning the bid in 1986 to host the 1992 Summer Olympics. Renowned designers and famous architects from all over the world had old structures restored, especially in the Raval district, to create new and exciting developments, including the airport and the television tower on Mount Tibidabo. The architects and designers also made sure that Barcelona would face the sea again. Ugly factory and warehouses were torn down and replaced by beautiful sandy beaches and harbour districts, ideal for walks and going out.

21ST CENTURY

2002	Gaudí Year
2004	Weltforum der Kulturen
2010	Pope Benedict XV elevates the Sagrada Família to papal basilica.

New projects and events In 2002, Barcelona celebrated the **Gaudí Year** in honour of the 150th birthday of the famous Catalan architect. Two years later the **Universal Forum of Cultures 2004**, under the patronage of UNESCO was a five-month event where citizens and representatives of international social, religious, cultural and public institutions exchanged ideas on war, environmental pollution, globalization, etc. Although Barcelona is bursting at the seams, squeezed between ocean and mountains, there appears to be no end to the city's construction frenzy. Since the 1992 Olympics, Barcelona's innovative urban architecture has been considered ground breaking, as the Venice Biennale in 2002 approvingly proclaimed. The city wants to continue living up to this reputation, and the next major project has already been realised: the former industrial area in Poblenou, situated between the Olympic village, the coast, and the Besòs river, has been transformed into an entirely new district called **@22**, complete with apartment blocks, shopping and leisure centres, convention halls and parks, that has attracted IT, media and high-tech industries.

In 2010 Pope Benedict XVI consecrated Gaudí's church of the Sagrada Família and thereby elevated it to a papal basilica. A year later, after the bullfighting ban was introduced in Catalonia (2010), La Monumental, the only bullring in Barcelona, was closed.

Like elsewhere in Spain, Barcelona has been hit by the financial crisis that began in 2008, though not quite as badly as other parts of the

People from all over the world visit Barcelona

country. In 2012 the national unemployment rate was 24.2%, while in the Catalan metropolis 20% of people eligible for work were without a job.

In October 2014 a **referendum to grant independence** to Catalonia was blocked by the Spanish Constitutional Court. Nevertheless the regional government continues its campaign and preparations for independence.

Art History

In the two thousand years of its eventful history, Barcelona has been shaped by a variety of cultures. The architectural styles that most dominate the cityscape are the Gothic and Modernisme, both of which were created in periods of great economic prosperity for the Catalan capital.

InRoman times Barcelona, unlike Tarragona situated further south, was a rather insignificant town, which is also why there are hardly any remarkable archaeological finds from the first centuries of the city's history. Relics from the ancient city wall, however, can still be discovered in the Barri Gòtic district, where the Roman Barcino once stood. Also worth seeing are the three pillars of the Temple of Augustus in the courtyard of a slightly hidden house at Carrer del Paradis 10, in a curve between the cathedral and Plaça Sant Jaume. The **excavation site** of the foundations of old residential buildings underneath the ►Museu d'Història de Barcelona is fascinating, not so much in an aesthetic sense, but because it gives good insight into Roman utilitarian architecture and way of life.

Roman art

The Visigoths, Moors and Franks who successively ruled in Barcelona did not leave any visible architectural traces.

Early Middle Ages

Besides Modernisme, the Romanesque style is the most prominent architectural style in Catalonia with more than 2,000 Romanesque monuments, including castles, palaces and a wealth of churches. In Barcelona itself, however, only the church of **Sant Pau del Camp** offers an example of Romanesque architecture. The most impressive works of 11th- and 12th- century **Romanesque murals** are no longer in the rural churches where they were originally painted, but exhibited at the ►Museu Nacional d'Art de Catalunya in the Palau Nacional on Montjuïc.

Romanesque

What the Catalan metropolis lacks in Romanesque architecture, Barcelona's Barri Gòtic district makes up for with Spain's **largest assembly of Gothic buildings** (13th–15th century). These monuments, symbolizing Barcelona's former political power and economic heyday, count among the best preserved in all of Europe. Represented are all types of buildings: churches (including the **cathedral**), monasteries with marvellous cloisters and city palaces with magnificent halls

Gothic

Christ Pantocrator: apse fresco from Sant Climent de Taüll in the Museu Nacional d'Art de Catalunya

(**Saló de Tinell**), government buildings (**Casa de la Ciutat** and **Palau de la Generalitat**) and artisan houses. The neighbouring district La Ribera also has some beautiful Gothic buildings, royal palaces, the stock exchange (**La Llotja**) and the church of **Santa Maria del Mar**, one of the Gothic highlights of the city. The **Drassanes Reials** (royal shipyards) by the harbour were built in Gothic times (today the Museu Marítim), and the Poor Clares convent **Monestir de Pedralbes** outside the city centre is also a Gothic monument. Fine arts during the Gothic era were largely influenced by French, later Italian and, in the 15th century, also Dutch painters. The **Barcelona School of Art** was established in the 15th century under the influence of the Dutch. In the works of Luis Dalmau, Bartolomeo Vermejo and Jaime Huguet its characteristic features shaped by distinct realism and rich detail already come to the fore.

Renaissance, Baroque, neoclassical

In Barcelona there is hardly any noteworthy evidence of Renaissance, Baroque or neoclassical art. As the population was too busy rebelling against the centralized power of Spain, the city (and Catalonia as a whole) was neither economically nor culturally productive during that time.

The façade of the **Palau de la Generalitat** and the **Palau del Lloctinent** date back to the Renaissance; the **Església de Betlem** on the Ramblas is from the Baroque period, and the **Palau de la Virreina** is neoclassical.

Modernisme

With the economic recovery stimulated by industrialisation during the second half of the 19th century, Catalonia revived its own cultural identity, which also led to the region's artistic revival. Modernisme, or **Catalan Art Nouveau**, emerged in the 1880s (►MARCO POLO Insight, p.180), and the heyday of this first distinctly Catalan art form, found mainly in the Barcelona district of **Eixample**, lasted until around 1920. It represented a change in artistic direction, beginning with the rediscovery of Catalan Romanticism by the architects Elies Rogent (Universidad de Barcelona, restoration of the Ripoll Monastery) and Pere Falqués (triumphal arch, street lanterns at Passeig de Gràcia), and then continuing and developing with the work of the three most famous Modernista architects, **Lluís Domènech i Montaner**, **Josep Puig i Cadafalch** and **Antoni Gaudí**.

Gaudí (►Famous People) was the main exponent the highly decorative and playful Modernisme style. It was inspired by medieval architectural elements and organic natural forms, and combined new techniques and materials with traditional craftsmanship (ironwork, carpentry, ceramics, glazing). Straight lines were anathema to Gaudí; his buildings had to evince soft, flowing forms – colourful Moorish-style tiles, stained glass that resembled petals or the wings of a butterfly, arched balustrades and wrought iron railings, curved stairs,

Magnificent glass dome of the Palau de la Música

and ventilation shafts and chimneys turned into anthropomorphic sculptures.

With economic growth there also emerged a prosperous middle class that had sufficient funds to show off its newly found self-confidence in the form of representative structures. So Modernisme developed into a culture of the haute bourgeoisie, which because of its close association with power and money was sharply criticized by the successor movement, Noucentisme. But Modernisme did have a social reform side to it. Many architects, for example, strived to create more humane designs for factories and workers' housing, where of course aesthetics played an important part

Pablo Picasso (1881–1973), founder of Cubism and probably the most prominent artist of the 20th century, can almost be considered a Catalan painter. He spent his first years at the Academy of Art in Barcelona before he moved to Paris in 1904. His early works were noticeably influenced by the city and its surroundings, as can be witnessed at the Museu Picasso. Although **Joan Miró** (▶Famous People) lived in Paris for some time, where he joined the Surrealist movement that emerged in the 1920s, his art is present in this city more than any other – from murals at Barcelona airport to a colourful mosaic on the Rambles, or his logo design for La Caixa bank. The new art of the young Spanish avant-garde, led by **Antoni Tàpies** (▶Famous People), developed a radical modern painting style, which entirely forgoes descriptive image motifs and rules of composition. Tapiès combined the most varied of styles with his attempt to create dramatic effects by the use of different materials. Like Picasso, Miró and Tàpies are represented by their own museums in Barcelona..

Contemporary architecture and design

Following the city's successful bid to host the 1992 Summer Olympics in 1986, there began an unparalleled redesign of Barcelona's squares, which also included a comprehensive makeover of entire districts. Renowned Spanish and international designers and **famous architects** participated in this urban transformation, which still continues today. Spaniard Santiago Calatrava designed the telecommunications tower near the Olympic Stadium, Arata Isozaki from Japan created the sports venue Palau Jordí directly next it. British architect Sir Norman Foster designed the TV and radio transmitter on Mount Tibidabo, American Richard Meier built the Museu d'Art Contemporani and Ricardo Bofill from Barcelona designed the Teatre Nacional de Catalunya. The Fòrum 2004 was built according to the plans of the Swiss architects Herzog and De Meuron and the 32-storey Torre Agbar (2001–2004) was designed by the French architect Jean Nouvel.

Visitors to Barcelona will also not fail to notice the city's **enthusiasm for any kind of design**. Over the past 15 years, highly motivated designers let their creativity run wild, mainly in pubs, nightclubs, cafés and shops. Their most prominent representative, **Javier Mariscal**, is also internationally acclaimed (▶MARCO POLO Insight, p.50). Naturally, the city offers a wide range of designer shops and even design schools. Since the 1990s at the latest, design trends have been evolving and changing in rapid succession. Typical of the city are also the minimalist elitist-looking interiors of shops, restaurants and hotels that can be seen in the Eixample district, as are the les restrained forms of retro, anarchist or anti-design in the districts Raval, Born and Grácia.

But the Mediterranean city still produces plenty of architectural surprises, evident for example in the »W Barcelona« and »Mandarin Oriental« hotels which opened in 2010 (▶Enjoy Barcelona, Accommodation).

Language

Catalonia's autonomous status has not only had an impact on politics but also on language.

Catalan

Catalan (català in Catalan, catalán in Spanish) is **one of the four languages of Spain** alongside Castilian (español or castellano), Galician (galego in Galician, gallego in Spanish) spoken in northwest Spain, and Basque (euskara in Basque, vasco in Spanish) spoken in the Basque Country. Besides Spanish and Portuguese, Catalan is also the most important language on the Iberian Peninsula. Like Spanish,

Portuguese and Galician, **Catalan is a Romance language**, meaning it is of Latin origin. Catalan is spoken by some six million people and is spread well beyond the borders of Catalonia, from the French Department of Pyrenées Orientales in the north, across Catalonia and Valencia in Spain, down to Murcia and the provinces of Huesca, Zaragoza and Teruel to the west. Even the Balearic Islands belong to the Catalan-speaking area, and Catalan is also the official language of Andorra. The Catalan language, which is related to Provençal in France, can be traced back to the 12th century. Although the dictator Franco prohibited the use of Catalan after the Spanish Civil War (1936–39), the language never became extinct, as »català« was still spoken among families and friends.

In 1990 the European Parliament recognised Catalan as a European language. In Catalonia, on the Balearic Islands and in the Province of Valencia Catalan is the official language alongside

Mosaic lizard at Parc Güell

Spanish, and dominates regional media, from radio to magazines. Texts on maps, menus and official documents are often only written in Catalan. **It currently seems that the Catalan government is planning to make Catalonia a monolingual country.** All civil servants must have some knowledge of Catalan. Since 2003, business owners have been required by law to write their shop signs in Catalan only and customers must be served in Catalan first (who may of course answer in Spanish).

The numerous non-Catalan residents of Catalonia (40 % of Barcelona's population is not Catalan) are disadvantaged by the rigorous language politics and often have no choice but to attend a Catalan language course in order to retain their career. **Foreigners are not expected to speak Catalan.** Everywhere in Catalonia, tourists who can speak Spanish get by just fine.

Literature

Many big name contemporary Spanish authors hail from Barcelona. The first works of literature were created here in the Middle Ages.

Middle Ages The first documented Catalan literature dates back to the 12th century. Mostly historical works and chronicles, old Catalan literature also comprises numerous translations from Classical Antiquity and the scientific works of Moorish culture. **Troubadour poetry** from the French Provence had an enormous impact on Catalan literature. It thrived in the 12th and 13th centuries, when many Provencal words entered the Catalan language.

A central figure in Catalan language and culture was **Ramón Llull** (Latinized: Raimundus Lullus; 1235–1316), a highly educated man born in Mallorca. His works became enormously significant to the thinking of the entire Occident, and Catalan thrived as a language of culture like it never would again. Lullus wrote his novels, poems and tracts not only in Latin and Arabic but also in the idiomatic language of his home country. Joanot Martorell extended Lullus' guide on courtly life called Llibre de Cavalleria and perfected the chivalric novel (*Tirant lo Blanch*, around 1455).

Modern times In the 15th century, the Iberian Peninsula began to orientate itself toward Castile and the Castilian language, and Catalan suffered a similar fate to the Provencal dialect, which was outstripped by Northern French. It kept its function as a spoken language, but in written language and particularly **in high literature it was replaced by Castilian**.

In 1714, a decree by King Philipp V prohibited the official use of Catalan, which made it virtually impossible for original Catalan literature to spread.

During the Romantic period, the awareness of a previously distinct national culture (**Renaixença** = rebirth) finally led to a revival of the Catalan language, entering circles of intellectuals and authors and finding support from sponsoring societies, as well as becoming a subject for philological and linguistic research.

Linguist Maria Aguiló (1825–97) compiled the first Dictionary of original Catalan, Tomás Forteza (1838–89) wrote the Gramàtica Catalana, and Joan Alcover published the Diccionari de la Llengua Catalana in 1906.

19th-century literature is primarily concerned with bourgeois subjects. Writers worth mentioning are the poet Jacint Verdaguer i Santaló (1845–1902), humorist and comedy author Emili Vilanova

(1840–1905), as well as Pere Corominas (1870–1939, known as Enrique Mercader), who became well-known as a political and philosophical writer and freedom fighter during the Spanish Civil War. In 1975, with the end of the Franco regime, Catalan was reinstated as an official language and **Catalan literature experienced an unprecedented boom**. The most notable representatives of contemporary Catalan literature are Mercè Rodoreda and Manuel Vázquez Montalbán (both under ►Famous People), Enrique Vila-Matas, Carlos Ruiz Zafón and Alicia Giménez-Bartlett (under ►MARCO POLO Insight, p.50), Juan Marsé, born 1933, and Eduardo Mendoza, born 1943 (both under ►Practicalities, Recommended Reading). Some of these authors write in Spanish rather than Catalan.

Traditions and Customs

In Barcelona and Catalonia there are some festive traditions and dances peculiar to the city and region.

The sardana is a typical Catalan **circle dance** in 3/4 or 6/8 time. The music is based on folkloric tunes from the 16th and 17th centuries. The dancers hold hands in a circle and dance slowly and cautiously to a particular sequence of steps. There is even a special band called the cobla, which usually consists of flute, wait-pipe, trumpet, trombone, drum and double bass. **Everyone can join the dance**, although the step sequence is rather complex. The sardana, **symbolising the Catalan sense of community** and once prohibited under Franco, is not only danced at every village fair but also in Barcelona itself (►p.44). Sardana

In Barcelona the sardana is performed at the following locations: on the square in front of the cathedral, every Sunday and holiday at midday in July, and from September to November; on the Plaça Sant Jaume every Sunday at 6.30pm; in the Parc de la Ciutadella every Sunday at noon in January and February; every Friday at 7.30pm in the de l'Espanya Industrial from mid-April to the end of September; every second and fourth Sunday in the Parc Joan Miró from December until March, and at noon every first and third Sunday in April, October and November.

The city's folkloric highlights include the **gegants**, giant puppets dressed in noble costume. They are brought along on festive processions for important holidays, particularly for the celebration of St John in mid-June. These festivals are also a good opportunity to Festive customs

Castells – Catalonia's Human Towers

An unusual spectacle can be seen at large festivals in Catalonia: Castellers building their human towers, the Castells. They originated around the late 18th cent. out of a folk dance which ends with a small human tower. The dance comes from the rural region of Valls, which explains why the human towers have only been at home in the city of Barcelona since 1969.

▶ **Castellers' lexicon**
5de8 (Cinc de Vuit): »The Cathedral« is five men strong and eight levels high. The first number refers to the number of Castellers per level while the second number refers to the number of levels.
The tower: Castell (castle)
The groups: Colles
The individuals: Casteller

Scarf:
Protects against hair-pulling at the base of the tower

Shirt colour:
symbolizes team membership

Cloth around wrist:
aids in climbing at the b[...]

Sash:
aids in climbing

Waistband:
protects lumbar spine

Traditionally rolled up **white** trousers to aid in climbing

Espardenyas, traditional foot covering

The typical red handkerchief with white dots identifies the function of the Castellers.

▶ **Dates**

15. August	Mare de Déu (Mother of God) in Bisbal del Pened[è]
30. August	Sant Fèlix in Vilafranca del Pened[e]
24. September	Mare de Déu de la Mercè in Barcelo[n]
1st Sunday in October	»Castells« contest in Tarragona (every two year[s]
Sunday after 22. October	Santa Úrsula in Va[l]
1. November	Tots Sants (All Saints) in Vilafranca del Pened[e]
3rd Sunday in November	Feast of the Minyons in Terras[sa]

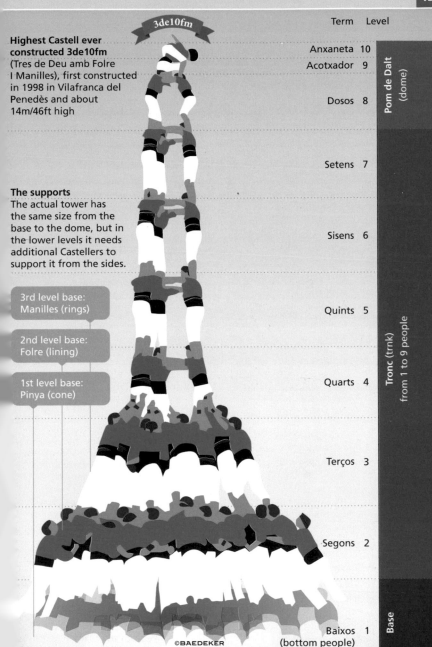

3de10fm

Highest Castell ever constructed 3de10fm (Tres de Deu amb Folre I Manilles), first constructed in 1998 in Vilafranca del Penedès and about 14m/46ft high

The supports
The actual tower has the same size from the base to the dome, but in the lower levels it needs additional Castellers to support it from the sides.

3rd level base: Manilles (rings)

2nd level base: Folre (lining)

1st level base: Pinya (cone)

Term	Level	
Anxaneta	10	Pom de Dalt (dome)
Acotxador	9	
Dosos	8	
Setens	7	
Sisens	6	
Quints	5	Tronc (trnk) from 1 to 9 people
Quarts	4	
Terços	3	
Segons	2	
Baixos (bottom people)	1	Base

©BAEDEKER

The »castellers« pile up to 10m/30ft high.

watch the amazing **castellers** (►MARCO POLO Insight, p.42), groups of festively dressed men acrobatically creating human towers. Like the sardana, the up to 10m/30ft high castells represent the Catalans' sense of community. The strongest men in the group form the lower circle of the tower, then the next group climbs onto their shoulders, and so on. Finally a small boy climbs on top of the pyramid. If he manages to stand up straight for three seconds the human tower was successful.

Highlight of many festivals is the **correfoc**, a fire run that traces its origins in the legend of St George. This is also when groups dressed up as devils, dragons or other horrific figures roam through the city throwing fireworks and making a huge racket until Sant Jordi, the dragon killer, appears and puts an end to it all (better take shelter!.

In 2004, despite the large bullfighting arena (La Monumental), Barcelona was the first city in the history of Spain to **abolish bullfighting**. In the summer of 2010, the Catalan Parliament approved a law that came into force in 2012, prohibiting the »corrida de toros« in the Autonomous Community of Catalonia. In contrast, supporters of bullfighting regard the spectacle as part of the Spanish identity, a cultural heritage that is worthy of protection. For staunch Catalans that is like showing a red rag to a bull.

Bullfighting

PAU CASALS (1876 – 1973)

Pau (Pablo) Casals was the greatest cellist of his time. Born in the   Cellist
Catalan town of Vendrell (Tarragona Province), he began to study at
the Music Conservatory of Barcelona in 1887. In 1905, he founded a
string trio with Alfred Cortot and Jacques Thibaud, whose outstanding interpretations soon became internationally renowned. The trio
played together for over thirty years. In 1919, Casals founded his own
orchestra in Barcelona, which performed all over the world, and he
was the first solo cellist to go on tour. He also became known for his
work as a **conductor** and **composer** of primarily spiritual music. His
major interest, however, lay in the revival of Johann Sebastian Bach's
solo works.
The artist emigrated in 1937, during the Spanish Civil War (1936–
39), and lived in exile for 45 years. His first home in exile was the
Pyrenean town of Prades, about 25km/15mi north of the Spanish-
French border. Like-minded Catalans even tried to convince the ex-
patriate, a staunch opponent of Franco, to become leader of the
Catalan government, whose president had been executed by the
Francoists. Casals refused. In 1958 he performed in front of the UN
in New York, which he used to publicly demonstrate for more humanity in the world and against the threat of nuclear war. Overnight,
the cellist became an ambassador for peace and was even nominated
for the Nobel Peace Prize. Married for the third time to a woman 59
years his junior, Casals died at the age of 97.

ANTONI GAUDÍ (1852 – 1926)

Born in Reus (Tarragona Province) Antoni Gaudí is by far the most   Barcelona's
famous Spanish architect in recent history and today's **most signifi-**   flagship
cant cultural figurehead of Barcelona and Catalonia. During his   architect
lifetime, however, the ingenious and obsessive architect was ridiculed
and even despised. He died after being hit by a tram in Barcelona in
1926.
Gaudí lived at a time when European architecture was dominated by
historicism and particularly by the neo-Gothic style. His vision was
the revival of a lighter, more colourful and Mediterranean Gothic
style, which is why Gothic forms are so prominent in many of his
schemes.   His creative legacy was the development of an entirely new
style, which can be described as Catalan Modernisme and mixes historical forms with the intertwining plant-like details of Art Nouveau.
Antoni Gaudí's major works (including Casa Milà and Casa Batlló)

**Joan Miró was a disciplined worker and remained modest despite
worldwide fame**

are all to be found in Barcelona. Gaudí was greatly supported by the duke Eusebi Güell, who commissioned him to build a residence for him (Palau Güell at the southwestern edge of Barcelona's Old City).

Gaudí's most famous building is the **Templo de la Sagrada Família** in Barcelona, where he lies buried in the crypt. The project took up most of the architect's working life, but even now this massive »church of the poor«, as Gaudì called it, is still being completed.

RAMÓN MERCADER (1914 – 1978)

Assassin   They had got to know each other, but Trotsky didn't really trust the new acquaintance who had ingratiated himself via friends. The **former Soviet revolutionary leader, who as an opponent of Stalin had gone into exile in Mexico**, said to his wife: »Maybe he is a fascist agent, we would do better not to receive him in our house«. But Trotsky did let him into the house again, and that was his undoing. Once in Trotsky›s study the guest showed him a newspaper article, and as Trotsky began to read it, he struck him from behind with an ice axe, in the head. The stricken Trotsky called out to the bodyguards rushing to his aid: »Don›t kill him, we need him to talk!«

The founder of the Red Army died of his injuries the following day. The assassin in Mexico was about 26 years old at the time, but he didn›t give away his true identity. A Mexican court sentenced him to 20 years in prison, which he had to serve out fully because he showed no remorse. It wasn›t until 1953, after a comparison of fingerprints, that it was revealed who had actually killed the most prominent enemy of Joseph Stalin: Jaime Ramón Mercader del Río Hernández, born in Barcelona in 1914 (his gravestone has the year 1913).

Early on, just like his mother, Mercader was a Communist sypathizer, and, also like his mother, he was recruited in 1937 as an agent of the NKVD, the notorious People›s Commissariat for Internal Affairs, a wing of Stalin›s secret police. In 1938 the NKVD selected Mercader for the task of eliminating Trotsky, who was living in a village just outside Mexico City. Trotsky had become a thorn in the side of Stalin, who wanted to be rid of him. After gaining the confidence of Trotsky›s supporters, Mercader finally got access to the villa of his »victim« on 20 August 1940, and did the deed. He was released from prison in 1960. Czech authorities issued him with a passport under a false name, which he used when living briefly in Havana, Prague, Moscow and allegedly also in the GDR before returning to Havana, where he died of cancer in 1978. At the request of his widow, he was buried in Kuntsevo cemetery in Moscow under the name of Ramón López Ivanovich. As early as 1940, Stalin had him appointed Hero of the Soviet Union and awarded him the Order of Lenin, one of only 21 people who were not citizens of the USSR to have received the honour.

JOAN MIRÓ (1893 – 1983)

Joan Miró was the second 20th-century Catalan painter after Salvador Dalí to become world famous. Born in Montroig, near Barcelona, the artist drew his first creative inspirations from French Realism and particularly the newly emerging Cubist style, which he was introduced to in Paris, during his first visit in 1919. Soon afterwards, Miró signed the **Manifesto of Surrealism**. In 1923, he turned away entirely from outdated painting styles and even the previous attempts of Cubism to create his own characteristic style.

Painter

His paintings are compositions of strong, calligraphic, emblematic lines with intense colours, which are not entirely abstract and encourage various different graphic associations. The artist also became greatly involved in graphic techniques, ceramics and sculptures. His work will forever be associated with the city of Barcelona. His art is omnipresent: printed on t-shirts, in the logo of La Caixa bank, and in the pavement on the Ramblas. One of his most famous sculptures is the bronze Solar Bird. Miró was a disciplined, hard-working, reliable and punctual man, and had a modest lifestyle. Despite his international reputation, his financial situation was always precarious. Mirò lived in Barcelona until the beginning of the Spanish Civil War, then in Paris until 1940. As German troops moved towards the French capital that year he fled back to Spain. He returned to France in 1944 after the liberation of Paris by the Allied Forces. After the end of the war he settled in Mallorca, where he died in 1983.

MERCÈ RODOREDA (1908 – 1983)

Mercè Rodoreda is the most acclaimed Catalan writer. Born in Barcelona, her first books were published in the 1930s and included the novel Paloma (1938), which won the Creixells Prize. Then for 20 years Mercè Rodoreda disappeared entirely from public view. She lived in Paris and Bordeaux, later near Geneva. In 1962, she published her novel **The Time of the Doves** (including an epilogue by the Colombian-born Nobel Laureate, Gabriel García Márquez, who died in 2014). The story depicts the ordeal of a young Catalan woman from the Barcelona district of Gràcia at the time of the Spanish Civil War (1936–39). Translated into 20 languages, it is her most fa-

Most important Catalan novelist

Stars from Barcelona

Barcelona has produced many famous people in numerous spheres, ranging from the visual arts, architecture and design, to music, literature, and the culinary arts.

The Architect

Whether in Tokyo, Paris, Metz, Houston, Chicago, Brussels, Madrid, Warsaw or Luxemburg, **Ricardo Bofill** sets architectural standards regardless of whether it is a building, such as the Catalan National Theatre in Barcelona, Barcelona airport, or an entire city, such as Antigone in southern France. Bofill, born in Barcelona in 1939 and educated at the School of Architecture in Geneva, has offices in Barcelona and in Paris that employ architects, engineers, and even sociologists and philosophers. The Catalan star architect is currently working on a scheme commissioned by the Algerian government to develop an ultra-modern city for 350,000 people in a practically uninhabited area at the northern edge of the Sahara desert, 200km south of the capital city of Algiers. He designed the W Barcelona Hotel, otherwise known as the Hotel Vela, at the tip of Barceloneta, which was completed in 2009. Completely clad in glass, the 26-storey five-star hotel looks like an enormous sail. Bofill also designed the Terminal 1 building at Barcelona Airport, which again opened in 2009.

The Prima Donna

Montserrat Caballé, along with Maria Callas and Joan Sutherland, is one of the most distinguished post-World War II sopranos, and one of the best-known celebrities in Spain. Born in Barcelona in 1933, the opera singer received her first musical training at the age of eight, at a conservatory in her hometown. She had her stage debut in 1956, at the Municipal Theatre in Basle, where she was under contract until 1959. From 1959–62, she was engaged by the Municipal Theatre of Bremen. In 1962 she returned to Barcelona. Until then, the soprano, who is fluent in German, had considered herself a singer of German works, an interpreter of the operas by Richard Wagner and Richard Strauss. Suddenly, however, she began to explore the Italian repertoire and sang Bellini, Verdi and Donizetti. In 1964, the Prima Donna married Spanish tenor Barnabé Martí. She achieved her international breakthrough in 1965, when she replaced Marilyn Horne at New York's Carnegie Hall in a concert performance of Donizetti's Lucrezia Borgia without any prior rehearsals. With her beautiful and versatile voice mastering all vocal techniques, Montserrat Caballé has sung at all major opera houses and concert halls throughout the world. The soprano, however, is not only restricted to opera. In 1987 she released a duet album with her friend, the late Freddy Mercury of the rock band Queen

(1946–91), and in 1988 they performed live together in Barcelona as part of the celebrations for city being chosen to stage the 1992 Olympic Games. The congenial singer has received countless international honours and awards, including being named Honorary Ambassador for the UN.

The Authors

Born in 1948 and based in Barcelona, **Enrique Vila-Matas** is one of the most significant living authors from Spain and Latin America. He is particularly popular in Mexico and Argentina, where he is considered a kindred spirit. Since 1973, Vila-Matas has written countless essays, short stories and novels, which have been translated into 15 languages and received numerous awards. In 2001, he received the international Ròmulo Gallegos literary prize. Vila-Matas is not easy to categorize. He often writes between genres, has a tendency towards anti-text and the absurd, and is not always easy to read. His works border between fiction and reality, hero and antagonist, and observer and observed are often blurred. Though born in Catalonia, the stubborn author composes his works in Spanish, as Vila-Matas believes he can more aptly express irony and distance by writing in a language that is not his mother tongue. Some works by the immensely well-read author have also been translated into English, such as the critically acclaimed Bartleby and Co (2001), Montano's Malady (2007), Dublinesque (2013) and Never Any End to Paris (2014). At times readers are faced with absurd questions such as: when committing suicide, can one be represented by someone else?

Alicia Giménez-Bartlett (born 1951) is regarded as one of today's most successful female Spanish authors. Her series of novels featuring the Barcelonan police inspector Petra Delicado was made into a 13-part TV series in Spain in 1999. Some of her books have been translated into English.

Carlos Ruiz Zafón (born 1964) received the Spanish »2002 Novel of the Year« award for The Shadow of the Wind. The suspenseful tale (translated by Lucia Graves and available in Phoenix paperbacks) is set in grey, post-Civil War Barcelona, and depicts the story of the young man Daniel and his quest for the vanished author of a mysterious book. This was the first of Zafón's »Cemetery of Forgotten Books« trilogy, the others being The Angel's Game and The Prisoner of Heaven.

The Designer

Cobi, the mascot of the 1992 Summer Olympics in Barcelona, is one of **Javier Mariscal's** best-known works. Born in Valencia in 1950, he moved to Barcelona in 1971, where he studied graphic design. In 1989, he and other graphic designers founded the Studio Mariscal, which is located in a former leather factory in Barcelona. His studio works in various different areas, such as textile and furniture design, interior design, and graphic illustration. Mariscal also publishes in countless magazines. In 1979, he designed the BAR CEL ONA poster, which became an emblem of the city. He has also been successful outside Spain, with exhibitions in Paris and at the Documenta in Kassel, for example. He created the new logo for the Swedish Social Democrats (1993) and a porcelain service for Rosenthal (1994). Furthermore, he has designed posters, brochures, decorations, TV commercials and cartoons.

Ferran Adrià ...

The Chef

He has been called the »most ingenious, craziest and most original chef in the western world«, the American magazine »Gourmet« even named him the »Dalí of the kitchen«, and in 2004, the French newspaper »La Monde« dubbed him the »World's Best Chef«. **Ferran Adrià** (born 1962) was until 2011 the head chef of the »El Bulli« restaurant near Roses, with its three Michelin stars. Adrià, son of a plasterer from a poor suburb of Barcelona, found his way into the culinary arts at the age of 18 when he worked as a dishwasher in a restaurant while studying business management. He taught himself, especially on his travels to France, and by the age of 22 he had be-

come the head chef of a high-class restaurant. Today, the Catalan is regarded as one of the most innovative chefs in the world, inspiring many other famous international cooks. Adrià's philosophy is to surprise the palate with unexpected flavours and contrasts in temperature. His menus – 30 tapas first developed while he was at »El Bulli« – are mainly comprised of jellies, purées, foams and sorbets. He used new techniques from medical and food science for his new and unusual creations. Since 2011, together with his brother Albert he has been running the »Tickets« tapas bar in Barcelona (Avinguda del Paral·lel 164) and the neighbouring »41°« cocktail bar. Meanwhile »El Bulli« has been converted into the »elBullifoundation«, intended as a place where cooks and gastronomic experts can develop new products and concepts.

The Female Chef

If Ferran Adrià is often known by the unquantifiable title of "best chef in the world", so there is little doubt about who deserves the ac-

... runs now the »Tickets« tapas bar

colade amongst female Spanish chefs – **Carme Ruscalleda** (born 1952). She is now internationally recognised as one of the very best in the business. Entirely self-taught, in 1988 she opened the Sant Pau restaurant together with her husband Antoni Balam in Sant Pol de Mar, a town to the north of Barcelona. It soon became clear that this farmer's daughter had an exceptional talent for the culinary arts. Just two years after opening, the Michelin Guide Rouge awarded the restaurant one star. It got its second star in 1996 and the third one came in 2006.

»Cooking is art, communication and culture,« says Spain›s only female three-star chef who, as well as the local Catalan cuisine also likes Japanese food culture. In Tokyo, she runs another restaurant that has been awarded two Michelin stars. The creations of Carme Ruscalleda are delicate works of art, perfect little bites that always look light and colourful. Her credo is very much »healthy eating meets enjoyment«, and she has even managed to make the passage of time itself slow down: for the »Moments« restaurant at the Hotel Mandarin Oriental Barcelona she has developed an anti-aging menu. Because she can›t be everywhere at once, her most faithful student works his magic there: Chef Raul Balam, her son.

The Fashion Designer

Custo Dalmau is Spain's most successful fashion designer. On a motorbike trip across the USA with his brother David, the former architecture student encountered, amongst other things, surfing fashion in California. Back in Barcelona, from 1996 the creative brothers began designing colourful shirts and t-shirts, to start with only for men. The bright and bold creations were well received in the States. In Los Angeles they positioned their clothing in shops whose customers included Hollywood stars.

The Catalans' big break came when their fashion featured in the TV series »Sex and the City«. With the all-over floral patterns, Japanese Manga comics motifs and patchwork elements, Custo Barcelona has developed its own style which is also admired by stars such as Christina Aguilera. »Custo Barcelona« now has outlets in about 40 counties.

mous work. Other publications include the poetic and surreal prose work Journeys and Flowers (1980), the family epic A Broken Mirror (1982) and Death and Spring (published posthumously in 1986), a disturbing parable on life in the closed world of a remote village.

ANTONI TÀPIES (1923–2012)

Artist Antoni Tàpies, who was born in Barcelona in 1923 and died there in 2012 is among the most important artists of modern times. His early works were strongly influenced by exponents of Surrealism, espe-

cially by Joan Miró ("Famous People), who was a close friend of his. At the beginning of the 1950s Tàpies encountered the newly emerging Tachism style (French tache = stain or blotch of colour), a variation of informal art that leads from Surrealism to total abstraction. Tapies' creations – he often worked with coloured mortar, ceramics and similar materials that are more malleable than paintable – are distinctive for their extremely alien language of signs and symbols. Tàpies also worked as a graphic designer and illustrator. The Fundació Antoni Tàpies in Barcelona, which the artist founded for the promotion of modern art ("Sights from A to Z), displays selected works from its extensive inventory in temporary exhibitions.

Two years before his death, in 2010, the artist received the hereditary title of Marqués de Tàpies.

MANUEL VÁZQUEZ MONTALBÁN (1939–2003)

Author Born in Barcelona in 1939, the vastly productive lyricist, novelist, essay writer and journalist Manuel Vázquez Montalbán counts among the most successful Spanish contemporary authors. Following his degree in journalism and humanities, the cult writer (»I'm just good at two things: writing and cooking«) worked as an editor for several newspapers.
He published more than one hundred novels, specialized books and cookery books, as well as volumes of essays and verse. His murder mysteries starring Detective Pepe Carvalho, a former communist and

CIA agent, whose adventures reflect Spain's political and social reality since Franco's death, made Vázquez Montalbán world famous. His thrillers, including Murder in the Central Committee and The Birds of Bangkok are some of the most successful in world literature. For his work he was awarded numerous international literary awards. Manuel Vázquez Montalbán died in 2003 in Bangkok.

ENJOY
BARCELONA

Where to go in the evening? What are Barcelona's specialities?
Where is shopping enjoyable? How can you explore the city?
Read about it here– ideally before you start the journey!

Accommodation

Way Up High

Just how popular Barcelona has become can be seen in the increase in bed capacity. In 1990 there were approx. 20,000 hotel beds available, now there are almost 70,000.

The average occupancy of 75% shows that there are not too many hotel establishments in the city. Therefore, it is recommended not to travel without a reservation, no matter what the season. If you do however arrive without a booking you can enquire about accommodation at the information points of the Barcelona Tourist Office at the airport and at the Plaça de Catalunya.

Book before you go!

Alongside the shared rooms or dorms in **youth hostels**, family-run pensions and hostels are the cheapest places to stay in Barcelona. Hostals are often located on one or more floors of a residential building. The rooms are generally smaller than in a hotel, but usually come with air conditioning and TV. Depending on the features and price, there is a shared bathroom in the hallway or in a private room. A one- or two-star hotel doesn't necessarily offer any more comfort and quality. For a double room in hostal expect to pay between €50 and €80. **Bed and breakfast** is also becoming increasingly popular, and there is a wide range of **apartments** and **holiday flats** to choose from.

Inexpensive accommodation

Nowadays you'll seldom find a hotel room for under €100. However there is a big choice of accommodation up to the €150 mark, and it shouldn't be a problem to find a room at that sort of price in the desired area. In addition to the district and price and quality of amenities, the location is extremely important. It isn't only on wide streets that you have to expect noise; it can be loud until early in the morning even on the narrow the streets of the Old City.

Hotels

The number of hotels in the luxury **four- and five-star category** has grown significantly. For a double room you usually pay €200 and upwards. They range from classic comfort hotels to business, boutique and design hotels, whereby the individual categories are not always clearly defined. Many establishments at this end of the market include swimming pool, fitness room, roof terrace, excellent restaurants and fashionable bars.

Depending on the day, season, availability and hotel booking website, room rates can vary considerably and deviate from the normal prices given here.

Hotel Catalonia Eixample in the Eixample quarter

Beauty Sleep

The new design hotels in Barcelona are cool-looking towers. They are relaxed and luxurious and almost always have an excellent restaurant and a spectacular bar.

❸❷ W Barcelona €€€€

The lift purrs to the 9th floor of the W Barcelona hotel. Completed in 2010, this five-star establishment has what it takes to be a real landmark. Located on the tip of Barceloneta, it is a 98m/322ft high sail made of glass, reflecting the sea and the sky. Designed by renowned architect **Ricardo Bofill**, it is somewhat reminiscent of the Burj al Arab in Dubai. Perhaps this is intentional, and Bofill wanted to create the Burj Barcelona.

Steeping out of the lift, you get to your room along the corridor that is red from floor to ceiling. It tapers outwards as you go along it to even out the perspective, i.e. appears to have no perspective at all. Opening the door you stop and gaze in amazement. It is evening already and Barcelona is lit by millions of lamps, windows and headlights. The darkening

Hotel W Barcelona was designed by star architect Ricardo Bofill

sky still has a blue cast over the sea; the water reflects the scattered light and the sky, heightening the feeling of being in a coastal metropolis. The view is literally sucked through the huge window of the fabulous room. The bed is in the middle of the room, with a generously proportioned desk behind it, and perfectly aligned towards the »Super TV« of night-time Barcelona. Instead of a sofa there's a comfortable seat along the length of the panorama window. A cocktail tray is at the ready.

Plaça de la Rosa dels Vents 1
tel. 93 295 28 00
www.w-barcelona.com

㉝ *ME Barcelona* €€€€

From the W to the ME. The clientele is the same – young people looking like models, business people and tourists who want to have a bed with a view. The ME Barcelona is situated on the Avenida Diagonal. The broad avenue leads to the Parc del Fòrum, where the trade fair of 2004 provided property developers with new possibilities for their drab schemes. The ME is an exception, standing tall over the low apartment buildings and workshops of Sant Martí. The Frenchman **Dominique Perrault** designed the 120m/394ft high, 29-storey building. It is composed of two slender structures that appear to have shifted against each other, creating a cantilever 20m above ground level and the entrance.

Diagonal / Pere IV 271-286
tel. 93 367 20 50
www.mebymelia.com

㉟ *Hesperia Tower* €€€

The Hesperia Tower by **Richard Rogers** is also among the architects' hotels of Barcelona. It isn't just the design that's courageous. The five-star business hotel stands guard over the suburb of L'Hospitalet de Llobregat, where low-income immigrants from southern Spain and other regions traditionally live. It looks like a UFO has landed on the roof of the hotel. This is where the Michelin-starred EVO restaurant treats its customers with a good head for heights.

Gran Via 144
tel. 93 413 50 00
www.hesperia-tower.com

⑭ *Omm* €€€€ **Insider Tip**

To get to the origins of design hotels in Barcelona, it's best to stroll up the elegant Passeig de Gràcia and look out for a building whose facade resembles stacks of open books. Jordi Maestro is the director of the Omm, which, although only opened in December 2003, has already become a classic. »The design is a must, one of the pillars of the hotel, its very foundation«, he says. Maestro sees the Omm as a pioneer of lifestyle hotels in Barcelona. A five-star hotel with a lounge that is also popular among non-residents, the Omm was the first establishment where the philosophy of opening up to the city has been successfully implemented. The hotel lobby and the multifunctional café and bar area are very pleasant. You just feel at ease, which is largely thanks to the abilities of **Isabel López and Sandra Tarruella** who were responsible for

the design. The rooms also achieve the right balance: the natural materials of floor, furniture and fabrics create a pleasing indoor environment while the satellite plasma TVs provide minimum interference with the design.
Rosselló 265
Tel 93 445 40 00
www.hotelomm.es

❺ *Mandarin Oriental* €€€€

The Mandarin Oriental opened a little further down Passeig de Gràcia in 2010. An entrance ramp, which gives the guest an almost Pharaonic feeling, leads up to a pure white patio that provides access to the core of the building. The design does away with the excessive orientalism that is typical of other hotels in the chain. Minimalist and with details done to perfection, the interior design lends the hotel a restrained elegance.
Passeig de Gràcia 38–40
tel. 93 151 88 88
www.mandarinoriental.com

❷❼ *Casa Camper* €€€€

Let's stay on Passeig de Gràcia for a moment. There at number 96 is the Vinçon design department store. When it comes to striking and well-designed furniture, accessories, kitchen appliances and more, this has long been a cherished institution. The team also takes orders for interior design projects. To get an idea about their style it's worth taking a look at the Casa Camper near the MACBA Museum in the Raval district.
The designers clearly had a lot of fun with this project. The Camper is playful, easy and creatively improvised. From a plain brick wall they created a vertical garden, or the serial experience provided by similar species of plants. The room layout is also unusual. The guest inhabits two separate spaces, a small living room with a hammock on the Old City alley side and a bedroom with bathroom overlooking the peaceful courtyard.
Elisabets 11, tel. 93 342 62 80
www.casacamper.com/barcelona

❸❹ *Grand Hotel Central* €€€

The Grand Hotel Central on the busy Via Laietana between the Barri Gòtic and La Ribera is another of the city's newer hotels. You make almost no noise at all as you approach your room on the sound absorbent carpet. The clear, restrained design matches the architecture of the townhouse dating from 1926. The bathrooms are also well-designed, semi-transparent glass compartments within the main space of the room. And the roof terrace is really spectacular. Each of these hotels has a roof terrace or a bar at dizzying heights but the view from the roof of the Grand Hotel Central surely deserves an award. Across an infinity pool you look over the rooftops of the Old City district of La Ribera. The backdrop doesn't look like a distant panorama, but so close that you only have to take a few steps out of the hotel to explore the alleyways.
Via Laietana 30, Tel 93 295 79 00
www.grandhotelcentral.com

RESERVATIONS
Gremi d'Hotels de Barcelona
tel. 0034 93 301 62 40
www.barcelonahotels.es

Barcelona On Line
tel. 0034 93 343 79 93
www.barcelona-on-line.es

Oh-Barcelona
Open House Barcelona
Apartments, private accommodation
tel. 00 34 93 467 37 79
in the UK
tel. 0203 499 5148
www.oh-barcelona.com

CitySiesta
Apartments and private rooms
tel. 00 34 646 713 179
www.citysiesta.com

Apartments BCN
tel. 93 456 16 19,
tel. 65 259 94 80
www.apartmentsbcn.net

PRICE CATEGORIES
Hotels (price for a double room)
€€€€ more than €250
€€€ €140–€250
€€ €80–€140
€ up to €80

Recommended hotels (▶map, p.104/105)

LUXURY HOTELS

㉔ Alma €€€€
Mallorca 271
tel. 93 216 44 90; 72 rooms
www.almabarcelona.com
Barcelona's newest five-star luxury establishment illustrates once more the importance of contemporary design and service. Whether from a fitness trainer or shopping consultant, the discerning guest will get all the help he/she needs. Over seven floors, modern materials combine with the historical substance of a townhouse from the early 20th century. The best Italian furniture and natural materials create a pleasant atmosphere in the rooms. The spa and an excellent restaurant are almost self-evident.

❸ Eurostars Grand Marina €€€€
Moll de Barcelona
tel. 93 603 90 00; 273 rooms
www.grandmarinahotel.com
This hypermodern five-star luxury hotel has been integrated into the large, representative building complex of the World Trade Centre on the Moll de Barcelona, offering every kind of luxury, contemporary elegance and state-of-the-art technology. The hotel includes several restaurants, a piano bar, a pool and a business centre. Right next to it stands the steel lattice mast of the harbour cable car.

❻ Arts Barcelona €€€€ Insider Tip
Carrer de la Marina 19–21
tel. 93 221 10 00; 482 rooms
www.ritzcarlton.com
International jetsetters like to meet at this five-star luxury hotel located right next to the Olympic marina. Spread across 44 floors in one of the two avant-garde towers at the Port, the hotel is marked by its high-tech elegance

Claris is a hotel for art lovers

and exclusive design and houses outstanding restaurants, bars, a fitness centre, pool and sauna, as well as meeting rooms. The elegantly furnished rooms, some of which are decorated with beautiful sculptures and paintings, as well as the balconies provide a breathtaking view of the ocean and the city.

❹ Casa Fuster €€€€
Passeig de Gràcia 132
tel. 93 255 30 00; 96 rooms
www.hotelescenter.es
The northern end of the Passeig de Gràcia is dominated by a building which Lluís Domènech i Montaner designed in 1908. The Casa Fuster was opened as a five-star hotel in 2004. Woody Allen was so impressed with the ambience of the Cafe Vienés with its columns that he shot scenes from his film Vicky Cristina Barcelona here. The rooms are tastefully designed,

with dark colours and highlights in red, violet and gold as well as curved forms mimicking Modernisme. In the evening the café is transformed into a jazz club. From the wonderful roof terrace with its pool you have a view along the entire Passeig.

❷ Claris €€€€
Pau Claris 150
tel. 93 487 62 62
124 rooms
www.derbyhotels.com
This five-star hotel, a member of Small Luxury Hotels of the World group, is in Eixample. It owes its reputation among other things its innovative design. The rooms are individually designed and furnished with pieces of Roman, Egyptian or Hindu art. Several restaurants, a bar, gym, spa and a rooftop swimming pool are at the guests' disposal, as well a beautiful views.

㉒ Hotel Neri €€€€

Sant Sever 5
tel. 93 304 06 55; 22 rooms
www.hotelneri.com

The location of this hotel alone, on the enchanting Plaza Sant Felipe Neri near the cathedral, is wonderfully romantic. Housed in a building dating from the 18th century, it is characterised by carefully applied, understated contemporary design, lending it an intimate and very pleasant character. Facilities include an excellent restaurant, a library and a sun terrace on the roof.

❼ Le Meridien Barcelona €€€€

Rambles 111
tel. 93 318 62 00
212 rooms
www.lemeridienbarcelona.com

This luxurious five-star hotel is often the preferred choice of film and pop stars. Double-glazed windows protect the modernist-style building from loud traffic noise. It is conveniently located near the main sights. Facilities include the Le Patio restaurant, a piano bar (with frequent live music in the evening) and fitness area.

COMFORTABLE HOTELS

❶ Catalonia Eixample €€€

Carrer Roger de Llúria 60
tel. 93 272 00 50
www.hoteles-catalonia.com
124 rooms

This four-star establishment, formerly known as the Catalonia Berna, is in a building erected in 1863–64, whose facade (►picture p.58) was painted by the Italian artist Raffaelo Beltramini. Very pleasant rooms, the best ones being those with the large balconies on the 6th floor.

❽ 1898 Hotel €€€

La Rambla 109
tel. 93 552 95 52; 173 rooms
www.hotel1898.es

Occupying a central location on the Rambles, this four-star boutique hotel offers much in the way of comfort. The spacious rooms in the former headquarters of the Philippine Tobacco Company reflect the colonial heritage of the building. Nice indoor pool in the vaulted basement, spa and roof terrace.

⓫ Alimara €€€

Berruguete 126
tel. 93 427 00 00; 156 rooms
www.alimarahotel.com

Away from the hustle and bustle, this multi-storey four-star hotel is located a 15-minute metro ride from Passeig de Gràcia. It offers a relaxing bar, a garden and suites with panoramic views.

❿ Condes de Barcelona €€€

Passeig de Gràcia 73–75
tel. 93 445 00 00
183 rooms
www.condesdebarcelona.com

This four-star hotel is housed in two facing buildings with landmarked façades and multi-level inside atriums. The interior has been luxuriously decorated with marble. The hotel features a roof terrace with a pool, as well as brasserie, bar and lounges. Also belonging to the Condes are the 2-star Lasarte restaurant (►Food and Drink) and the highly recommended Loidi bistro.

Insider Tip

A room in the Condes de Barcelona

⑯ Catalonia Porta de l'Àngel €€€
Portal de l'Àngel 17
tel. 93 318 41 41
74 rooms
www.hoteles-catalonia.com
Despite its central location in the pedestrian zone near Plaça de Catalunya and the cathedral, this three-star establishment is a good place to relax and unwind. Guests have a patio with large pool, garden and terrace at their disposal. The premium rooms in the historic 19th-century building have recently been renovated and done out in tones of dark grey and brown.

⑳ Husa Oriente €€€
La Rambla 45
tel. 93 302 25 58; 142 rooms
www.hotelhusaoriente.com
Traditional three-star establishment built around a Franciscan monastery in the 19th century, which has catered to famous guests including Arturo Toscanini, Maria Callas and George Orwell. Except in the impressive foyer and restaurant (with glass ceiling) the charm of this former Belle Epoque grand hotel has faded slightly. The rooms have recently been renovated, however, and anyone concerned about noise from the Rambles should opt for a room overlooking the open courtyard.

⑫ Expo Hotel €€
Carrer Mallorca 1-23
tel. 93 600 30 20; 423 rooms
www.expohotelbarcelona.com
This four-star hotel is located at Sants station, just a short walk from the convention centre and therefore particularly suitable for business people. With its beautifully redesigned interior, the hotel has several restaurants, a piano bar, sauna, solarium, hairdressers and a roof terrace with swimming pool.

⑲ Pulitzer €€€
C/ Bergara 8
tel. 93 481 67 67; 86 rooms
www.hotelpulitzer.es
The popular four-star boutique hotel is centrally located and conveniently close to the Plaça Catalunya. The style of the bright communal spaces with plenty of white furniture and a mix of contemporary, colonial and Asian elements is repeated in the well-equipped and comfortable rooms. Indoor pool, spa and fitness room.

⑮ Rivoli Rambles €€€
La Rambla 128
tel. 93 481 76 76; 125 rooms
www.hotelrivoliramblas.com

This hotel, housed in a restored Art Deco building on the Rambles, features a rich and varied interior design. Some rooms are tastefully classic, others done out in Catalan Modernista style, others in contemporary style and still others like in distant Japan. Original works of art decorate the rooms and communal spaces.

MODERATE

❾ Avenida Palace €€
Gran Via de les Corts Catalanes 605-607
tel. 93 301 96 00; 151 rooms
www.avenidapalace.com
Not far from the Rambles this traditional four-star hotel features an impressive spiral staircase and grandiose hallways that lead from the main lobby to the various lounges. The rooms are kept strictly classical in style, without concessions to modernity.

㉓ Catalonia Born €€
Carrer Rec Comtal 16–18
08003 Barcelona
tel. 93 268 86 00
90 rooms
www.hoteles-catalonia.com
Renovated in 2001, this three-star hotel is housed in a historic building in the Old City. The three to four-storey residence (including side wings that were formerly used as factory halls) surrounds a large and bright patio made of white marble, which is occupied by the restaurant, bar and lounge.

㊱ Barcelona Sants €€
Plaça dels Països Catalans
tel. 93 503 53 00; 377 rooms
www.barcelosants.com

This postmodern block at Sants station has recently been renovated. Sants is a good place to be for business people, trade fair visitors or anyone who needs good transport connections. As well as comfortable and practically designed rooms with panoramic windows, guests have a sauna, fitness room, office facilities and much else at their disposal.

⓭ Colón €€
Avinguda de la Catedral 7
tel. 93 301 14 04; 145 rooms
www.colonhotelbarcelona.com
Guests should like flowery wallpaper and textile patterns to fully enjoy the charm of this classic hotel. The four-star establishment lies right opposite the main portal of the cathedral. If you want a room with a view of the square and the cathedral, you may have to pay a bit more.

⓭ Granvia €€   *Insider Tip*
Gran Via de les Corts Catalans 642
tel. 93 318 19 00; 53 rooms.
www.hotelgranvia.com
The 19th century lives on in this magnificent Art Nouveau palais. The three-star hotel, with its beautiful staircase, dining rooms and lounges, opened its doors in 1935 following comprehensive renovation work. Some of the rooms have period furniture, but are otherwise quite plainly appointed.

⓱ Hesperia Metropol €€
Ample 31
tel. 93 310 51 00
71 rooms

www.hesperia.com
This three-star hotel occupies a former palais near the Passeig de Colom. The location at Port Vell will appeal to travellers who want to be close to the harbour. The rooms are unexciting, but bright and modern.

㉑ Sant Agustí €€ Insider Tip
Plaça Sant Augustí 3
tel. 933181658; 75 rooms
www.hotelsa.com
This three-star family-run hotel housed in a 17th century former monastery building, not far from the Rambles, offers good service and excellent value for money. The rooms, some of which come with a balcony, are simple and modern, yet comfortable. Many overlook the relatively calm square of the same name, which was revamped several years ago. Special family rooms are available. Good restaurant.

INEXPENSIVE
㉖ Antibes €
Diputació 394
tel. 93232 6211; 71 rooms
www.hotelantibesbcn.com
This dependable two-star hotel is located in the Modernisme district of Eixample, near the Sagrada Família. Alongside the comfortable rooms and friendly service, the fact that the hotel has its own car park might be a consideration.

㊲ Balcón del Born €
Rera Palau 2, Primero 2a
tel. 93 295 41 28; 5 rooms
elbalcondelborn@gmail.com
In recent times a number of pleasant and congenial B&Bs have opened up in the city. The Balcón del Born is run by a nice couple, and as its name suggests, is located in the trendy Born district. The rooms are clean and tastefully furnished. And the view out of the windows is as romantic as the interior.

㉕ Condestable €
Ronda de la Universitat 1
tel. 93 318 62 68
78 rooms
www.hotelcondestable.com
This two-star hotel is nicely and centrally located near Plaça Catalunya. The rooms are plainly furnished, but some of them offer a good view. Good value for money, especially if you book a few days in advance.

㉘ Hostal Agua Alegre €
Roger de Lluria 47
tel. 93 487 80 32
10 rooms
www.aguaalegre.com
This hostel lies in a parallel street to the Passeig de Gràcia. The Old City and shopping areas are easily reached on foot. The rooms of the historic building are spacious and simply furnished but very charming.

㉙ Hostal Oliva €
Passeig de Gràcia 32
tel. 93 488 01 62
www.hostaloliva.com
Good location on the Passeig de Gràcia. The family-run pension with en-suites or shared bathrooms is on the 4th floor, reached with an old wooden lift. Some rooms offer good views of the Passeig. No breakfast provided.

㉚ Lloret €
La Rambla 125
tel. 933173366
52 rooms
www.hlloret.com
Charming hotel on the Rambles, whose lobby and lounges feature details of the originally Art Nouveau building. The simple rooms all include a bathroom, TV, A/C, and some also a balcony. The loud street noise might make the view of the Rambles less enjoyable.

㉛ Peninsular €
Sant Pau 34
tel. 93302 31 38
59 rooms
www.hotelpeninsular.net
The Peninsular is a nice little hotel in Raval, housed in a former Carmelite convent, complete with a romantic courtyard. The atmosphere is relaxed and the rooms very simple and plain, looking out into the courtyard.

㉘ Barcelona BB €
Mallorca
tel. 63 797 72 63
4 rooms
www.barcelonabb.com
Anyone who takes a room in this pleasant B&B run by John and Kiku will almost feel like they're visiting friends. The furnishings in what used to be a flat in this Modernista building are luxurious compared to the spartan surroundings of other hostels. Style doesn't have to be expensive and there's a delicious breakfast too.

YOUTH HOSTALS
Alberg Mare de Déu de Montserrat
Passeig Mare Deu Coll 41-51
(in the Gràcia district)
tel. 93 210 51 51

Alberg Kabul
Placa Reial 17
(Barri Gòtic)
tel. 93 318 51 90
www.kabul.es

Alberg Pere Tarres
Carrer Numància149-151
(in the Les Corts district)
tel. 93 410 23 09
www.peretarres.org

CAMPING
Camping Masnou
Ctra. N-II km 633 Camil Fabra 33
08320 - El Masnou
tel. 93 555 15 03
Campsite located 15 km/9 mi northeast of Barcelona. With the regional FGC (Rodalies) train it's just 25 minutes into Plaça Catalunya.

Children in Barcelona

A Colourful World

Barcelona has a multitude of beautiful buildings and has some very interesting museums; it offers its visitors a big range of accommodation and gastronomic options, and is a paradise both for shoppers and for night owls. And the city is also a great place for children, because there is so much for the little ones to do in the Catalan metropolis! There's a host of spectacular attractions including sporting activities, great rides, child-oriented departments in museums and places to see wild animals.

Lots to experience spectacle

Watch, wonder and even actively participate: at the computer and playing the scientist. At the CosmoCaixa Museu de la Ciència, a »hands-on museum«, you can leave the little ones to explore the secrets of the world on their own or do it together with them. Compared to the modern amusement parks, the one on Mount Tibidabo is quite different, namely quite old-fashioned. But which Ferris wheel and which carousel gets you such fantastic views as those from Barcelona›s highest mountain? The bustling Rambles are another place for the younger generation to discover. There are street musicians, pavement artists, jugglers, fire-eaters, mime artists, not forgetting the ubiquitous »living statues« (Roman soldiers, cowboys, magicians, etc.), which always fascinate the kids and only interrupt their rigid poses to acknowledge a cash contribution. Among the crowds of Barcelona›s most popular shopping street, one should, however, always hold the little ones firmly by the hand!

Sporting activities

There are lots of sports for kids to do in Barcelona. There are ice-skating rinks and swimming polls, they can go riding or inline skating, and even in the cold season the miles of sandy beaches are the perfect place for running around. And of course the city can be explored by bicycle, or perhaps more comfortably with a Segway (► Tours and Guides).

Fun trips

Adventurous trips by air and sea are always a nice way to occupy children, and there is plenty to see: a ride on the harbour cable car, then a trip on the funicular up to Montjuïc or a journey on the Tramvia Blue and then the rack-and-pinion railway up to Tibidabo, where they can visit the amusement park, is always an experience. Also exciting is a 40-minute trip around the harbour with a golondrina from Moll de las Drassanes (in front of the Columbus Monument). A trip

This merry-go-round is on Tibidabo

in a helicopter is also possible, and so of course are city tours with the Bus Turìstic, other bus companies, horse and carriage and various other means of transport (►City Tours).

Animals trips Children can watch the animals not only in the Zoo but also the Aquàrium, where interactive areas for children have been installed on the top floor.

EXCURSIONS
Zoo
The dolphin shows held several times per day provide nice entertainment. Sometimes there are special guided tours, for example, to see baby animals. There are several playgrounds and a small lake with rowing boats for hire.
Daily from 10am, winter till 5.30pm, summer 8pm
Admission €16.50, children (aged 3–12) €10
www.zoobarcelona.com

Parc d´Atraccions
A number of rides (Ferris wheel, rollercoaster, haunted castle, water slides, children's carousel etc.)
Opening times vary greatly depending on the season
Admission: €25.20, children (90–120 cm in height) €9
www.tibidabo.cat

Poble Espanyol
In the Spanish Village you can experience a whole country in an afternoon. Among the replicas of famous Spanish buildings children can have fun with arts and crafts, puppet theatre and other activities.
The current programme for children can be found at www.poble-espanyol.com
Mon 9am–8pm, Tue–Sun till 2am, Fri till 4am, Sat till 5am and Sun

till midnight. Admission €9.50, children (aged 4–12) €5.60, family (2 adults and 2 children) €20.

Parc del Laberint d'Horta
Day-trip destination at the foot of the Serra de Collserola. This labyrinth and surrounding park with statues, temples, canals and a goldfish pond is a perfect place to play hide-and-seek.
Daily from 10am till dusk

Trenet Parc de l´Oreneta
For thirty years, a miniature steam train on which one can ride has wound its way through the park in the Sarrià-Sant Gervasi district. And it isn't just children who enjoy the ride on the 200 m long route.
Parc del Castell de l'Oreneta
Passatge Blada - Parc del Castell de L'Oreneta (Bus: 34, 60, 66).
Sun and holidays 11am–2pm
www.trenparc.org

MUSEUMS
Museu Marítim
The wonders of shipbuilding up to the steamer are documented here. The history of seafaring, including maps and battles offers fascinating viewing material for interested children. Irresistible, however, is the authentic replica of the galley from the famous sea battle of Lepanto, which you can go aboard.

Daily 10am–8pm
Admission: €2.50, children (aged 7–16) €1.25
www.mmb.cat

Cosmocaixa Museu de la Ciència

This is a museum (►p.202) with hands-on science: playful experiments about weather, motors, light and lasers. There is also plenty to learn about human functions (the senses) and animals (boa constrictors), and there is a planetarium and a special section for children.

Museu Blau

Rocks and plants, a stuffed lion and many other animals await in the museum of natural history collection.
Pl. Leonardo da Vinci 4–5 (Parc del Fòrum)
Tue–Fri 10am–7pm, Sat and Sun 10am–8pm
Admission: €7, children €5
www.museuciencies.bcn.cat

Museu del FC Barcelona – Camp Nou

Explore the largest football stadium in Europe, see the changing rooms of the stars and what it's like to run through the tunnel onto the field – a thrill for both little and large soccer fans. The ad-joining museum is a great repository of goals, cups and legendary names.
Aristides Maillol, Mon–Sat 10am–6.30pm (mid-April to mid-Oct till 8pm), Sun 10am–2.30pm, admission: €22, children (aged 6–13) €16.50, www.fcbarcelona.com

Museu de la Xocolata

How chocolate is made and what you can do with it, is shown here in an illustrative way. Ideal for little foodies.
Comerç 36, Mon–Sat 10am–7pm, Sun 10am–3pm, admission €4.30, children aged 7 and under free, www.museudelaxocolata.cat

Museu de Cera

The highlight for children after viewing the wax figures is always a visit to the museum café Bosc de les Fades, a whimsical fairy tale forest with elves and dwarfs, babbling brooks and spiders' webs in the corners. Enjoy some coffee and cake in the dim light while seated on a tree stump among bare-branched trees and bushes.
Summer daily 10am–10pm, otherwise Mon–Fri 10am–1.30pm and 4pm–7.30pm, Sat and Sun 11am–2pm and 4.30pm–8.30pm, admission: €15, children (aged 5–11) €9
www.museocerabcn.com

Bustling Nightlife

The Barcelonans like to go out, preferring to meet up with their friends and acquaintances out on the town in a bar or at a nightclub than at home.

And if you go out you tend not to stay in the same place all the time. »Ir de copas« – moving from pub to pub – is the motto. After the tour of a few bars it's off – especially at weekends – to the nightclub or some other form of evening entertainment. There's always a good atmosphere in the bars and bodegas, student bars and designer clubs, jazz bars and other music clubs, cocktail bars and music halls. People chat, discuss, flirt and laugh, and there's a lot of eating and drinking. On the way home or on the way to the next pub it might be noisy but you'll hardly ever encounter drunken behaviour and rarely see anyone who is badly dressed.

»Ir de copas«

Except maybe in Gràcia where the dress code is more relaxed and alternative, the night owls of Barcelona like dressing up. Young and beautiful people in fashionable and often expensive clothes frequent the clubs and bars of the city. Even the more mature contingent is out and about and likes to dress immaculately. But because there are as always numerous tourists from England, Scandinavia, Germany, etc. in the city, each with their own preferences and ideas about what constitutes proper style or cool appearance, of course, there is ultimately quite a mix and in many places you can wear what you want.

Smart or casual?

The countless bars and nightclubs are spread across the entire city, with virtually every neighbourhood having its own nightlife zone. In the **Barri Gòtic**, the Plaça Reial is a good place to start. The most popular old city quarter – quite regardless of age – is currently **La Ribera**. There should head for the Passeig del Born and see what takes you fancy either on the square or in one of the side streets. Cafés and bars can be found in the **Raval** around the Museum of Contemporary Art. It gets nostalgic and a little crazy in the bars in the Barri Xinès in the Carrer Nou de Rambla and in the dimly lit streets towards the sea. Further south, along the Avinguda del Paral·lel, the »Broadway of Barcelona«, you will find some good music clubs. The restaurants and bars on Passeig Maritim in **La Barceloneta** are chic and international. In the otherwise rather quiet **Eixample** district Carrer de Muntaner is lively at night and is as it were the centre of the gay scene (»Gaixample«). Other places to head for are the clubs in

Nightlife zones

Stylish nightlife at »Otto Zutz«

Poble Espanyol on Montjuïc and the beautiful garden pubs on the slopes of **Tibidabo**. Between June to August, in cooperation with club operators, the city sets up enormous tents at the harbour, on Montjuïc in the stadiums and on the heights huge tents where open-air parties of up to 15,000 people take place. If clubbing is what you're after, it's not worth going out before 10pm. The clubs only really fill up at around 2 or 3am.

CULTURAL OFFERINGS

Music, theatre and cinema The cultural palette in Barcelona is outstanding. Friends of classical music and opera are in their element here. The theatre and cinema offerings will be of particular interest to those who can understand Spanish and/or Catalan; movies are mostly shown in their in Spanish versions, while the reverse is true for the theatre with most performances being in Catalan.

Flamenco Thanks to the many migrants, who came from Andalucía to Barcelona from the 1960s in search of work, there is a vibrant flamenco culture complete with its own venues, the tabalos.

Night spots (map p.80/81)

BARS
⑲ Boadas
Tallers 1 (El Raval)
Just a few steps away from the Rambles and Plaça Catalunya, serious-looking men in dark suits mix their excellent drinks just like they always have. Nothing much has changed in this little cocktail bar since Hemingway's days – an institution with a lot of charm.

❸ Dry Martini
D'Aribau 162–166
(L'Eixample)
www.drymartinibcn.com
The classic interior of wood-panelled walls and thick leather chairs with round wooden tables might have provided a location for a James Bond movie. The cocktails they mix here are second to none.

❹ Eclipse
Plaça de la Rosa dels Vents 1
(at the Hotel W Barcelona, Barceloneta)
Of course the views are phenomenal – after all the Eclipse is located on the 26th floor of Hotel W Barcelona. But the bar in this new hotel is also really nicely designed. Even the narrowfBoada access to the two club areas with its precise illumination from drawer-like cubes raises expectations. The Eclipse is a glamorous place for nights out over Barcelona.

❽ Gimlet
Rec 24
(La Ribera)
The cocktail of the same name is prepared at the Gimlet by sharply dressed gentlemen, who like the

bar itself guarantee a stylish evening with a touch of the bohemian.

⑳ Pastis
Carrer de Santa Mönica 4
(El Raval)
After 10pm it gets very crowded in this dimly lit existentialist bar with chanson soundtrack. The pastis is a classic in the once infamous Barri Xinès, which has no need of keeping up with current trends and fashions.

㉑ London Bar
Carrer Nou de la Rambla 34
(El Raval)
Steeped in tradition, this Art Nouveau bar was one of Picasso's favourite haunts. Seated at the bar until the early hours, guests can enjoy assorted entertainment, from flashy drag shows to jazz performances.

❼ La Luna
Carrer dels Abaixadors 10
(El Born)
Successful mix of restaurant, bar and lounge. Very good food, fantastic choice of cocktails and great music in the background.

㉒ Marsella
Carrer de Sant Pau 65
(El Raval)
The Bar Marsella has been around since 1820. So it's an establishment with a lot of patina, where, after being banned from time to time, Absinth is once again served. The powerful brandy vermouth is nowadays diluted and drunk with sugar. The fact that overindulgence resulted in dizziness and even hallucinations in-

Picasso loved the London Bar

spired the imagination of artists such as Paul Gauguin and Toulouse-Lautrec.

❾ Schilling
Carrer de Ferran 23
(Barri Gòtic)
From the outside this establishment with the German name looks like a coffee shop, and at lunchtime and in the afternoon that's exactly what it is. Towards the evening the Schilling becomes a bar, a place where people meet to organise their night out, or a gay couple tell each other how their day was.

CLUBS

⑩ Bikini
Deu i Mata 105 (Les Corts)
www.bikinibcn.com
Salsa, funk, disco sounds or sometimes a live concert – in Barcelona's classic disco venue people are busy dancing in all three halls from Wednesday to Saturday.

⑪ Luz de Gas
Muntaner 246 (Eixample)
www.luzdegas.com
In this former theatre with its magnificent chandeliers, things only really get going at around 1am. Clubbers dance both on and in front of the stage to a varied music repertoire ranging from salsa to pop.

⑫ Magic
Passeig de Picasso 40 (La Ribera)
The Magic is a very popular, usually jam-packed club with dancing to the latest pop, Latin and rock. Sometimes with live music.

⑬ Moog
Arc del Teatre 3 (El Raval)
Barcelona is a major centre of electronic music. In the minimalist spaces of the Moog club, which gets its name from the legendary Moog synthesizer, predominantly techno, industrial and other types of electronic music are played.

⑭ Otto Zutz
Carrer Lincoln 15 (Gràcia)
www.grupo-ottozutz.com
This stylish nightclub covering three floors of an old textile factory has long enjoyed cult status. The motto is very much »see and be seen«. Sometimes there is live jazz. The bouncers take their job very seriously.

⑮ Razzmatazz
Carrer de Pamplona 38 (Poblenou)
www.salarazzmatazz.com
This music bar and club is a trendy institution. The huge loft with several areas for techno, pop rock, indie and other styles is situated some distance outside the centre in the industrial quarter of Poblenou. National and international bands also perform here, otherwise people dance like there was no tomorrow.

⑯ Sala Apolo *Insider Tip*
Nou de la Rambla 113 (El Raval)
www.sala-apolo.com
This beautiful ballroom, once Barcelona's largest vaudeville theatre, is one of the city's most interesting clubs. During the week the most varied of concerts and events take place (world music, Latin-American, Spanish or African music). On weekends the ballroom becomes the Nitsa Club with dancing and DJs.

⑰ Sutton
Carrer Tuset 13 (Sarrià-Sant Gervasi)
www.thesuttonclub.com
At the Sutton Club they tend to go for smarter looking, mainstream-style dancing. Up to 1400 people can enjoy themselves here from Thur to Sat from midnight.

LIVE MUSIC

⑱ Nits d´Estiu a la Pedrera
Casa Milà, Passeig de Gràcia 92 (Eixample)

Bikini Club is a classic disco venue

tel. 90 210 1 2 12
From mid-June to the end of August the roof terrace of the Casa Milà, better known as La Pedrera, is transformed into an atmospheric cocktail bar with live music. Listening to jazz and flamenco on the roof of one of Gaudi's buildings is a great way to spend a warm summer night.
Tickets in advance at:
www.telentrada.com

❶ Bel-Luna
Rambla de Catalunya 5
(Eixample)
www.bel-luna.com
The restaurant is open from 9pm and the musicians arrive on the stage from 10.30pm or 11pm. Every evening there are jazz concerts by local or internationally renowned artists. Those who don't want to dine have the cocktail bar. Modern ambience with club atmosphere.

❺ Harlem Jazz Club
Carrer de la Comtessa de Sobradiel 8 (Barri Gòtic)
tel. 93 310 07 55;
www.harlemjazzclub.es
Several artists have launched their careers at the Harlem, others who perform at this small venue have already established themselves as greats in the world of jazz or fusion.

❻ Jamboree
Plaça Reial 17
(Barri Gòtic)
tel. 93 319 17 89
Jazz and blues have been played at the cavernous Jamboree ever since Franco's time. Later on in the evening Barcelona's most famous jazz club is transformed into a jazz-free dance venue.

FLAMENCO
❷ Cordobés
La Rambla 35 (Barri Gòtic)
www.tablaocordobes.com
Flamenco actually has nothing originally to do with Barcelona. The passionate art form arrived with migrants from the south of Spain. Flamenco shows have been performed at the Cordobés since 1970, with famous artists sometimes making guest appearances.

Barcelona · Going Out

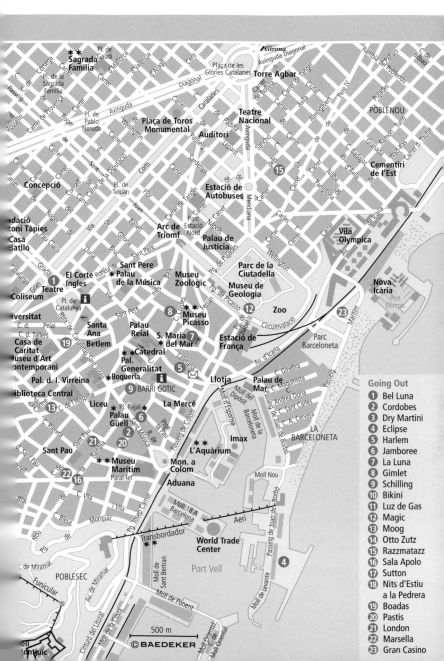

Going Out

1. Bel Luna
2. Cordobes
3. Dry Martini
4. Eclipse
5. Harlem
6. Jamboree
7. La Luna
8. Gimlet
9. Schilling
10. Bikini
11. Luz de Gas
12. Magic
13. Moog
14. Otto Zutz
15. Razzmatazz
16. Sala Apolo
17. Sutton
18. Nits d'Estiu
    a la Pedrera
19. Boadas
20. Pastis
21. London
22. Marsella
23. Gran Casino

Performances take place at 8.30pm, 9.30pm and 10.30pm. You can book them together with a meal or just a drink. From around 40 euros.

CASINO
㉓ Gran Casino de Barcelona
Carrer Marina19–21; Port Olimpic tel. 93 225 78 78
www.casino-barcelona.com.
At this casino gamblers can try their luck at roulette, poker or blackjack. A restaurant and dance floor are attached.

CINEMAS
The main streets for cinemas are Passeig de Gràcia and die Rambla de Catalunya. Multiplex cinemas can also be found in the Maremàgnum at Port Vell (Moll d´Espanya). Most films are shown in Spanish rather than Catalan. Films shown in the original are identified with »v.o.« (versión original).

THEATRE
Teatre Nacional de Catalunya (TNC)
Plaça de les Arts 1
(near Plaça de les Glòries)
www.tnc.cat
This theatre with two stages and one concert hall was opened in 1997. The temple to postmodernism was designed by the renowned architect Ricardo Bofill. The programme includes classical and modern plays in Catalan as well as dance performances.

Teatre Grec
Passeig de Santa Madrona 36
www.bcn.cat/grec
Every summer this amphitheatre on Montjuïc, which was built for the 1929 World Fair, is the venue for the Festival de Barcelona. The programme includes theatre performances, concerts and dance.

Mercat de les Flors
Lleida 59; www.mercatflors.org
This theatre is part of the Ciutat de Teatre, the »theatre city« in the old flower market near the convention centre on the flanks of Montjuïc. The modern stage is considered to be the top venue for dance theatre in Barcelona.

Teatre de Lliure
Passeig de Santa Madrona 40–46
Plaça Margarida Xirgu 1
www.teatrelliure.com
The »Free Theatre« is also part of the Ciutat de Teatre complex, the theatre city by the convention centre. There are two ultra-modern stages with contemporary and avant-garde theatre.

CLASSICAL MUSIC AND OPERA
Auditori
Lepant 150; www.auditori.org
Erected according to plans by Rafael Moneo, the Auditori is located just off the Plaça de les Glòries Catalanes. This concert hall is the home of the Catalan Symphony Orchestra.

Gran Teatre del Liceu
La Rambla 51–59
www.liceubarcelona.com
Even after its reopening in 1999, the auditorium of this renowned opera house remains an opulent feast for the eyes. The liceu can count itself among the leading

opera houses worldwide. Despite moderately modern tendencies, the productions are often classically grandiose.

Palau de la Música Catalana
Sant Francesc de Paula 2
www.palaumusica.org
Even if you're not there for a concert, this magnificent temple of Modernisme built by Lluís Domènech i Montaner is one of the highlights of Barcelona. When the Palau was built, Richard Wagner was one of the most respected composers among the art-loving bourgeoisie; the master of the Ring was as much a part of the programme as flamenco or guitar concerts.

PROGRAMME OF EVENTS
»Guia del Ocio« is the name of the weekly events programme (in Spanish), which provides a good overview of the current range of evening entertainment (from casinos to theatres, concerts, cabaret, pop and rock, all the way to striptease). The magazine is available at all newsstands and hotel receptions.
www.guiadelociobcn.es
www.atiza.com
At hotel receptions you can also find copies of the »What's On« magazine published in English and Spanish, as well as »Barcelona Prestige«, which also contain lots of information on nightlife etc.

TICKETS
Servi-Caixa, Telentrada
Tickets for concerts, theatre, shows and sporting events are available from all branches of the Caixa de Catalunya. Or online at:
www.servicaixa.com
www.telentrada.com

Puccini's _Turandot_ on stage at the Gran Teatre del Liceu

Festivals · Holiday · Events

Pure Enjoyment

Irrespective of the month or season you're visiting Barcelona, there's a strong possibility that some kind of festival will be going on in one of the barris (districts). It could take the form of a colourful folk festival with Sardana dancing, an open-air stage with local bands performing, or sporting events.

All of Barcelona is out and about when the city festival of **La Mercè** is celebrated in September, when fire-breathing dragons create pandemonium in a correfoc (firewalk), castellers build a human tower on the Plaça de Sant Jaume and gegants, giant figures in historical costumes, meander through the Old City. The spectacle goes on for four days and there is so much going on that that you'll need the 60-page programme in order not to lose track.

Exuberant spectacle

If you have the chance to experience the **Cavalgata dels Reis Mags** (procession of the three wise men) or the Diada de Sant Jordi, the festival in honour of the city's patron saint which is celebrated with books and flowers, will get to know Barcelona from its more exuberant, wacky side.

Sports fans will be interested to see what's going on at the **Montmeló** racetrack and whether **FC Barcelona** has a home game. However, getting a ticket to see Messi & Co play in a packed out Nou Camp stadium can be just as difficult as procuring one for the Liceu opera house. But both will make you happy.

Calendar of Events

PUBLIC HOLIDAYS
1 January: Any Nou (New Year)
6 January: Reis Mags (Epiphany)
19 March: Sant Josep (St Joseph's Day)
1 May: Diada del Treball (Labour Day)
24 June: Sant Joan (St John's Midsummer's' Eve)
29 June: Sant Pere i Sant Pau (Peter and Paul)
25 July: Sant Jaume (St James)
15 August: Assumpció (Assumption Day)

11 September: Diada Nacional de Catalunya (Catalonia's national holiday)
24. September: La Mercè (patron saint of the city)
12 October: Diada de la Hispanitat (Discovery of America)
1 November: Tots Sants (All Saints Day)
6 December: Dia de la Constitució (Constitution Day)
8 December: Inmaculata Concepció (Immaculate Conception)

The human towers are acrobatic masterpieces

25 December: Nadal (Christmas Day)
26 December: Sant Esteve (Boxing Day)

MOVEABLE HOLIDAYS
Good Friday, Easter Monday, Corpus Christi

FESTIVALS AND EVENTS
JANUARY
Cavalcata dels Reis Mags
Procession of the Three Magi. On the evening of 5 January the Three Kings arrive aboard an illuminated boat at the Moll de la Fusta, where they are ceremoniously greeted. The ships in the harbour sound their horns and the castle on Montjuïc fires a 21-gun salute. This is followed by the »cavalcata«, a horse parade through the city centre with music and dancing.

MARCH
Ralli Internacional de Cotxes d´Època
Vintage car rally from Barcelona to Sitges on the first Sunday in March. Since 1959 real museum pieces dating from 1900 to 1924 have chugged their way along the coast road from Sitges to Barcelona. By the way, the winner of the rally is not the fastest, but the team with the most original vehicle and whose attire is best suited to the vehicle.

MARCH / APRIL
Semana Santa
On Palm Sunday a market with palm leaves, Fira dels Rams, is held. The following Holy Week (Semana Santa) is marked by church services and celebratory parades.

APRIL
Diada de Sant Jordi
St George's Day (23 April), in honour of Catalonia's patron saint. It is the Catalan equivalent of St Valentine's Day, when loved ones are presented with flowers or a book. The Rambles is transformed into one huge market with flower and bookstalls, and shops also put out their books on Passeig de Gràcia.

Feria de Abril
Huge Andalusian folk festival with flamenco and culinary specialities at the Parc del Fòrum. Just like the original in Seville there are tents with sherry, dance and tapas as well as a fair. Dates vary between the end of April to early May.

MAY
Fira de Sant Ponç
Traditional honey market in the Old City, also selling cakes and spices.

JUNE
Sónar
This world-renowned festival for avant-garde music and video installations has been moved from the city centre to the suburb of L'Hospitalet due to its popularity.

Revetlles de Sant Joan
Mid-summer night festival with dancing and bonfires in many places, and a big fireworks display on Montjuïc, where the traditional coca cake is served; 23 / 24 June

Festival d'Estiu Grec
A cultural festival organized by the Institut de Cultura de Barcelona. Concerts, dance-theatre etc. from all over the world.

JULY
Processó Marinera de la Verge del Carme
The faithful pay homage to the Virgin in a boat procession, including city festivals in different quarters and the singing of sea shanties (habaneras).

AUGUST
Festa Major de Gràcia
Popular street festival with music, dance, theatre, cava and tapas in the district of Gràcia. www.festamajordegracia.cat

SEPTEMBER
Festa National de Catalunya (La Diada)
Catalan national holiday (11 September). Political rallies and demonstrations in remembrance of the conquering of Barcelona by the troops of Philipp V in 1714, a symbol of Catalan resistance. The Catalan national flag, the Senyera, is everywhere.

Fira del Llibre
Spain's most important book fair at the end of the month.

Festes de la Mercè
Insider Tip

Saints' day and the city's most important festival since 1977, with plenty of folklore, music and theatre performances, parades, acrobatic displays like the »castellers« (human towers), and performances by the fire spitting »gegants«.

Giant puppets called *Gegants* are part of many processions

Regional treats are also for sale, as well as fireworks etc. Held around 24 September.

LATE
OCTOBER / NOVEMBER
Festival Internacional de Jazz de Barcelona
Jazz sessions in the bars of the Old City, at the Palau de la Música and other venues. www.theproject.es

DECEMBER
Nadal – Christmas
For especially hardy swimmers there's the popular Copa Nadal race, which takes place in the harbour. Things get Christmassy from early December until 23 when the Fira de Santa Llúcia, the Christmas market, is held. Outside the cathedral Christmas decorations, crib figures, candles, incense sticks and other items are for sale.

Electro Sounds and New Design

Festivals large and small take place in Barcelona throughout the year.
The highlights, however, are reserved for the spring and the autumn.
Dance, design and lots of music are all part of the mix.

At the CCCB and the MACBA, the two centres for contemporary art and culture in the Raval district, young people sit in small groups on the ground. They smoke, talk among themselves or may be just taking a short break from an event. Many are waiting around for the next concert, others just want to be part of the scene – a picture of idyllic urban cool with the contrasting architecture of old and avant-garde as a backdrop.

Three Days

Every third weekend in June since 1997, Barcelona has been the centre of avant-garde music. The **Sónar Festival** is regarded as perhaps the single most important event in electronic music. The fact that a lot of multimedia art can also be experienced is thanks to open and progressive understanding of the scene, whereby art and music combine to create a massive event that has achieved cult status. 2014's event included Massive Attack, Rudimental, Boys Noize, Lykke Li and DJ Harvey. In addition to lots of well-known musicians and artists from around the world, many newcomers also turn up at the festival, which goes on for three days and is attended by around 80,000 people. The big Sónar party is usually held at the new **exhibition grounds on Gran Via** and goes on – how could it be otherwise – until the small

hours. Those who don't want to wait until the next festival in Barcelona have the option of other Sónar venues around the world at various dates, and can listen to Sónar radio any time they like.

Rocking

Bands and well-known DJs playing in the city every weekend. There isn't a city festival that doesn't have live music. In addition to Sónar Festival, another well-established music festival **is Primavera Sound Festival**. It takes place in early summer in May or June at the **Parc del Fòrum**. Unlike the Sónar programme, the sounds tend more towards rock, but in no way mainstream. Well-known acts such as the Neutral Milk Hotel, Queens of the Stone Age and The National appeared in 2014.

Sophistication

June is also when the **Grec Festival de Barcelona** starts, a programme of cultural events that goes on until the beginning of August, featuring theatre performances, classical music concerts, opera, dance theatre and other events. The appeal of the festival lies not just in its sophisticated programme but also its magical main venue, the **amphitheatre** at the foot of Montjuïc: the Teatre Grec was built for the World Fair of 1929, and is a replica of the ancient theatre of Epidauros in Greece. That the festival is now such an indispensable part of the city's cultural calendar is born out by the attendance figures: almost 120,000 people in 2013.

Dance Spectacle

Since 2009, another festival, the **Festival Dansalona** has taken place not far from the Teatre Grec, at the **Theatre Lliure**. This young international dance festival opens the cultural season after the summer break from late August to late September. In order that the Dansalona appeals to a broad audience, it features a whole spectrum of genres from flamenco to modern dance theatre to folk dances.

Exciting Design

Barcelona is a city of design. Fashion, furniture, interior design, product design, jewellery – the blend of »seny« and »rauxa«, of prudence and passion, inspired even the Modernista artists and architects to produce their unusual and independent creations. The atmosphere of the city, both cosmopolitan and steeped in tradition, has always had a positive effect on creative people. This is evident in the **Barcelona Design Festival**, which is celebrated with a variety of events, shows and exhibitions from July to October. The festival revolves around two main events, the FADfest and the Barcelona Design Week in October.
Independent of the festival and its various events you can check out the website of the BCD, the Barcelona Design Centre, where exciting design can be found.

All That Jazz

Jazz fans look forward every year to the autumn and the **Voll-Damm Festival Internacional de Jazz de Barcelona**. At least that's the official name of the Barcelona International Jazz Fesival, which has been sponsored by the Voll-Damm brewery for the last 12 years. It was in 1966, during the crippling Franco era, that this highlight of the jazz calendar began with a concert by Dave Brubeck. Now, with around 50 concerts performed by Spanish and international jazz greats, the festival is one of the most prestigious of its kind, with venues including clubs, dance halls and concert halls, such as the Auditori, Palau de la Música and JazzSí Club.

SonarRadio
www.sonar.es

Primavera Sound Festival
www.primaverasound.com

Grec Festival
www.bcn.cat/grec

Festival Dansalona
www.bcn.cat/barcelonacultura

Barcelona Design
Festival
www.barcelonadesignfestival.com

Barcelona Design Center
www.bcd.es/en/rutadisseny.asp

Voll-Damm Festival
International de Jazz de
Barcelona
ww.barcelonajazzfestival.com

Food and Drink

Diversity and Imagination

Gourmets can look forward to Barcelona: the city's experimental cuisine is world renowned. And whatever else, you should include a tour of some of the city's tapas bars. Among the most popular are the »tapas de autor«.

There are countless tapas variations. The simplest tapas are little bowls of olives or nuts that are usually served free with your drink. The more complex delicacies, freshly prepared each day - from meat, fish, seafood, potatoes or mushrooms - are usually lined up in glass cases at the counter. They arrive at the table in brown clay bowls or on small plates, and they are eaten with small forks or toothpicks. Of course, the small dishes can also be ordered as a »ració« – a bigger portion.

Tapas

In addition to the usual tapas there is a new type of appetizer called the »tapa de autor« – refined miniature dishes created by chefs of haute cuisine. At the forefront of this movement is the world-famous chef **Ferran Adrià**. His restaurant »El Bulli« at Roses on the Costa Brava is currently closed, but this means that the celebrity chef now spends more time in Barcelona than he did in the past: in the **Ticketsbar** (▶p. 108). Here he proffers culinary specialities that are meant to be an experience for all the senses: smell, taste, texture and appearance. Thus you can try out new sweet and savoury taste sensations with white chocolate and black olives in a single dish. Other places also offering exquisite »tapas de autor« are **Comerç 24** (▶p. 100) and **Dos Palillos** (▶p. 101) whose chefs once learned with Ferran Adrià.

Barcelona has transformed itself into a true gourmet destination. There are around 18 restaurants with one or two Michelin stars. However, the local cuisine is by no means an invention of recent years, nor the result of the innovative talent of just a few Catalan chefs. Rather, it can look back on a centuries-old tradition. »The cuisine of a country is its landscape in the pot«, the Catalan writer **Josep Pla** (1897–1981) once said. In fact, the diversity of the Catalonian countryside is reflected in the cuisine. The food on the coast, whose specialities are mainly fresh fish and seafood, are relatively light; hearty stews and dishes including sausage, game, mushrooms, trout, rabbit, lamb, partridge, pork and goat tend to come from the mountainous hinterland. Just how imaginative Catalan cuisine can be is

A true gourmet destination

Peix fregit, fried anchovis, are very popular throughout coastal Spain and of course in Barcelona.

Did you know?

It was the drug of choice during the Fin de Siècle – the »green fairy«. The poison-green absinth liqueur is said to have inspired Picasso and Van Gogh, but it has been a source of drama including death and injury due to thujon, the nerve poison found in the wormwood-based absinth, which is believed to cause hallucinations. For this reason, absinth was banned in nearly all European countries at the beginning of the 20th century. Since the early 1990s, the drink has once again been allowed in the EU, although now only with a fraction of the previous thujon content. Absinth bars are mainly found where Barcelona is at its most dimly lit – the Barri Xinès of El Raval: The Marsella Bar, London Bar and Bar Pastís (▶Entertainment).

also evident in the delicious combinations of fish and meat, which are called »mar i muntanya« (sea and mountain) in Catalonia.

Catalan cuisine experienced its first heyday in the Middle Ages, and so it is not surprising that the oldest Spanish cookbooks came from Catalonia and were also written in Catalan, such as the »Llibre de Sent Soví« of 1324. By the middle of the 15th century Catalan cooks were regarded as being amongst the best in the world.

Josep Pla, the great Catalan writer of the 20th century, also preached the still valid maxim that modern cuisine is inseparable from the traditional art of cooking, though of course there should always be some surprises in store. And you can look forward to them in the many restaurants and tapas bars of Barcelona. For the Mediterranean metropolis has always absorbed a variety of influences: the regional cuisines of its Catalan environs and hinterland, those of the Spanish migrants and all kinds of international concoctions that have found their way into local cooking pots via the sea and the harbour.

DRINKS

Alcohol free Local specialities can also be found among the drinks. A natural refreshing drink is the orxata xufla, a horchata served chilled that is available from the classic milk bars, the granjas, such as those along carrer portixol. In the cold season hot chocolate is also popular. It has the consistency of sauce and you eat it either with a spoon or by dunking in some freshly fried churros, those long spanish-style doughnuts made of choux pastry.

Coffee If it's cold outside, a »cremat« coffee flambéed with rum, makes a nice drink. Every type of Spanish coffee is made with espresso. »Café« is an espresso, »tallat« contains a shot of milk, and »café amb llet« is a half espresso and half milk.

Beer (cerveza) is now more popular than wine in Spain. People Beer drink Pilsner-style lager beer. To order a draught beer ask for »una caña«; for a bottle (botella), »una cerveza«. Among the best-known Spanish beers is San Miguel, while a popular Catalan brand is Estrella Damm, which is brewed in Barcelona. Numerous other lagers are also served in Barcelona, including popular German and Czech brands.

From the wine regions of Catalonia come wide range of wines: red, Wine white and rose wines as well as heavy dessert wines, brandies and sparkling wines. Catalonia has a total of eleven regions and districts which like all Spanish wine regions are protected by the D.O. (designation of origin/denominació d'origen) classification system: Catalunya, Alella, Conca de Barberà, Costers del Segre, Empordà Costa Brava, Montsant, Penedès, Pla de Bages, Priorat, Tarragona and Terra Alta.

Cava is the bubbly favourite drink of the Catalans – a sparkling Cava wine produced according to the standard French Champagne process of bottle fermentation. Around 95 % of Cava comes from Catalonia, and of that, some 90 % from the Penedès region southwest of Barcelona, primarily in the area around the town of Sant Sadurní d'Anoia.

RESTAURANTS

Breakfast in Spain is spartan and is normally taken between 8am and Breakfast 10am in a bar. It usually only consists of coffee with a slice of toast or a small piece of cake. However, hotels have adjusted to the needs of their guests and offer a varied breakfast menu or breakfast buffet. Unlike breakfast, lunch and dinner are more elaborate, with three courses being the norm for both meals. The »menú del día« (menu of the day) offered at nearly all restaurants is usually better value than ordering a la carte.

Lunch is never eaten before 1pm, and normally it is after 2pm. In the Lunch evening people meet for dinner at 9pm at the earliest, and more often at 10pm. Most restaurant kitchens remain open until midnight. In addition, there are many restaurants that serve hot meals all day. A large number of restaurants are closed on Sunday evenings and during August.

Despite the fact that the bill includes service charge, a tip of between Tipping 5% and 10% is still expected. In a bar it is normal to leave small change on the counter.

Typical Dishes

Barcelona's pubs have many delights to offer their guests. It is above all »little things« that delight the palate.

Pa amb tomàquet: the simplest dish in Catalonia, but certainly the most popular snack in the Catalan daily routine is the tomato bread Pa amb tomàquet: hearty rustic bread that is first toasted and then smeared with a halved, ripe tomato until the juice and seeds coat it, and topped off with a little olive oil and salt.

Tapas: Usally just a snak but each snack is a dish in itself. Among the most popular tapas are »Gambes a la Planxa« (fried shrimp with garlic), »Empanada de Pebrots i Tonyina« (baked tuna and paprika pie), »Escabetx de Sardines« (fried sardines in spicy vinegar marinade) and »Croquetes de Pollastre i Peril« (croquettes with chicken and ham).

Pintxos: at the forefront of the tapas movement in Barcelona were the numerous Basque pubs. Here the tapas were called »pintxos« (little snacks) – appertisers with fish, meat, vegetables etc. on a piece of white bread, all of it held together by a toothpick. The Pintxos are lined up on trays on the bar top and you can usually help yourself; the price is calculated according to the number of toothpicks.

Jamón: Like all Spanish people the Catalans love their ham. On the walls and ceilings of rustic restaurants hang hams by the dozen. The real classic is Jamón Serrano, which is salted and dried, and then aged for at least another twelve months. Even finer is the Jamón ibérico. Three months before being slaughtered pigs of the pata negra breed are fed exclusively on acorns, which lends the ham a nutty flavour.

Crema Catalana is the quintessential Catalan dessert. It is made of egg yolk, milk, sugar, cinnamon, vanilla and lemon zest and served cold in shallow clay dishes. Before serving, the creamy mixture is sprinkled with cane sugar, which is then quickly caramelised in the oven. The sugar is still caramelized in the traditional way, which involves melting it with a specially designed circular branding iron that has been heated over a flame. The sugar gets so hard that it's like a thin layer of glass that splinters when you eat it.

Dolços i pastissos: cakes and pastries – Barcelona has very fine confectionary. The importance of the role played by cakes and pastries here is demonstrated by the fact that Barcelona's first patisseria opened as long ago as 1382, while Paris only got its first one in 1608.

The Haute Cuisine of Chocolate

When star chefs such as Ferran Adrià revolutionized haute cuisine, the art of chocolate making also experienced a renaissance. The centre of this not always sweet art is Barcelona. Here they treat the dark cocoa masses as artistic material, something that has been imitated around the world.

More of an artist than patissier, **Oriol Balaguer** one of the stars among Barcelona's chocolatiers. Now in his early forties, he has collected so many awards, from the »Best Spanish Dessert Chef« to the »Best Dessert in the World« to the »Best Patissier in Catalonia«. There are branches in Barcelona, Madrid and Tokyo, which present the product of chocolate as if it were a piece of jewellery. Bows and silver paper are taboo. The new chocolate culture is classy and urban – perfect for the trendy city of Barcelona.

Perfectionist

Oriol Balaguer's shop lies off the beaten tourist track on Plaça Sant Gregori Taumaturg, southwest of the Old City. With its cool light and glass design it is reminiscent of a perfumerie. »We try to think of everything, not just about the product and how it looks«. Balaguer is convinced that the appeal of his creations is also influenced by the presentation of the packaging and the store design. »It is like in a museum, where there are precious paintings and the building itself is like a sculpture. Even if its just a feeling when you enter the shop you should be able to cherish the time you spend there«, says the maître.

Balaguer does not think in the display-window format of his confectioner guild. He is a perfectionist with great ambition. Why should there not be **Haute Cuisine for desserts**? Balaguer spent seven years working with the team at the famous »El Bulli« restaurant in Roses on the Costa Brava. »My time there was fundamental for my professional development. Adrià opened my eyes«, he explained.

»Xocalater«

When the **chocolate boom** began about ten years ago began and developed into a worldwide success, which was followed by the major chocolate manufacturers with fine cocoa and chilli chocolates and the like, Barcelona just took back what had been made famous by countries such as France, Belgium and Switzerland – the art of fine chocolate. The cacao bean and chocolate found their way to Europe via Spain. As long ago as 1550 hot chocolate was drunk at the royal court in Madrid. By the middle of the 17th century the Spanish had the monopoly on the trade in cocoa beans. In Catalonia and especially in Barcelona the profession of chocolatier, the »xocalater« as he is called in Catalan, has been around since the 18th century.

Patisseria Escribà produces wonderful pastries in a wonderful set

The inventions of solid chocolate in bars, milk chocolate and the refined variants such as filled pralines, were made in England, Belgium and Switzerland. It is not surprising that comparable developments can be found in 19th-century Barcelona. The Catalan capital was pretty much the only city on the Iberian Peninsula that emulated the fashion and trends as well as the technological and industrial innovations coming from the North.

True Artists

A tradition particularly popular with children are the so-called »Mona de Pasqua«, which can be approximately translated as »Easter Figures«. They can be artful chocolate eggs or even entire landscapes and scenes, which are painstakingly put together from special-

ly moulded chocolate bars.

That **Enric Rovira** – another maître of new chocolate art – can easily be cast in the Catalan tradition of the »monas« might seem puzzling at first. These creations of the Catalans are even more avant-garde than those of Oriol Balaguer. Rovira's working methods are similar to those of the modern gourmet kitchen: selection, deconstruction, minimalism. His style and his innovations, and even the design of the packaging, have been adopted by other chocolatiers.

At the beginning of his career the man with the twinkling eyes tinkered with little houses and figures just like his idols Antoni Escribà and Joan Giner. Then he went in search of architectural motifs of the Mediterranean city. So he moulded the small tiles, the »rajoles«, of which Barcelona›s sidewalks are paved, and recreated in miniature the floor tiles that Gaudí designed for the residential building »La Pedrera«. Over the years Rovira›s concepts have become ever more sophisticated. Artists are commissioned to come up with new shapes and textures. He even developed a planetary system from chocolate balls, that›s much too nice to simply pop in your mouth. And he has tried doing a gourmet version of John Lennon's *Imagine*; the sensations of the music are recreated on the tongue with different flavoured pralines.

The fashion of combining chocolates with unusual flavours such as ginger, pepper, corn, salt or olive oil has a long tradition in Catalonia, as Rovira is well aware. »A casserole without chocolate is not worth a potato«, goes a Catalan saying. When one thinks of squid with chocolate, a specialty from Tarragona, Enric Rovira›s fried pork belly pieces in chocolate are not all that unusual.

Strategically Located

Carles Mampel has also successfully joined the bandwagon of sweet delights. His »bubó« patisserie is strategically situated opposite the Church of Santa Maria del Mar and after a brief peek inside to survey of the rows of delicacies it's already too late. Suddenly you find you've ordered a coffee and an outrageously delicious morsel to go with it, such as the Xabina, an award-winning chocolate cake made with chocolate mousse, egg yolk, olive oil dough and vanilla.

Everything's Possible

The list would not be complete without the traditional family-run **Escribà**. This pastry shop on Gran Via is a Barcelona institution; its late maître Antoni Escribà, who died way back in 2004, a legend. It is difficult to imagine what has been invented in this establishment and all the incredible things from chocolate, sponge cake, marzipan and candy mass that have been created here. Whether it's a metre-high wedding cake or a chocolate sculpture that has to go round 12,000 guests, »tell us what you want and we make it«, explains Xavier Marco. Their own PR man leaves no doubt that nothing is impossible for the brothers Escribà. In addition to chocolate sculptures for which one needs a forklift, somewhere among the spectacular array there must even be cakes that explode at the touch of a button.

CHOCOLATE SHOPS
Oriol Balaguer
Plaça Sant Gregori Taumaturg 2
www.oriolbalaguer.com

Enric Rovira
Josep Tarradellos 113
www.enricrovira.com

Escribà
Gran Via 546
Rambla de los Flores 83
Ronda Litoral 42
www.escriba.com

Bubó
Caputxes 10
www.bubo.es

Recommended restaurants (map p.104/105)

PRICE CATEGORIES
Restaurants (price for a
main course)
€€€€ = more than €30
€€€ = €25 – 35
€€ = €15 – 25
€ = up to €15

GOURMET
㉘ÀBAC €€€€
Avinguda Tibidabo 1
tel. 93 319 66 00, 93 254 22 99
www.abacbarcelona.com
Closed Mon midday, all day Sun
This gourmet restaurant run by
the young chef Xavier Pellicer,
who learnt his trade at Can Fabes,
is not exactly cheap. The reward is
inventive yet not overly preten-
tious creations. A good tip both
for experienced gourmets and curious guests with a pioneer spirit.

㉖Gaig €€€€
Carrer d'Aragó 214
tel. 93 429 10 17
www.restaurantgaig.com
Closed Mon
This long established restaurant is
run by top chef Carles Gaig and is
situated in Hotel Cram. Once a bar
for truck drivers, it is now among
the city's best culinary addresses.
The variety and originality of the
traditionally Catalan to modern
Mediterranean dishes with Haute
Cuisine appeal and the heavenly
deserts have earned this place a
star in the Michelin guide.

❾Hofmann €€€
La Granada del Penedès 14 – 16
tel. 93 218 71 65
www.hofmann-bcn.com

This small, exclusive restaurant in
the Old City is run by the renowned top chef Mey Hofmann,
whose school has produced many
famous cooks. The selection of
primarily Mediterranean-styled
dishes and suitable wines is ac-
cordingly superb. Particularly satis-
fying is the flawless, extremely
courteous service.

❷Lasarte €€€€
Hotel Condes de Barcelona
Mallorca 259
tel. 934 45 32 42 93
www.restaurantlasarte.com
Closed Sun, Mon and during
August.
Martin Berasategui is one of the
great masters of Spanish cuisine.
He has been in charge of the
two-star Lasarte restaurant at the
Hotel Condes de Barcelona for
almost 10 years. The Basque's
creations are elaborated and
perfectionist, his desserts outstanding. The service befits the category.

❶Neichel €€€
Beltran i Rózpide 1-5
tel. 93 203 84 08
www.neichel.es
Closed Sun and Mon
This acclaimed restaurant, run by
the Alsatian top chef Jean-Louis
Neichel is in the centre of Pe-
dralbes, a posh residential area of
Barcelona. It offers stylishly served
French and Mediterranean cuisine.
It is known for its wide selection
of cheeses and desserts as well as
an exceptional wine cellar. It was
Neichel who built up Ferran
Adrià's »El Bulli« restaurant

Tragaluz is famous beyond Barcelona's limits

⓰ Via Veneto €€€€
Ganduxer 10 – 12
tel. 93 200 72 44
www.viavenetorestaurant.com
Closed Sat midday and Sun
A first-rate restaurant with some nostalgic charm. The classic Catalan cuisine, subtly elaborated upon by star chef Josep Muniesa, has made this a top address among Barcelona's establishment and a respected school for emerging master cooks for three decades. Notable wine list.

CHIC AND CREATIVE
❸ BRAVO 24 €€€
Plaça de la Rosa dels Vents 1 (W Hotel); tel. 93 295 26 36
www.w-barcelona.com/bravo-signature-restaurant
After the success of his Comerç24 and Tapas 24 restaurants, the star chef and Ferran Adrià student Carles Abellan has now taken over the management of the Bravo 24. Abellan uses the best ingredients of the region, whose taste he presents as pure and unadulterated as possible. The name of the stylishly elegant restaurant in the W Hotel says it all – »bravo« means wild or undaunted. Meat is grilled over different woods depending on its type and origin.

⓮ Comerç 24 €€€
Comerç 24
tel. 93 319 21 02

Closed Sun and Mon
This restaurant with hypermodern, mainly red and black decor, is run by Carles Abellán, a student of Ferran Adrià, and offers no less hypermodern minimalist cuisine featuring up to 30-course menus of inventive tapas creations. Not necessarily the place for a filling meal, but always good for surprises.

㉕ Dos Palillos €€

Carrer Elisabets 9
tel. 934 04 05 13
www.dospalillos.com
Closed Sun and Wed midday
This small restaurant next to the Camper hotel serves Far Eastern fusion cuisine in the Spanish tapas style. Takeshi Somekawa and Albert Raurich, who previously worked as head chef at »El Bulli«, are responsible for the unusual creations. Guests sit at a bar around the kitchen where the little delicacies are prepared.

㉚ Moo €€€

Hotel Omm Rosellón 265
tel. 934 45 40 00
Closed Sun
Like no other luxury hotel, the Omm manages to combine elegance and quality with effortless style. This also applies to the excellent restaurant. In a relaxed atmosphere, the Roca brothers astound their guests with accomplished Mediterranean dishes. The lunch menu is popular and highly recommended.

❽ Tragaluz €€

Passatge de la Concepció 5
tel. 93 487 06 21; open daily

MARCO ⊕ POLO TIP

! Sweet Menu *Insider Tip*

The ㉓ **Espai Sucre** €€ is in a way a restaurant just like any other. There is the starter, main course and dessert, a good selection of wine to go with the food and everything else you need for a good meal. Nevertheless one does dine rather differently here. With Jordi Butrón and his team the dessert has cast off its role of coveted, but if needs be also dispensable appendage of a sequence of courses, and takes centre stage. The whole variety of the dessert, from frothy, crispy or creamy texture to bitter, salty or acidic notes can be savoured from a menu that opens new sensations for the palate. The menu costs around €40.
Princesa 53, tel. 93 368 16 30
Tue–Thur 9pm–11.30pm, Fri and Sat in two sittings at around 8.30pm and 10.30pm.
www.espaisucre.com

www.grupotragaluz.com
This modern restaurant won an award for its inventive interior (created by the star designer Javier Mariscal), with guests seated beneath a sloping glass ceiling. The restaurant upstairs offers international dishes, while the entire downstairs is reserved for the bar serving drinks and tapas and an excellent patisserie.

COAST AND SEA

❼ Agua €€

Passeig Marítim de La Barceloneta 30
tel. 93 225 12 72
www.grupotragaluz.com

This pleasant little fish restaurant with its terrace right on the sea is of better quality than many others in the area. The simple yet inviting dishes are fresh and well prepared, whether you're ordering just tapas or an entire menu.

㉗ Cal Pep €€
Plaça de les Olles 8
tel. 93 310 79 61
www.calpep.com
Closed Mon midday, Sun and holidays
Fish and seafood are served at the very busy bar of this popular fish restaurant, from where it is interesting to observe the preparation of the various tapa dishes. Those wishing to eat in the comfortable, usually jam-packed restaurant area in the back should definitely reserve a table. The daily lunch menu of traditional dishes is also much in demand.

❺ Cal Pinxo €€
Plaça Pau Vila 1
tel. 93 221 22 11
www.calpinxo.com
This restaurant is located in the Palau de Mar at the north end of the old harbour. Delicacies from the sea, prepared in a variety of ways, are served in a cultured atmosphere.

⓲ Can Costa €€
Passeig Joan de Borbó 70
tel. 93 221 59 03
www.cancosta.com
Closed Wed, Sun evening
The famous Can Costa is among the most traditional establishments of the Barceloneta fishing quarter. In addition to fish, they serve magnificent rice dishes. Guests can watch the food being prepared.

㉑ El Cangrejo Loco €€
Moll de Gregal 29 – 30
tel. 93 221 05 33
www.elcangrejoloco.com
Open daily
This good restaurant with relatively moderate prices at the Port Olímpic was opened for the 1992 Olympic Games. The kitchen is visible from both dining areas. Upstairs offers a lovely view across the harbour.

HEARTY AND TRADITIONAL

⓳ Agut €€
Carrer Gignàs 16
tel. 93 315 17 09
Closed Sun evening, Mon
A classic among Barcelona's restaurants. Located in a narrow street in the south of the Old City, this down-to-earth restaurant was established in the 1920s. An old haunt for artists, as proven by the pictures on the walls, the restaurant serves Catalan dishes including excellent fish specialties, exquisite starters and desserts. It is good value for money and the tables are full every evening, so book in advance.

㉙ Can Culleretes €€
Carrer Quintana 5
tel. 93 317 30 22
www.culleretes.com
Closed Sun evening, Mon
The oldest restaurant in the city, opened in 1786, is a bit stuffy, but pleases guests with a solid Catalan menu. Paintings and tiles

decorate the walls, wooden beams on the ceilings.

⑥ Can Travi Nou €€€€

Jorge Manrique
tel. 93 428 03 01
www.gruptravi.com/nou
Closed Sun evening

This down-home restaurant with garden is in an old country manor house at the foot of the Serra de Collserola, serving traditional, regional fare.

⑪ I Qué? €

Topazi, Gràcia
tel. 93 416 07 533

Cosy restaurant in Gràcia. Try the tapas, patatas bravas (with Guacamole, eggplant puree or homemade salsa) or marinated chicken wings.

⑩ Els Quatre Gats €€

Carrer de Montsió 3 bis
tel. 93 302 41 40

www.4gats.com
Open daily

A hundred years ago, the legendary »Four Cats« was a well-known meeting place for artists (Pablo Picasso had his first exhibition here in 1900). Today the large, well-attended dining room serves traditional Catalan dishes (also in smaller portions). With its authentically restored Art Nouveau interior, the place is also well worth a visit just for a drink.

⑳ Los Caracoles €

Escudellers 14
tel. 93 302 31 85
www.loscaracoles.com
Open daily

As the name suggests, snails are the speciality at this warren-like traditional restaurant (a favourite of Dalí) near the Rambles. They also offer excellent, rustic Catalan cuisine and a notable selection of grilled dishes.

Picasso started his career at Els Quatre Gats

Barcelona · Restaurants, Hotels, Cafés and Tapa Bars

Where to stay

1. Catalonia Eixample
2. Claris
3. Eurostars Grand Marina
4. Casa Fuster
5. Mandarin Oriental Barcelona
6. Arts Barcelona
7. Meridien Barcelona
8. 1898 Hotel
9. Avenida Palace
10. Condes de Barcelona
11. Alimara
12. Expo Barcelona
13. Colón
14. Omm
15. Rivoli Ramblas
16. Catalonia Porta de l'Angel
17. Hesperia Metropol
18. Granvia
19. Pullitzer
20. Husa Oriente

21. Sant Agustí
22. Neri
23. Catalonia Born
24. Hotel Alma
25. Condestable
26. Antibes
27. Casa Camper Barcelona
28. Hostal Agua Alegre
29. Oliva
30. Lloret
31. Peninsular
32. W Barcelona
33. ME Barcelona
34. Gran Hotel Central
35. Hesperia Tower
36. Barcelona Sants
37. Balcón del Born
38. Barcelona BB

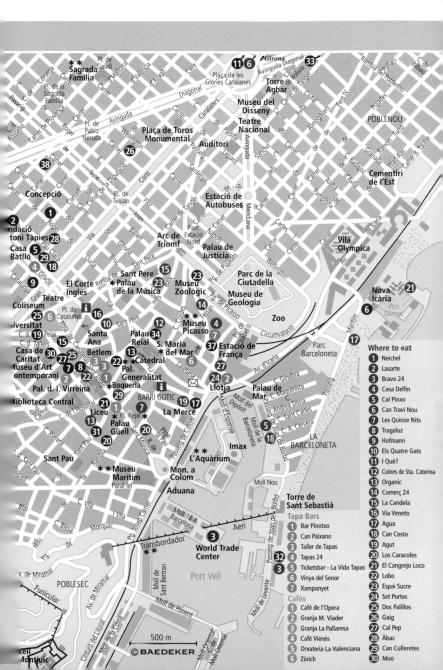

Where to eat
1. Neichel
2. Lasarte
3. Bravo 24
4. Casa Delfin
5. Cal Pinxo
6. Can Travi Nou
7. Les Quinze Nits
8. Tragaluz
9. Hofmann
10. Els Quatre Gats
11. I Qué?
12. Cuines de Sta. Caterina
13. Organic
14. Comerç 24
15. La Candela
16. Via Veneto
17. Agua
18. Can Costa
19. Agut
20. Los Caracoles
21. El Cangrejo Loco
22. Lobo
23. Espai Sucre
24. Set Portes
25. Dos Palillos
26. Gaig
27. Cal Pep
28. Àbac
29. Can Culleretes
30. Moo

Tapa Bars
1. Bar Pinotxo
2. Can Paixano
3. Taller de Tapas
4. Tapas 24
5. Ticketsbar - La Vida Tapas
6. Vinya del Senor
7. Xampanyet

Cafés
1. Café de l'Opera
2. Granja M. Viader
3. Granja La Pallaresa
4. Café Vienés
5. Orxateria La Valenciana
6. Zürich

© BAEDEKER

㉔ Set Portes €€€
Passeig Isabel II 14
tel. 93 319 30 33
www.7portes.com
Open daily
This restaurant near the north end of the old harbour (Port Vell) was opened in 1836 and counts among the city's most traditional establishments. The delicious paella is definitely worth trying here.

CHEAP AND CHEERFUL

⑫ Cuines de Santa Caterina €   Insider Tip
Avinguda Francesc Cambó 16
tel. 932 68 99 18
www.grupotragaluz.com
With its curving roofs the Santa Catarina Market is not just an architectural highlight but also well worth a visit for those who like their food fresh from the market. The contemporary rustic decor of the restaurant is just as successful as the concept of a Mediterranean fast food restaurant.

❼ Les Quinze Nits €
Plaça Reial 6,
Passatge Madoz
tel. 933 17 30 75
www.lesquinzenits.com
Open daily
This attractive, stylishly decorated traditional restaurant in the Old City offers excellent value for money. Try to get a seat upstairs near the windows overlooking Plaça Reial. The traditional Catalan dishes with a dash of Mediterranean place an emphasis on the quality of ingredients fresh from the market. There is also an extensive wine selection. The service is courteous and well organized. The only disadvantage is that there are often long queues.

Snails are the specialty of Los Caracoles

㉒Lobo €

Carrer Pintor Fortuny 3
tel. 934 81 53 46
www.grupotragaluz.com
Urbane café-restaurant near the
Rambles. Particularly busy at
lunchtime when the menu del dia
is on offer. They serve substantial
neo-Mediterranean dishes.

❹Casa Delfin €

Passeig del Born 36
tel. 93 319 53 33
One could very well imagine this
classic restaurant, with its large
dining room and terrace, to be in
a Spanish provincial city. As down
to earth as the restaurant is its
cuisine: here they serve fresh local
ingredients with little in the way
of finesse but very well prepared.

⑬Organic €

Junta de Commerç 11
tel. 93 321 75 64
www.antoniaorganickitchen.com
The name does as it promises. In a
casual atmosphere you can enjoy
salads, pasta and other dishes from
organically produced ingredients.
Near La Boqueria covered market.

⑮La Candela € Insider Tip

Plaça de Sant Pere 12
tel. 93 310 62 42
This friendly little restaurant is just
as a much an insider tip as the romantic Plaça de Sant Pere, which
still hasn't been overrun by visitors. It serves fresh modern Mediterranean cuisine.

THE WORLD OF TAPAS

❶Bar Pinotxo

La Boqueria, Stand 466–467
La Rambla 89

Almost as famous as the Boqueria
market is the counter at the Bar
Pintoxo. (Coming from the Rambles keep to the right once you're
in the market.) Lots of visitors to
the market crowd in here, or people that simply want to have a
tasty snack.

❷Can Paixano

Reina Cristina 7
www.canpaixano.com
In this Champagne bar at Port
Vell, every evening (except Sunday) you can find out for yourself
just how happy lots of people can
get, even in the smallest of spaces. Of course they don't drink
Champagne here but Cava, which
comes from the nearby wine
growing area of Penedès. There
are delicious tapas to go with it.

❸Taller de Tapas

Plaça Sant Josep Oriol 9
www.tallerdetapas.com
There are now three of these tapas workshops in Barcelona. The
restaurant at the secluded Plaça
de Sant Josep Oriol/Plaça del Pi in
Barri Gòtic was the first of its
kind. You can either sit out on the
Plaça or indoors between bare
stone walls. The tapas selection is
huge. Prices range from €1.50 to
€10 per tapa.

❹Tapas24 Insider Tip

Diputació 269
tel. 93 488 09 77
www.tapac24.com
Gourmet tapas bar run by Carles
Abellan, who worked at »El Bulli«
with Ferran Adrià. Uncomplicated
and anti-elitist atmosphere and of
course delicious tapas made with

fresh ingredients. There are delicious croquettes, foie burger, trempó, a Catalan vegetable dish that is served here as omelettes, and more. It›s also worth coming to this tapas temple for breakfast.

❺ **Ticketsbar – La Vida Tapas**
Avinguda Paral·lel 164
Reservations at
www.ticketsbar.es
Ferran Adrià is a tireless genius. Together with his brother and the proprietors of the Rias de Galicia restaurant he has created a kind of concept bar, in which cinema, cuisine and going out are combined into a visual feast. Along with the delicious tapas, which are just as creative as they are unusual, the playful ambiance might set a new trend after all the stylish designer bars. You'll barely stand a chance of getting in without a reservation. Tapas cost €4-€16.

❻ **Vinya del Señor**
Plaça Santa Maria del Mar 5
This romantic wine bar has long been crowded out by ever more new places. But the original remains one of the best tapas bars in the Ribera district. It's impossible to say whether it's nicer inside at the bar or outside on the plaça overlooking the main portal of the church of Santa Maria del Mar. The very good selection of wines and cavas obscures the fact that the tapas are not the cheapest of their kind.

❼ **Xampanyet**
Montacada 22
This simple champagne bar has been a popular meeting place for years. People come here to get back into the swing of things after work with a glass of cava, or to mark the start of a night out.

GRANJAS, CAFÉS AND ORXATERIAS

❶ **Cafè de L'Opera**
Rambles 74
www.cafedelaoperabcn.com
This café is a haven of peace and nostalgia in the tumult of the Rambles. The clientele changes according to the time of day.

❹ **Cafè Vienés**
Passeig de Gràcia 132
(Hotel Casa Fuster)
www.hotelcasafuster.com
The Casa Fuster, built by Luis Domènech i Montaner, is the only hotel in the city that is housed in a UNESCO World Heritage Site. The Café Vienés on the ground floor is an elegant place with curvy sofas on which you can enjoy a chat over a coffee just as much as an evening cocktail.

❷ **Granja M. Viader**
Xuclà 4; www.granjaviader.cat
Granjas are milk bars. In these historic institutions Barcelonans enjoy thick hot chocolate with or without cream, sweet pastries and cream cheese with honey or yogurt. It's nice to spend a little longer in the beautifully preserved interior of this granja.

❸ **Granja La Pallaresa**
Petrixol 11
www.lapallaresa.com **Insider Tip**
The Carrer Petrixol is known for sweet treats. The La Pallaresa milk bar is a wonderfully old-

There is a plenty of restaurants in Barceloneta

fashioned and simple place where you can enjoy yourself over almond milk, dipping churros into thick, hot chocolate (churros con chocolate) or mató de Pedralbes, the latter being a kind of Crema Catalana made from milk, eggs, sugar, cinnamon and lemon – delicious.

❺ Orxateria La Valenciana
Aribau 16
www.lavalenciana.com
By the university on the corner of Aribau and Gran Via, this Orxateria has supplied the neighbourhood with specialities from the re-

gion of Valencia since 1910. In this traditional establishment they are proud that the former mayors and later Prime Ministers Jordi Pujol and Pasqual Maragall once bought their nougat and drank their Orxata here.

❻ Zürich
Plaça de Catalunya
Even if it doesn't look like it, the Zürich is one of the most traditional eateries in Barcelona. The new building the café had to move into lacks a certain atmosphere, but its location on Plaça Catalunya couldn't be more central.

World-class

More than 50 museums can be found in the Mediterranean metropolis. They include small and sometimes curious collections as well as internationally renowned institutions, the latter including the MNAC with its outstanding collection of Romanesque and Gothic art, the Picasso Museum and the Miró Foundation.

The most visited museum in Barcelona is now the **Museu Picasso**. When it opened, General Franco, who ruled Spain as a dictator from 1939 to 1975, is said to have foamed with rage at this tribute to the hated artist (Picasso was an implacable opponent of Franco). Revenge was inevitable: the authoritarian regime made sure that Picasso's name did not appear at the museum entrance.

City of museums

But Barcelona's museums don't just focus on modern or contemporary art. The city's own history comes to the fore in museums such as the **Museu d'Història de Barcelona** (City Museum) and the **Museu d'Història de Catalunya**, which has in-depth coverage of the history of Barcelona and the region on its four levels. In the latter, the visitor is transported from one floor to the next on huge, silvery escalators; it has the finest parquet flooring and no expense has been spared with the exhibits – after all representing your own history also means giving a good impression. In the **Museu Marítim** (Maritime Museum) visitors will be impressed by the faithful reconstruction of the magnificent galley Real, the flagship of the fleet that defeated the Turks at the Battle of Lepanto in 1571; with the Audioguía you will get a vivid impression of the sad fate of the convicts who did the rowing (their stench – they had to relieve themselves where they sat – carried for miles). And in the museum you will also encounter an underwater world, as may have been experienced by Narcís Monturiol in 1859 on the dives he undertook with his homemade submarine.

Whimsical exhibits await visitors to the **Museu de Carrosses Fúnebres** (Sancho d'Àvila, 2), where a collection of historic hearses can be admired. You should not expect too much, however, from the **Museu de l'Eròtica** (La Rambla, 96 bis), whose exhibition – including erotic art from all over the world and from the Barri Xinès of the 1930s – does not come across as being particularly erotic.

The city's most visited museum after Museu Picasso is not devoted to art, history or oddities, but to football – more precisely to the history

Picasso's portrait of Marie-Thérèse Walter from 1937 is owned by the Museu Nacional d'Art de Catalunya

'of FC Barcelona, its many triumphs and its players. Visitors to the **Museu del Futbol Club Barcelona** have the added bonus of direct access to the upper tiers of the Camp Nou stadium, which with its almost 100,000 seats is one of the biggest football stadiums in the world.

Price reductions

Guests who see the city aboard a **Barcelona Bus Turístic** tour bus are eligible for discounts of between 10–25%, while the **Barcelona Card** qualifies you for free admission or discounts. The **ArtTicket** enables you to get in to the seven major art museums for €25. For historical and archaeological enthusiasts the **Arqueoticket** is the best choice, while the Maritime Museum and the museums d'Historia de Barcelona, Egipci, Barbier-Mueller and Archeology are accessible for €14. The tickets can be bought at the tourist office or be ordered online at discount http://bcnshop.barcelonaturisme.com.

Opening times

Most museums are closed on Sunday afternoons and Monday.

Wax figures of Miró, Dalí and Picasso in the Museu de Cera

Important Museums

ART
Casa-Museu Gaudí
►Parc Güell

Caixaforum
►p.165

Centre de Cultura Contemporánia de Barcelona (CCCB)
►Museu d'Art Contemporani, Casa de Caritat

Fundació Antoni Tàpies
p.183

Fundació Fran Daurel
►Poble Espanyol

Fundació Francisco Godia
►p.183

Fundació Joan Miró
►p184

Fundació Suñol
Contemporary art from the Josep Suñol collection
Passeig de Gràcia 98
www.fundaciosunol.org
Mon–Sat 4pm–8pm

Gabinet de les Arts Gràfiques
►Museu del Disseny de Barcelona

Museo Real Círculo Artístico
44 sculptures by Salvatore Dalí done in the 1970s.
c/Arcs 5
www.dalibarcelona.com

Museu d'Art Contemporani de Barcelona (MACBA)
►p.200

Museu Barbier-Mueller d'Art Precolombi
►p.198

Museu de la Catedral
►Catedral

Museu Diocesà de Barcelona (Pia Almoina)
►Catedral

Museu de l'Eròtica
Displays of erotic art from all over the world.
La Rambla 96 bis
Metro: Catalunya (L 1, L 3), Liceu (L 3)
Daily 11am–10pm

Museu Frederic Marès
►p.214

Museu Nacional d'Art de Catalunya (MNAC)
►p.217

Museu Picasso
►p.221

Sagrada Família Museu del Temple Expiatori
►Sagrada Família

ARTS AND CRAFTS
Museu de les Arts Decoratives
►Museu del Disseny de Barcelona

Museu del Calçat
►p.204

Museu de Cera
►Museu de Cera

No doubt – Picasso

Museu de Ceràmica
►Museu del Disseny de Barcelona

Museu de Carrosses Fúnebres
Hearses dating from the 19th and 20th centuries are on display in the vast vaulted cellars of the municipal undertakers.
Sancho d'Àvila
Metro: Marina (L 1); Mon–Fri 10am–1pm and 4pm–6pm, Sat and Sun 10am–1pm

Museu del Disseny de Barcelona
►p.205

Museu Tèxtil i d'Indumentària
►Museu del Disseny de Barcelona

SCIENCE
Casa-Museu Verdaguer
p.169

Museu de la Ciència
►p.202

Museu Blau
►Fòrum

Museu d´Arqueologia de Catalunya
►p.199

Museu Egipci de
Barcelona
►p.212

Museu Etnogràfic
Andino-Amazònic
►p.213

Museu Etnològic
►p.213

Museu d' Història de
Catalunya
►Port

Museu d'Història de Barcelona (MUHBA)
►p.211

Museu-Monestir de
Pedralbes
►Monestir de Pedralbes

Museu Marítim
p.216

Institut Municipal d'Història
►Barri Gòtic

Museu Tauri
►Plaça de Toros

Museu de la Xocolata
Chocolate museum housed in a
former Augustinian monastery,
devoted to the history of choco-
late.
Comerç 36
Metro: Jaume (L 4),
Arc de Triomf (L 1)
Mon–Sat 10am–7pm
Sun 10am–3pm

SPORT
Museu de l'Esport Dr Melcior
Colet
►Museu de l'Esport Dr. Melcior
Colet

Museu del Futbol Club
Barcelona
p.207

Museu Olímpic i de l'Esport
►Anella Olímpica

OTHER MUSEUMS
Museu dels Autòmats
►Tibidabo

Museu de la Música
►p.203

Shopping

Shopper's Paradise

Barcelona is a shopper's paradise. The best shopping can be found along the »Barcelona Shopping Line«, which stretches 5km/3mi from Maremàgnum at the old harbour via the Rambles and the Barri Gòtic, Plaça de Catalunya, Passeig de Gràcia and Avinguda Diagonal to the Ciutat Universitaria. The shopping line includes shops recommended by Barcelona›s tourist information office. To help you find your way around there is the folding »Shopping Map« from the Tourist Information Office.

It's hard to find such a large number of **exclusive fashion and design shops** concentrated in such a small area as you have in the Eixample district. It's best to focus on the Rambla de Catalunya, the Passeig de Gràcia including the side roads, equivalent to the area of covered by the Quadrat d´Or, the part of the district that is so worth seeing on account of its Modernista buildings. Alongside international luxury brands like Armani, Burberry, Cartier, Escada, Lacoste and Versace, the entire range of famous and successful Catalan designers such as Ana Bofill, Antoni Miró and Lydia Delgado is also represented.

Eixample and Diagonal

The second shopping area is the almost entirely pedestrianized Old City, and in particular its northern section between Plaça de Catalunya and Carrer de la Palla. In the small, crowded streets you will find fashion, leather goods, sports and jewellery shops. Many shops concentrate on young people. Above all, the area is known for its **rustic, sometimes quirky shops**, some of which might have been around for a century or more and sell items such as handmade oil cans, hand dipped candles or colonial goods. Those who like antiques will also find plenty of interest in the shops lining Palla, Pi and Banys Nous streets.

Barri Gòtic

The Ribera district was formerly known for its textile workshops. Today, the trendy district is a great place to find a nice souvenir to take home from one of the many boutiques with fashion by Spanish or international designers. La Ribera is also the right place to be for those who want to delve into delis for good wines, the finest oils or local cheeses and cold meats.

Ribera

In the once dilapidated district of El Raval there are now art galleries, shops with creative trinkets or design pieces as well as fashion bou-

El Raval

The Boqueria is Barcelona's largest market hall

tiques of mostly Spanish textile designers. The shops in the upper part of the district around the CCCB and MACBA arts centres are youthful, urban, creative and also mostly alternative. In the lower part towards the harbour they are simpler and more international with Chinese textile shops, Indian-run electronics outlets and shops for daily needs.

Shopping centres

It's also worth dropping by the **Maremàgnum** at the Old Harbour, not just for the shopping, or even the cinemas and restaurants, but for its wonderful location. Even the **Arenas** mall, the former bullring at Plaça Espanya is worth a visit. True shopping havens are the branches of El Corte Inglés, Spain's largest department store chain, offering almost everything money can buy. They can be found at Plaça de Catalunya, Portal de l'Àngel 19–21 and on Avinguda Diagonal (Plaça de Francesc Macià and Plaça de Reina Maria Cristina). Another shopping centre is **El Triangle** with the reopened Café Zürich, located on Plaça de Catalunya. On Avinguda Diagonal, east of Plaça Reina Maria Cristina, the huge, modern **Illa Diagonal** shopping centre contains over 130 exclusive in-house shops and a market hall as well as restaurants, a hotel and a nightclub (Diagonal 557). **Les Glòries**, at Diagonal 208, is a classic shopping centre with 200 shops.

There is much junk sold at Mercat Sant Antoni

l'Illa is a shopping centre at Avinguda Diagonal

Municipal market halls can be found in all districts of Barcelona. Nearly all of the around 40 market halls provide a wide range of fruit, vegetables, dairy products, meat, fish and seafood. Particularly recommended are the **Boqueria** on the Rambles (▶Mercat de Sant Josep), the **Mercat de Santa Caterina** (Plaça d'Antoni Maura; ▶MARCO POLO Insight, p.120), as well as the **Mercat de Sant Antoni** at the southwestern edge of Raval.

Market halls and markets

Many Barcelonans consider the **Mercat de Galvany**, housed in a church-like building (on the corner of Madrazo/ Santaló in Sarrià-Sant Gervasi), to be the best market in town. The biggest flea market is **Els Encants**, Plaça de les Glòries Catalanes (Mon, Wed, Fri, Sat), with more than 400 vendors, open spaces and canopied alleys and booths. Also interesting are the surrounding shops (furniture, lamps, art, books). On weekends, the **Mostra d'Art** artisan market on Plaça Sant Josep Oriol, at the Santa Maria del Pi church, is where members of the Art Society present their latest watercolour and oil paintings. **Numismática y Filatelia** on Plaça Reial is the market to see for collectors of coins and stamps (Sun and holidays, mornings).

If that's not enough, you can head for La Roca Village, an **outlet shopping centre** 30 km/18 mi outside Barcelona with around 100 exclusive brand boutiques. The Shopping Express bus departs for La Roca from C / Fontanella 2 (Plaça Catalunya) at 9am, 11am, 4pm and 6pm, the return journey costing €12.
www.larocavillage.com

La Roca Village

In Spain, there are no legally defined closing times. Shops are usually open from 9am to 1pm and from 4.30pm to 8pm, and during summer they are often open until late at night. Large department stores and shopping centres are usually open all day, Mon–Sat 10am–9pm; many shopping centres are also open on Sundays and holidays.

Opening times

In the Belly of the City

Every district in Barcelona has its market hall. Most of the around 40 halls were built at the end of the 19th century and beginning of the 20th. Little by little the historic markets have been renovated, or new halls with bold designs such as the Mercat de Santa Catalina have been created. Just how important and lively the markets still are, is evident at the world famous Boqueria market.

It is a paradise – no heavenly one but of this world and down to earth – that reveals itself just a few steps back from the Rambles. Framed between art and the church, between the Liceu Opera House and baroque Església de Betlem, the protective canopy of the Mercat de Sant Josep, better known as **La Boqueria**, spans over 300 stalls. With its 2583 sq m/ 27,803 sq ft, the indoor market is not just the largest in the city, but is the one place guaranteed to send every hobby cook or chef, house husband or housewife, gourmet or kitchen gardener into astonished raptures. And what a wealth of products, fruit and vegetables, fish and seafood, meat and poultry there is here! Like Pepe Carvalho, the detective and gourmet from the detective novels by Manuel Vázquez Montalbán, one just wants to take bag loads of fresh produce home or to the holiday apartment, get hold of the odd bottle of wine and perfect the art of cooking and indulgence.

La Boqueria is a **place for locals and tourists**. Some take pictures and buy individual portions of fruit salad, practically packaged salads and freshly squeezed fruit juices, while others are drawn towards the back of the steel structure dating from 1914, where they can get all the fresh produce they need for their own kitchen. The visit can be rounded off with a snack at one of the bars or kiosks, an indispensible feature of any market hall. After all, markets are not just places where food is sold; they are also places to exchange information and gossip, a lively barometer of the mood of a city and a meeting place for the local neighbourhood.

Indispensible

In Barcelona, as in any other major city in Spain, there is a market hall to be found in virtually every neighbourhood. The supermarkets and even the discounters have been unable to make a dent in their popularity, not least because their range of fresh produce is usually more expensive.

La Boqueria is not the only notable market in the city. At the other side of the Barri Gòtic, beyond the Via Laietana, the **Mercat de Santa Caterina** provides more evidence of Barcelona's innovative city planning. In the middle of the 1990s the authorities began to upgrade the at the time problem districts of Santa Catalina and Ribera through a series specific measures. The Santa Caterina market hall has benefited from this development, not only being transformed into an architectural gem, but also a social

Freshness is obligatory

hub that helps the district to realise its own identity. The architect Enric Miralles (together with Benedetta Tagliabue) provided the restored base of the building with a wavy roof design that both evokes the shapes and colours of the Catalan landscape and can also be seen as an abstract work of art. Meanwhile the roof, with its colourful honeycomb pattern, has become one of the many landmarks of Barcelona.

No cause for Nostalgia

That a market hall doesn't need to be a place of misplaced nostalgia is evident in the **Mercat de la Concepció** in the smart Eixample district. This steel construction between Aragó and València streets dates from 1888. It has been carefully restored and combines on two levels a traditional market and a supermarket. Antoni Rovira i Trias, the architect of the hall, was also responsible for the Mercat de Sant Antoni, the largest indoor market in Barcelona. Opened in 1882, the complex takes up a whole block of Ildefons Cerdà's Eixample grid plan. It is currently undergoing renovation (reopening scheduled for 2016). Also well worth seeing, although currently closed, is the **Mercat del Born** at the edge of the Ribera district adjacent to the Parc de la Ciutadella. Erected in 1876, the hall was closed down back in the 1970s. The plan at the time was to convert the building into a district library. During the work they came across the foundations of the Gothic Old City, dating from well before the time the Castilian central power erected their citadel here (sometime after 1714, no longer in existence). With the conversion work having been delayed for so many years, all the signs are that the Mercat del Born construction site will soon be finished, the hall set to be used as an open-plan museum and exhibition space.

Interesting shops

ANTIQUES
El Bulevard dels Antiquaris
Passeig de Gràcia 55–57
(im Bulevard Rosa)
More than 70 antique shops (for Art Nouveau furniture and breath-taking crystal chandeliers, porce-lain and jewellery) and art galler-ies are joined in this circular-canopied shopping ar-cade. Also the Centre Català d'Artesania is located here, where genuine handicrafts from all over Catalonia are for sale. The centre is meant to promote traditional arts-and-crafts. With a focus on good quality and fair prices, this shop is a good choice.

DESIGN
Dos y Una
Rosseló 275.
Barcelona's oldest high-end souve-nir shop, through which Xavier

Mariscal has also become well-known.

Vinçon
Passeig de Grácia, 96 (Eixample)
The Art Nouveau palace built by Ramón Casas houses one of the most renowned shops for modern interior decoration. Kitsch articles, whimsical and avant-garde furni-ture, fabrics, kitchen and bath-room items, gifts such as elegant candles and lamps make this an excellent place for browsing. It's worth seeing the furniture on the first floor, with contemporary items displayed in the original rooms of the building. Vinçon also runs a Tincon for bedroom furni-ture, right around the corner.

DELI / GOURMET FOOD
Caelum
Carrer de la Palla 8 (Old City)

A design shop in the Raval quarter

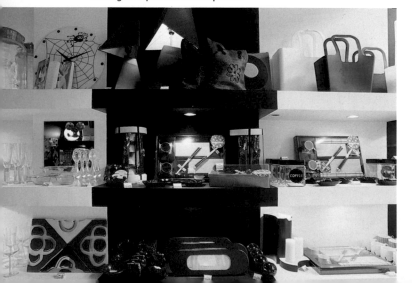

Located in the vaults of an old thermal bath in the Jewish quarter. Besides wine, tea and liqueurs this shop also sells all kinds of sweet treats and traditional specialties from Spanish monasteries, which can also be tasted, including honey, pastries, etc.

Pastisseria Escribá
La Rambla 83 (Old City)
Gran Via 546
Here you will find the finest pastries (great cakes and petit fours creations), all exhibited in the most beautiful Art Nouveau showcase in the city (Cristian Escribà). In the summer there are tables out on the terrace so you can sample the goodies on the spot.

Queviures Murria
Roger de Llúria 85 (Eixample)
Founded in 1890 in Modernista style, this shop was decorated by the artist Ramón Casas. For sale are 200 different types of cheese, sausages, tinned delicacies – and everything that gourmets enjoy. The in-house wine shop with its outstanding selection is sure to provide the right wine to match.

Formatgeria La Seu
Daguería, 16 (Old City)
This cheese shop right in the heart of the Barri Gòtic is one of the oldest in town. Not only does it sell the finest cheeses of Catalonia and Spain, it also provides excellent and knowledgeable service. Some of the impressive old machines can still be seen here.

Vila Viniteca
Agullers 7 (Ribera)

Wine lovers will be happy in the well-stocked rooms. The wine shop is located in the district of La Ribera, and Vila Viniteca also operates a deli with small bar next door.

FOOTBALL
La Botiga del Barça
There are branches in the Mare-magnum shopping centre, next to Sagrada Familia (C/Provença 439), at Sants station, at Ronda Univeridad 37 and at C/ Jaume I 18 in the Old City.
In the botigas you can get the official kits, flags, scarves, etc. of FC Barcelona. This megastore at the Camp Nou stadium has the size of a department store.

HANDICRAFTS
Art Escudellers
Escudellers 23–25 (Ribera)
This shop sells Spanish handicrafts and wine. At the adjacent workshop visitors can watch how earthenware is manufactured and those who wish can even have a go at some creative pottery.

Cerería Subirà
Insider Tip
Baixada Llibreteria 7 (Old City)
Candles and all varieties of other wax items have been produced here since the 18th century. Some of the particularly artistic pieces can cost up to several thousand euros. They can also make individual items on request.

FASHION
Armand Basi
Passeig de Gràcia 49 (Eixample)
This internationally known Catalan brand is particularly popular

A nostalgic herb shop in Barri Gòtic

for the lightness of its carefully knitted and processed fabrics and for its well-chosen combinations.

Cortana
Carrer Flassanders 41
www.cortana.es
(Ribera-Born)
The small shop in the Born is just as enticing as the feminine creations of Rosa Esteva. The native Mallorcan studied fashion design in Barcelona and creates light, naturally elegant looking women's fashion.

Desigual
Las Ramblas 136, Las Ramblas 140 (Outlet)
This Barcelona-based brand is now also represented in other European cities. The promise of fashion that is often youthfully colourful and flashy is proving popular: whoever wears it will be different,

individual and urban. Currently, there are 15 shops in the Catalan metropolis alone.

Custo
Plaça de Olles 7
Centre Comercial L'Illa Diagonal
Diagonal 557
(Eixample)
The brothers Custo and Dalvis Dalmau began developing fashion at the time of the Movida in the 1980s, initially focusing on printed tops and T-shirts inspired by the looks of Californian surfers. They opened their first shop in 1996. The shrill, individual and creative designs immediately stood out. The fact that actresses like Julia Roberts and Penelope Cruz were seen in Custo creations is a measure of just how beneficial the flight of the brand from Barcelona has been.

Loewe
Diagonal 570 and Passeig de Gràcia 35
(Eixample)
Traditional Spanish chain for leather goods (since 1846) selling the finest leather bags, jackets and accessories at correspondingly high prices.

Lurdes Bergada
Centre Comercial L'Illa Diagonal
Diagonal 557
(Eixample)
The Flagship store at the L'Illa Diagonal shopping centre is currently one of the most remarkable examples of contemporary store design. It was planned by Deardesign. Barcelona-born Lurdes Bergada's fashion is simple and usually restricted to subtle and muted shades of grey.

Sombreria Obach
Call, 2
(Old City)
A hat shop from the good old days with exclusive service and various kinds of hats for gentlemen.

SHOES
Camper
Rambla Catalunya 122 (Eixample) and other branches
This brand's chic and comfy shoes are international bestsellers. Originally from Majorca, the sneakers are still relatively inexpensive here.

La Manual Alpargatera
Carrer d' Avinyó 7
(Old City)
Old shoe shop that sells handmade espadrilles in all colours (in-

cluding accessories). Manufacturing can be watched; like many famous customers, one might want to order a bespoke pair of the linen shoes with hemp soles.

Munich
Centre Comercial L'Illa Diagonal
Diagonal 557
The brand with the X logo was founded in Barcelona in 1939. The new flagship store is a gem of interior design. Asymmetric and hard-edged cubes of light wood interspersed with stylized trees in the otherwise black interior provide the stage for Munich's footwear.

TOBACCONISTS
Casa Gimeno
La Rambla 100
Legendary tobacconists dating from 1920, which every lover of tobacco should visit at least once. Cigarettes, cigars, tobacco from around the world along with all kinds of accessories. You will find the finest Cuban cigars stored in the basement. Across from the Boqueria market.

LATE OPENING
Open25
C/ Aribau 149
Food, snacks and ready meals. Open round the clock.

Opencor
Amongst others:
Gran Via 407
Calle de Calvet 33
Ronda de Sant Pau 34
Unusual mix of foods, drugstore products, baked goods and music.

Tours and Guides

Spoiled for Choice

Special buses, harbour boats, funiculars, gondolas, a tourist tram, tourist train, helicopter, horse-drawn carriages as well as guided sightseeing tours on foot and by bike, Segways with or without guides – there are numerous ways to get to know the city.

When the weather's nice, which is often the case in Barcelona, the **Bus Turístic** is a practical and relaxing way to get around. Sitting on the open top deck you can watch the city go by along three different routes. There are bus stops either at or near the most important attractions where you can hop on and off as desired. The Blue Route covers the south of the city, the Red the north and the Green the new urban areas in the northeast. During the journey you can follow the explanations with headphones. The buses run on average every 10 to 20 minutes. In addition, holders of a ticket are eligible for all sorts of discounts, including on tickets to museums or when buying food in fast food chains. Bus tickets can be bought on the bus itself, at tourist information offices and at the TMB Contact Points.

If you are at the Plaça de Catalunya and see that a long queue has formed again at the Bus Turístic stop, just go to their competitor **Barcelona City Tours**, which operates similar routes but seems to be less crowded.

Bus Turístic: www.barcelonabusturistic.cat
Barcelona City Tours: www.barcelonacitytours.com

Tour buses

> ## ? MARCO POLO INSIGHT
> *The king didn't want to*
>
> Mount Tibidabo is the oldest leisure destination in Greater Barcelona. The summit was home to an amusement park as long ago as 1900, the first in all of Spain. The funicular to the summit was constructed in 1901. Visitors usually get to the base station by taking the vintage Tramvia Blau. One man, however, refused to take it: on his visit to Barcelona the Spanish king Alfonso XIII (1902–31) strictly objected to using the »blue tram«. Instead, for whatever reason, a car brought him to the base station of the funicular.

A trip on a Golondrina is very pleasant. Die »swallows« cast off at the old port just a stones throw from the Columbus Monument for a 30-minute round-harbour tour (MARCO POLO Insight, p. 238).

Golondrina

Those wanting to take the Transbordador Aeri, the harbour cable car (►Port), should have a head for heights. The venerable gondola traverses the harbour from Barceloneta to Montjuïc.

Transbordador Aeri

No cycling on the Rambles!

Exploring the City on two Wheels

Comfortable and yet close to the action – on a guided bike tour you will experience Barcelona directly and don't have to be restricted to a small section of the city.

Barcelona is a city made for cyclists. Unlike in the Spanish capital, Madrid, the two-wheeler is not regarded as an exotic form of transport in the Mediterranean metropolis. In recent years the environmentally friendly mode of transportation has not just become popular, it is now part of the zeitgeist. While in 2006 there were an estimated 50,000 cycle journeys per day, now the number has risen to more than twice as many. New bicycle lanes, the mostly good weather and few gradients of note within the centre make the bike an ideal way of exploring Barcelona. This also applies to guided city tours.

Six Tours

The Barcelona Tourist Office currently has six guided bicycle tours in its programme. For a good overview there is the **BikeTour Barcelona**. The group of maximum 25 participants visits the Old City, Port Vell, Barceloneta, the Port Olímpic and the grand boulevard Passeig de Gràcia. The tour stops repeatedly for the guide to talk about the city and its attractions. It takes between two and three hours and can be booked in English, French or Spanish for €24.

The **Barcelona Ciclo Tour** is a similar undertaking. It also takes in the Old City with the museums in the Raval district, the Port Olímpic and several buildings by Gaudí. The tour starts at 11am every day from Plaça de Catalunya (€22).

Of course there is also a tour devoted solely to Catalan Modernisme. The offer from Budget Bikes is called the **Gaudí-Tour**. It departs daily at 10.30am from Calle Estruc 38, near Plaça de Catalunya. The programme includes the highlights of the Catalan Belle Epoque. As the name suggests, the tour takes in famous buildings by Antoni Gaudí – the Sagrada Família and the Casas Milà, Calvet and Batlló. But less well-known gems of Modernisme like the Castle of the Three Dragons in Parc de la Ciutadella, the Hospital Sant Pau and the La Monumental bullring are also visited (€22).

BornBike concentrates its operations along the coastal strip.

The **Beach Bike Tour** starts daily at 11am from C. Marquesa 1 in the Ribera. Three hours are enough for a relaxed cycle ride on car-free tracks along the city's beaches, all the way from the Columbus Monument to the Parc del Forùm (€22).

For those wishing to get out of the city and cycle, the **Collserola Bike Tour** could be the answer. Every Friday at 9.30am from April to October they meet up at Terra Diversions Bike Tours at C. Santa Tecla 1. A minibus takes the group into the Collserola hills, from where there is a magnificent view of the city. The tour sounds hard work but it isn't

– the route is suitable for all ages (€38).

Outside Barcelona

If you want to venture further into the countryside, you should look at what **Terra Diversions** has to offer. For families for example there is a day excursion along one of the Vías Verdes. In Spain, that's what cycle ways that have been created along disused railway lines are called. The organizers will arrange for transportation to the start and return transportation from the destination point and provide bicycle and helmet. More demanding MTB tours in the mountains surrounding Barcelona start from the office in Carrer Tecla.

Interesting for children

Apart from those offered by Terra Diversions, all tours can be booked via the Barcelona Tourist Office or www.barcelonaturisme.com. Most of the cycle tours are also suitable for parents with small children. In order to avoid disappointment, you should let the operator know beforehand so that they can have a child seat at the ready.

OUTSIDE BARCELONA
Terra Diversions
Carrer Tecla 1
tel. 93 416 08 05
www.terradiversions.com

BIKE RENTAL
Without guided tours

Barcelona Rent a Bike
Tallers 45 (Raval)
tel. 93 317 19 70
Passeig de Joan Borbó 35

Cycling on the beach is permitted

(Barceloneta)
tel. 93 221 27 90
www.barcelonarentabike.com
2 hours €6, 24 hours €15
Citybikes, folding bikes, tandems, children's bikes.

Bike Rental Barcelona
Rauric 20 (Barri Gòtic)
tel. 666 057 655
www.bikerentalbarcelona.com
2 hours €6–20, 24 hours from €22
Citybikes, folding bikes, MTB, single speed

Budget Bike
Unió 22 (Raval)
Estruc 38 (bei Plaça Catalunya)
Plaça de la Llana 3 (Ribera)
Passeig Joan de Borbó 80
(Barceloneta)
tel. 93 304 18 85
www.budgetbikes.eu
2 hours €6, 24 hours €16

Reaching
Montjuïc

▶Montjuïc, Barcelona's »local mountain«, can be accessed by a variety of means. The Funicular de Montjuïc starts its climb on Avinguda del Paral·lel. At the top station you can switch to the Telefèric de Montjuïc cable car and effortlessly continue up to the castle. In the high season, to the delight of children, the Tren Turístic de Montjuïc operates on Montjuïc.

Reaching
Tibidabo

The climb up ▶Tibidabo is an experience if you take the Tramvia Blau tram (between Avinguda Tibidabo and Plaça Dr. Andreu). At the terminus you catch the Funicular del Tibidabo (between Plaça Dr. Andreu and Plaça del Tibidabo ▶Tibidabo). Practical but without any nostalgic appeal is the Tibibus, which runs from Plaça de Catalunya directly to Plaça del Tibidabo on the mountain plateau.

MARCO ⊕ POLO TIP

! *Barcelona by sidecar* **Insider Tip**

The tours offered by the Bright-Side company are both individual and unusual. For your tour of Barcelona you can have an itinerary lasting between 1.5 and 9 hours put together. The means of transport is a classic motorbike with sidecar. Driver and guest communicate with each other via an intercom system (in English). From € 55. tel. 647 761 522 www.ridebrightside.com

GUIDED TOURS

Anyone interested in a guided city tour will be spoiled for choice. It depends what you want to see and whether you want run, cycle, go by scooter, Segway, rickshaw or a motorized tricycle, take a ride in an old motorcycle sidecar or simply learn more about Barcelona while out on an early morning jog. Almost all offers, even from third parties, can be booked through the Turisme Barcelona website.

ON FOOT
Walking Tours
www.barcelonaturisme.com
Programme of the Barcelona Tourist Office. Walking tours through the Barri Gòtic, through Picasso's Barcelona (including a visit to the Picasso Museum), to Port Vell, to the highlights of Modernista architecture or to traditional markets and delicatessens in the Old City. The 1.5 to 2-hour tours take place at weekends and are given in Catalan, Spanish or English. The starting point for all tours is the Plaça de Catalunya, where you can also sign up.

Sightjogging-Barcelona
2 joggers / 1 hour €50
www.sightjogging-barcelona.com
The sportiest way to get to know the city. A 60- or 90-min early morning or evening jog through the Old City, around Montjuïc or along the Rambles.

BY BIKE
Guided cycle tours can also be booked through the Tourist Of-

fice. Excursions include Gaudí's buildings and along the city beaches (▶MARCO POLO Insight, p. 128) and last 2–3 hours.

RICKSHAW
Trixi Tours
1 hour for 2 persons €18
www.trixi.com
Explore the city aboard a futuristic rickshaw while the driver talks about Barcelona and its highlights in Spanish, Catalan, German or English. So that the driver doesn't get too out of breath, his vehicle is equipped with an auxiliary electric motor.

SEGWAY
1.5 or 2 hours; from €45
tel. 670 48 40 00
www.barcelonasegwayfun.com
The tour begins at Plaça Sant Jaume, and then from Port Vell to Barceloneta and to Port Olímpico and back.

SCOOTER
3 hours on a 125cc: €50; departure: Thur 3.30pm, Sun 10.30am from Cooltra at Pg. Joan de Borbó 80–84
Instead of bicycle or Segway it's possible to organise a city tour on a motor scooter.

VESPA
tel. 626 77 33 61
www.vesping.com
A similar deal is available through Vesping, in this case astride a 1950s Vespa.

TRICYCLES
GoCar
C/ Freixures 23 Bisbajos; from €35
www.gocartours.es
The small tricycles powered by 50cc engines are called GoCars. The vehicles are equipped with GPS, and as you approach a sight you receive the relevant commentary through your headphones. You can choose your own route and go for as long as you like.

HORSE AND CARRIAGE
Take a carriage ride along the Rambles and Port Vell.

HELICOPTER
Costa Tour
Start: Passeig l'Escullera helicopter pad (Moll Adossat) at the harbour
tel. 93 224 07 10
www.cathelicopters.com
5-minute flights. CAT helicopters along the coast to the Parc del Fòrum and back (€50 / person).

TOURS

You can get to know Barcelona quickly and comfortably aboard a sightseeing bus. But tours on foot through the Catalan metropolis are more exciting and varied.

Tours through Barcelona

Four tours taking in some of the most interesting attractions of the Catalan metropolis

Tour 1   Barri Gòtic and the Rambles
From the historic Gothic Quarter to
Barcleona's most famous pedestrian boulevard
page 137

Tour 2   Montjuïc
Barcelona's local mountain and favourite
excursion destination has both sports and culture
page 139

Tour 3   Eixample
Jewels of Modernisme
page 141

Tour 4   Architecture and Sea
Beaches, a new district and contemporary
architecture
page 143

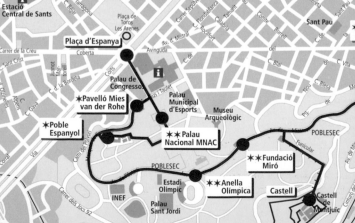

Girona ↗

Plaça de les
Glòries Catalanes

Avinguda Diagonal

Parc Diagonal Mar

Edificio Forum

Torre Agbar

Diagonal

**Museu
del
Disseny**

POBLENOU

**Teatre
Nacional**

Plaça de Toros
Monumental

Auditori

**Parc
del
Poblenou**

**Cementiri
de l'Est**

**Estació de
Autobuses**

Meridiana

Av. del Bogatell

Ronda del Litoral

rc de
riomf

**Palau de
Justícia**

**Vila
Olímpica**

**Museu
Zoològic**

**Parc de la
Ciutadella**

**Museu de
Geologia**

Zoo

Port Olímpic

Circumval·lació

**Museu
Picasso**

Port
Olímpic

Ronda del Litoral

lau
ial

**Museu
Tèxtil**

**S. Maria
del Mar**

**Estació de
França**

Parc
Barceloneta

Llotja

at

**Palau de
Mar**

GÒTIC

La Mercè

La Barceloneta

LA
BARCELONETA

Palau Güell

Mirador de Colom

Imax

L'Aquarium

PORT VELL

**Mar
Mediterrània**

Aduana

**Torre de
Sant Sebastiá**

Transbordador

★**Transbor-
dador Aeri**

**World Trade
Center**

Port Vell

500 m

©**BAEDEKER**

Getting Around in Barcelona

Barcelona was one of the first European cities to be serviced by low-cost airlines. With its typically Mediterranean climate, the Catalan metropolis is an attractive destination all year round; it's even worth coming for a long weekend as the city has much to offer. There are countless examples of historic architecture, especially from the Gothic and Modernisme periods, the latter being the Catalan version of Art Nouveau. Barcelona even has two entire quarters that emphasize these specific architectural eras: the **Barri Gòtic** around the Gothic cathedral, and the **Eixample**, some parts of which feature whole rows of impressive Modernista buildings. Art lovers and football fans alike will get their money's worth in the museums spread around the city. Boulevards such as the Rambles, Passeig de Gràcia or the Diagonal are ideal for a leisurely stroll. The countless shops and boutiques provide shopping galore – from whimsical shops selling bric-a-brac and antiques, all the way to chic boutiques. Barflies and night owls will find nonstop entertainment, and those looking for lively beaches will be more than satisfied. Nice and sunny days at any time of the year can be spent on the outdoor terraces of street cafés, ideal for enjoying a snack and people watching. Many of the interesting architectural highlights – as well as the lively boulevards, lovely shops and trendy bars – can be easily reached **on foot**, as they are mostly concentrated within a relatively small area in the city centre, around Plaça de Catalunya. Places of interest that are slightly further away can be reached by public transport, such as metros, city buses, trams (to the outer districts), trains, taxis or sightseeing buses that stop at all the main sights and parks. To reach Barcelona's two local mountains, take the nostalgic Blue Tram followed by the funicular railway for Mount Tibidabo, and harbour cable car, funicular railway and cable car for Montjuïc. Travelling around the city **in your own car or in a rental car is not advisable**. Traffic is always busy during the day, the road network involves a lot of one-way streets, and street signs leave much to be desired. Finding a place to park can try your patience, car parks are not all that cheap, and vehicles with foreign license plates and rental cars are tempting targets for theft.

MARCO ⊕ POLO INSIGHT

? *Did you know?*

Most of the commercially available city maps of Barcelona, including the large overview map in this guidebook, are not oriented to the north, as is common for most maps; instead the right-angled streets of the Eixample run parallel to the lines of the map's grid. This takes some getting used to and can be somewhat confusing. The cartographically correct situation is shown on the city map found on pages 134–135of this book.

Barri Gòtic and the Rambles   Tour 1

Starting Point: Plaça de Catalunya
Finishing Point: Museu Marítim   **Duration:** 3 hours.

This tour from Plaça de Catalunya, through the Gothic Quarter, along the Rambles and down to the old harbour, is a classic amongst the following suggested routes through Barcelona. Nearly all tourists visiting the Catalan capital take a stroll through the Barri Gòtic and wander along the world-famous boulevard.

Starting point is the expansive ❶**Plaça de Catalunya** on the northern edge of the old quarter – which is also the main traffic junction and hub of the metropolis. The Rambles, Barcelona's famous boulevard through which all life in the city is channelled, starts at the southeastern side.

Opposite the Church of Bethlehem, a former Jesuit monastery and one of the few Baroque buildings of the city, the lively Portaferrissa shopping street leads directly to the heart of the Barri Gòtic, where the Gothic ❷ ****Cathedral** towers majestically. The Gothic Quarter, with its narrow and sometimes dark alleys, is one of the most historically dense quarters of the city.

Impressive medieval buildings surrounding the cathedral were built at a time when Barcelona was still a world power. Two of the buildings still serve as governmental offices (City Hall and the seat of the Provincial Government); other buildings house interesting museums including the Museu Frederic Marès and Museu d'Història de Barcelona. From Plaça Sant Jaume take Carrer del Call or Carrer de Boqueria to return to the Rambles. A definite must is visiting the covered ❸****Mercat de la Boqueria** across the street, if only for the atmosphere.

Continuing towards the harbour, visitors walk on a famous work of art – the pavement mosaic by Miró. Finally, pass the ❹**Gran Teatre del Liceu**, the largest opera house in Spain and Barcelona's pride and joy.

Directly opposite the Liceu is the Café de l´Opera, a coffee house that has maintained the atmosphere of the early 20th century. On the same side of the street, walk through an archway to the ❺***Plaça Reial**. Surrounded by arcades, it is the most beautiful square in the city. Taking time out at one of the many cafés provides a relaxing break from the hectic bustle on the Rambles. Return to the Rambles and turn into Nou de la Rambla across the street; a few yards along it stands the beautiful ❻***Palau Güell** by Antoni Gaudí, long recognized as a UNESCO World Heritage site.

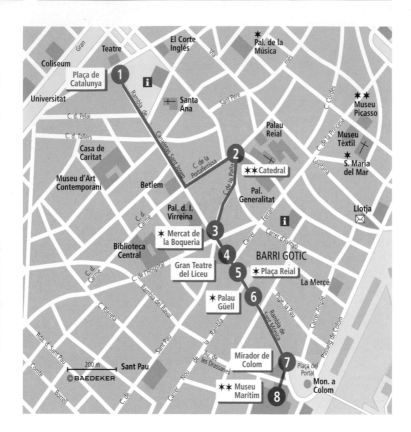

From the Rambles, a quick visit to the Museu de Cera (wax museum) is definitely worthwhile, before arriving at the **❼Mirador de Colom** (Monumento a Colom). An overwhelming panoramic view of the city and the old harbour can be enjoyed from the very top of the 60m/200ft Columbus Monument.

From there, it is only a few steps along the Rambla del Mar, a wide pontoon bridge, to the Moll d'Espanya, where the shops and restaurants, as well as the Aquàrium of the Maremàgnum, make for a nice stroll.

The nearby **❽**Museu Marítim** (Maritime Museum) makes an excellent conclusion to this tour. The museum, accommodated in the former royal shipyards, contains spectacular ships and testaments to the country's maritime past, including the galley of Don Juan d'Austria, under whose command the Turkish fleet was defeated in 1571, near Lepanto..

The Ramblas flower market – one of the prettiest sections of Barcelonas's magnificent boulevard

Montjuïc

Tour 2

Starting Point: Mirador de Colom
Finishing Point: Plaça d'Espanya   **Duration:** 4 hours.

Montjuïc, one of Barcelona's two local mountains, is a popular excursion destination close to the city. The many gardens on top of the hill offer serenity and relaxation from the noise and hectic bustle of the city; numerous spots on the hill provide wonderful views of Barcelona, its harbour and the sea. Yet Montjuïc has even more to offer: the summit is home to the main sporting venues of the 1992 Olympic Games, and those interested in culture will also get their money's worth.

From the ❶**Mirador de Colom** on Plaça del Portal de la Pau (easy to reach with public transport including the metro) walk to the inter-mediary stop of the Transbordador Aeri (harbour cable car), which is located at the ❷**World Trade Centre** on the Moll de Barcelona. Then take the ❸**✳✳Transbordador Aeri** to Plaça de l'Armada, half-way up Montjuïc. This square is located at the top entrance of the Jardins Costa i Llobera, which are known for their elaborate collection of cacti and succulent plants. From Plaça de l'Armada walk to the entrance of the cable car leading up to the ❹**Castell** at the top of Montjuïc and enjoy some delightful views of the city along the way. The ❺**✳✳Fundació Miró** beneath the castle is an art centre which received a special award from the Council of Europe in 1977, as the world's best museum of the year. Then visit the expansive ❻**✳Anella Olímpica** with the 1992 Olympic stadium and, nearby, the Palau Sant Jordi sporting arena. The Old Botanical Gardens are worth seeing on the way to the ❼**✳Poble Espanyol**, a Spanish village built for the 1929 World Fair, with numerous bars and restaurants and featuring representative and impressive examples of traditional architecture from the various regions of Spain. Further along, take a look at the ❽**✳Pavelló Mies van der Rohe**, which the architect built for the 1929 World Fair. Due to its perfect shapes and contours the architectural world considers it a »paradigm of modern architecture«. Montjuïc is also home to the Archaeological Museum, the Ethnological Museum and the Greek Theatre built in 1929 and based on the ancient theatre of Epidaurus in Greece. Particularly interesting, however, is the Palau Nacional with its world-famous ❾**✳✳Museu Nacional d'Art de Catalunya** (MNAC, National Art Museum of Catalonia), which contains outstanding collections from all periods of Catalan art history. A stairway from the Palau Nacional to the grounds of the convention centre (Fira de Barcelona), where the Avinguda de Reina Maria Cristina, lined by fountains, forms part of the main axis on the grounds and continues on towards ❿**Plaça d'Espanya**, where the metro (line 3) runs back to the Portal de la Pau (the starting point of this tour).

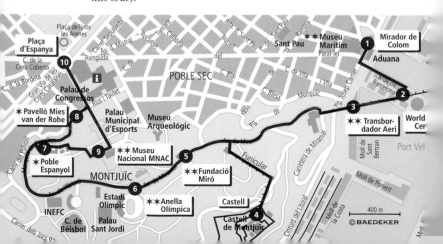

Eixample   Tour 3

Starting Point: Plaça de Catalunya
Finishing Point Sagrada Família   **Duration:** 2-3 hours.

This tour features the most beautiful and curious-looking buildings of Modernisme, the Catalan Art Nouveau period – including the unfinished Sagrada Família by Barcelona's most
renowned architect, Antoni Gaudí. On the way you can
browse some smart shops, particularly along Passeig de
Gràcia. And there's no shortage of chic tapas bars and high-
class restaurants.

As with the first route, the starting point for this tour is ❶**Plaça de
Catalunya**. This is where the wide, prestigious Passeig de Gràcia runs
northwest into the Eixample district, an urban expansion project that
started in the 19th century. Its most prominent architectural monuments can be found in the Quadrat d'Or – the area around Passeig de
Gràcia. On the left side of Passeig de Gràcia, the »mansana de la
discòrdia« (»block of discord«, or rather, »apple of discord«) comes
into view, which is comprised of three very different houses: Casa
Lleó Morera (No 35) by Lluís Domènech i Montaner, Casa Amatller
(No 43) by Josep Puig i Cadafalch and the unmistakeable ❷****Casa
Batlló** (No 43) by Antoni Gaudí, with its »animal bone facade« –
named after the appearance of the balcony.

Take the street to the left after Casa Batlló for another creation of architect Domènech i Montaner (Aragó, 225). The building with the
wire sculpture on the rooftop is now home to the ❸***Fundació Antoni Tàpies**, a centre of modern art.

The most important Modernista house in Eixample, however, is located on Passeig de Gràcia, 92. Gaudí's ❹****Casa Milà** looks more
like a sculpture than a house and has suffered a fair amount of mo-
ckery in its time. Constant changes to the design leading to conside-
rable delays in construction, as well as quarrels between Gaudí and
the owner, soon gave the building its derogatory name: »La Pedrera«
(»the quarry«). Today, it attracts so many tourists that there's nearly
always a queue outside.

Those who find shopping or pub crawling along the busy Passeig de
Gràcia too hectic and noisy can slip over to the parallel Rambla de
Catalunya on the southwest side – the continuation of the Rambles
(▶Tour 1). This rather elegant street is also home to jewellery shops
and Haute Couture boutiques; the numerous street cafés on the wide
central reservation provide for a relaxing break, and the many cinemas are also an attraction. Best of all, this Rambla is practically
devoid of tourists.

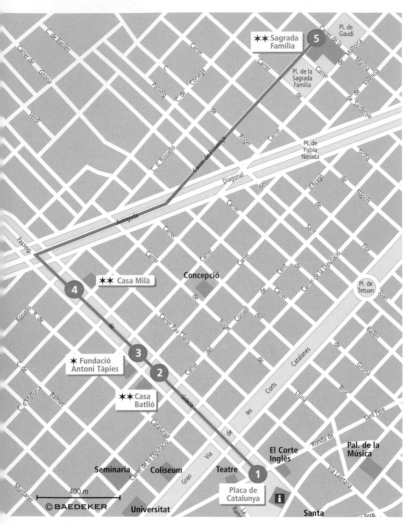

On the other side of the wide Avinguda Diagonal, which is always crammed with dense traffic, the Passeig continues as the considerably narrower Carrer Gran de Gràcia.

Slightly hidden in a maze of alleys in the former suburb of Gràcia is one of Antoni Gaudí's relatively early works: Casa Vicens. From there, the metro at the nearby Fontana stop (line 3; change trains at Diagonal, take line 5 towards Horta and get off at the second stop) runs directly to the church of ❺**Sagrada Família** (Temple Expiatori de la Sagrada Família), Barcelona's most famous monument and symbol of the city.

From the Sagrada Família metro stop return to Plaça de Catalunya, the starting point of this tour (line 5 to Diagonal; then change to line 3 in the direction of Zona Universitaria).

Architecture and Sea   Tour 4

Starting and finishing Point:
Arc de Triomf   **Duration:** 3 hours.

With a rented bicycle explore the beaches and coast, La Barceloneta, the Parc del Fòrum and the new district of 22@. On the way there are green open spaces as well as lots of modern architecture to discover.

For this tour a bicycle is ideal. Almost the entire route can be travelled on bike paths. The starting point is the ❶**Arc de Triomf**, the gateway to the World Fair of 1888 that took place in the ❷**Parc de la Ciutadella**, a well-kept park where a romantic pond and the »Castle of the Three Dragons« are among the attractions. Via the Avinguda del Marqués de l'Argenataria and past the ❸**Estació de França**, worth a short stop to admire the iron and glass structure of the station, you continue along the Old Harbour towards ❹**La Barceloneta**. On the right is the Museu de Catalunya d'Historia.

When you arrive at the W Hotel, which arches like a giant sail on the promontory between the harbour and the sea, you can enjoy a break on the terrace just to the south of the impressive building, which was designed by Ricardo Bofill (▶MARCO POLO Insight, p.50). Traditional fish restaurants with outdoor patios in La Barceloneta provide for a long lunch. The route now follows the Passeig Marítim towards the ❺**Port Olimpic**. Anyone interested in modern architecture should take a look at the barrel-shaped building before you get to the two striking highrise towers that dominate the marina.   Completed by EMBT Arquitectes in 2006 according to the designs of Enric Miralles (died 2000), the Gas Natural Headquarters is one of the most unusual

! Insider Tip

Great beaches

MARCO POLO TIP

Barcelona's 4.5 km kilometres of beach begin just below Barceloneta and extend as far as the Riu Besòs river in the north. The seven beaches are well maintained and equipped with showers, restaurants, beach bars and sports facilities. They also have lifeguards. The city's longest beach is Platja de Barceloneta with a length of 1 km.

Barcelona's 4.5 km kilometres of beach begin just below Barceloneta

modern buildings in Barcelona, featuring a floating horizontal section jutting out from the main tower (Plaça del Gas 1).

Between the sea and the Parc del Poblenou you reach the spacious grounds ❻**Parc del Fòrum** with the striking sun sails and the Museu Blau, a building completed by architects Herzog and De Meuron in 2004. EMBT was also responsible for the unusual and modern ❼**Parc Diagonal Mar** featuring a lake with water-spurting sculptures, raised walkways over the water, curved tubular structures and a children's play area. There is also a large shopping centre adjacent.

From here it's a relaxing ride into town following the cycle path along the Avinguda Diagonal. Even from a distance you can see the ❽**Torre Agbar**. Designed by Jean Nouvel and completed in 2004, the tower has become the new landmark of the city. It looks particularly impressive in the evening when the circular facade begins to glow blue and red. There is one exciting modern building after another. Rising above the low-rise apartment blocks and commercial buildings of the Sant Marti district is the ME Barcelona hotel. The Frenchman Dominique Perrault designed the 27-storey building, which is composed of two slender structures that appear to have shifted against each other. Passing the futuristic Disseny Hub design centre at Plaça Glories Catalans one passes two classics of contemporary Spanish architecture on Avinguda Meridiana, the Auditori (1994) with the Museu de la Música by Rafael Moneo and the Teatre

Literature Tour

In Don Quijote, Miguel de Cervantes talks of the »most beautiful city in Spain«. Especially in the 20th century, Barcelona established a firm place in Spanish and to an extent international literature. Whether crime novel, bestseller or literary masterpiece, the »city of wonders« can be read like a book.

It is early afternoon. The crowds along the Carrer Canuda in the Gothic Quarter have abated somewhat. It's time for lunch, and anyone who can afford the time takes a siesta. At the Canuda bookshop only the front room is open. Floor to ceiling shelving units, replete with antiquarian books disappear into the dark hallway, where there look to be many more books and shelves. »Visit our graveyard of books« says the notice above the closed curtain. Only later, when the owner comes back from his lunch break, is the repository duly opened, but then it just turns out to be a basement full of books.

Haunted House

The Canuda bookshop could have inspired **Carlos Ruíz Zafón** to his »graveyard of lost books« in his bestseller *The Shadow of the Winds* (2002). Sometimes the author still drops by, says the bookseller Pere Anton Torres, but he »doesn't like crowds«. You can encounter the shadow of the winds a few doors further on at No 6. This is the home of the Ateneo, a private cultural institution with about 150 years behind it. The venerable old reading room provides a wonderful setting for one of the scenes in the book, whose plot will also lead you to Plaça Felipe Neri or the more distant Avinguda de Tibidabo. There at No 32 is a villa, which in the book is an overgrown haunted house.

The historical novel *Cathedral of the Sea* also became a bestseller, in which the author, the lawyer Ildefonso Falcones, travels back in time to the Barcelona of the 14th century. On a walk through the Ribera district you can easily imagine the life Arnau, the simple load carrier who advances from being the son of a slave to a very wealthy man.

Place of Humanity

The detective novels of **Manuel Vázquez Montalbán** are also imbued with lots of local colour. Private detective Pepe Carvalho is on the hunt for small-time crooks in the Raval and Barri Xines districts in his efforts to catch the big fish with houses in the Zona Alta offices in Eixample. Montalbán grew up in the Raval. Poverty and prostitution and the patina of grime and crime that permeate his detective stories leave no doubt that the Raval district, despite its seamier side, is also a place of humanity which draws the author and his characters back again and again. Until his death in 2003, you could regularly spot the author at the Boadas (Tallers 1) or the Casa Leopoldo restaurant (Sant Rafael 24).

Barcelona is the scene of numerous novels

Loved by Authors

The topography of Barcelona is not only etched, so to speak, in the books of Monatalbán, but also the works of Eduardo Mendoza, Juan Goytisolo and Francisco González Ledesma. While Eixample and the higher-lying districts are the embodiment of money, prosperity and tradition, as well as boredom and puritanism, the districts of the Old City are places of secret indulgence and excess, of poverty and repression. There is hardly a novel about Barcelona in which this pattern does not appear.

In the novels of **Mercè Rodoreda** the gulf between what people need and reality of what's there is dealt with in a more subtle way. Among the outstanding literary novels to be set in Barcelona is *La Plaça del Diamant* (1962). Anyone who has read the book and is on a visit to Barcelona will probably want to go up to Gràcia to check out what of the novel can be found at the real Plaça del Diamant. It's at that point that you might come to the realization that one should never travel to Barcelona without book.

The town centre of Girona oozes medieval charm

Nacional de Catalunya (1991) by Ricardo Bofill. Through this exciting and rapidly changing urban landscape, the tour returns past the North Station to the Arc de Triomf.

Excursions

There are plenty of charming and interesting excursion destinations all around Barcelona. The towns listed below can all be reached by train (either from Sants Station or, if travelling north, from Passeig de Gràcia or Plaça de Catalunya).

**Montserrat Montserrat is the number one destination from Barcelona. The fantastically located mountain monastery is described in greater detail in the »Sights from A to Z« section.

Costa Brava An approx. 60-minute train ride leads to the northern coastal town of **Calella**. The most popular holiday town on this 50km/31mi stretch of Costa del Maresme features a beautiful beach. Further north is Blanes, the southern-most holiday town on the Costa Brava and a place marked by idyllic coastal landscapes and large tourist centres. At **Blanes**, which has an excellent beach and has managed to maintain its old charm in the town centre, the train leaves the coast. Further inland, **Girona**, capital of the province of the same name and therefore also the capital of the Costa Brava, is one of the most enticing cities of Catalonia. The wonderfully tangled streets of the historic centre transport visitors back to medieval times.

The country town of **Figueres**, north of Girona, is a true cultural gem with southern French flair. Every year several hundred thousand tourists come here to visit the Teatre-Museu of the eccentric artist Salvador Dalí. Once a year thousands of people also travel to Montmeló very close to Barcelona, where the world's best Formula One drivers compete for the Spanish Grand Prix on the **Circuit de Catalunya** (▶ MARCO POLO Insight, p.287).

Fine sandy beaches similar to those in Calella can also be found on the **Costa Daurada**, on the Golden Coast south of Barcelona. **Sitges**, especially, has become a popular holiday town. Discovered by artists in the early 20th century, it was quickly appropriated as a summer getaway by rich Barcelonans. During the summer months, this elegant seaside resort never sleeps and its well-known liberal attitude has made it one of Europe's favourite holiday destinations for the gay scene.

A very different world is found in **Tarragona**, located further south. Numerous buildings in this town, located in the province of the same name, testify to the fact that it was once the most influential Roman city on the Iberian Peninsula.

A visit to the hinterland is also worthwhile. **Penedès**, for example, has excellent wine, which is processed to bubbling cava, the Catalan version of sparkling wine. In fact, the over one hundred sparkling wine cellars of cava producers are the main attraction in this region, including those belonging to the families of Codorníu and Freixenet in **Sant Sadurní d'Anoia**.

SIGHTS FROM A TO Z

Colourful districts for shopping and nightlife, grand monuments and exciting museums, lively boulevards, splendid parks and a good deal of modernisme: that's Barcelona.

✳ Anella Olímpica

✦ C – D 7

Location: Montjuïc
Metro: Paral·lel (L 2, L 3), continuing
by funicular; Espanya (L 1, L 3),
Bus: 50

❶ April – Sept daily
10am–8pm,
Oct–March till 6pm
Admission free

**The summer games of the XXV Olympiad in 1992 took place
in Barcelona. Almost all the competitions were held within the
city area. Where possible, already existing stadiums and halls
were used.**

Olympic Stadium The main centre of Olympic activities was the extensive area of the Anella Olímpica (Olympic Ring) on top of Montjuïc. The original stadium was inaugurated in 1929, but the present Olympic stadium (Estadi Olímpic) holds 56,000 spectators. In 1936, the so-called »People's Olympics«, the Olímpic Popular, was going to be held here, as a peaceful protest against the Olympics in Nazi Germany. More than 5,000 athletes from more than 20 nations arrived, but the Spanish Civil War broke out the night before the opening ceremony. During the following years the stadium gradually deteriorated until it was finally completely renovated. Today, the façade is the only surviving part of the original structure. The stadium is partially open to the public.

Museu Olímpic i de l'Esport The Museu Olímpic i de l'Esport, located at the southern gate of the stadium is an exhibition and documentation centre for the Olympic games in Barcelona and for the history of modern Olympics.
❶ Tue–Sat 10am–8pm (Oct–March till 6pm), Sun 10am–2.30pm, admission €4.50, www.museuolimpicbcn.cat

Palau de Sant Jordi, Torre de Calatrava The Olympic grounds are worth visiting even without a sporting event taking place, if only for the avant-garde architecture. Named after Catalonia's patron saint Sant Jordi, the sports arena with a capacity of 17,000 was designed by Japanese architect **Arata Isozaki** and is located next to the Olympic stadium. Thanks to its good acoustics, the arena is now mainly used for concerts. Japanese artist Aiko Miyawaki used the open space between the stadium and the arena to construct a forest of stone columns.
Just beyond that rises the most spectacular and dynamic construction on Montjuïc: the **Torre Telefónica**. Architect Santiago Calatrava conceived this 136m/446ft high tower unlike any previous such concepts the structure is said to be reminiscent of an athlete holding the olympic torch, a javelin thrower and a kneeling figure. Ricardo Bofill created the facilities for the adjacent INEF sports academy.

The façade is the only original surviving part of Estadi Olímpic Lluís Companys

Arc de Triomf

✦ H 7

Location: Passeig Lluis Companys
Metro: Arc de Triomf (L 1)

This Neomudejar-style triumphal arch was erected for the World Fair of 1888. It provides the main architectural focus along the palm-lined Passeig de Lluis Companys.

Josep Vilaseca designed this representative main entrance for the World Fair, which was held on the site of the present-day Parc de la Ciutadella. Typical for that time and for early Modernisme, the Catalan version of Art Nouveau, are the Neomudejar stylistic elements (Mudejar is the name given to a Spanish style of architecture that combines Gothic and Arab elements and emerged in the 14th century). The approx. 30m/100ft high structure is made of red brick and is decorated by friezes depicting allegories of trade, industry, agriculture and art. If you look closely, you will also be able to make out several bats carved in stone. The animal was said to be a lucky charm of King Jaume I (1213–76).

Triumphal Arch for the World Fair

Barceloneta

✴ G/H 8

Location: northeast of the harbour
Metro: Barceloneta (L 4)

No district of Barcelona is as closely linked to the sea as La Barceloneta. Fishing boats, which also supply the restaurants of the district, tie up at the Moll de Pescadors. On the seaward side are the popular local beaches of La Barceloneta and Sant Sebastià.

Little Barcelona district Barceloneta stretches along a narrow promontory to the northeast of the harbour basin. Walking along, you will appreciate the special character of the district with harbour on one side and the open sea on the other. La Barceloneta is characterized by its densely packed buildings with almost uniform residential areas and the strong sense of neighbourhood. Investors have long had their eyes on the area but without much success – at least as far as the centre of »little Barcelona« is concerned.

La Barceloneta is known for its sandy beach

Along the harbour promenade in contrast, things look positively sophisticated. Expensive yachts and motor yachts are berthed along the Moll de la Barceloneta, while just a few metres away, on Joan de Borbó, lounge bars, bicycle rental shops, traditional fish restaurants and snack bars lie cheek by jowl. Continuing along the Passeig towards the south you'll arrive at the Moll de Rellotge and its compact fishing harbour with the **Torre de Sant Sebastià** rising above it. From this 96m/315ft high steel lattice mast, the **Transbordador Aeri** cable car sails high over the port to Barcelona's local mountain, Montjuïc.

At the end of the mole, between the port and the sea, the **W-Hotel** looks like an inflated sail. This luxury hotel was designed by the Catalan architect Ricardo Bofill. Just to the south steps lead up to a large viewing terrace, while to the side facing the sea are Barcelona's beaches. All along the fine sandy beaches of Platja Sant Miquel, Sant Sebastià and Barceloneta runs a broad pedestrian promenade complete with cycle way that to the north extends as far as Port Olímpic and the Parc del Fòrum created in 2004.

From 1753, La Barceloneta was built on a regular grid layout with streets intersecting at right angles – typical for Baroque schemes of the day. The district was created for the residents of the La Ribera district, in which fishermen and harbour workers traditionally lived. In the early 18th century a part of the district had to make way for a citadel to house the troops of the Bourbon king, Philipp V (the citadel no longer stands, having stood on the site of the present-day Parc de la Ciutadella).

Only a few of the simple, two-storey houses that were built for fishermen and harbour workers in the 18th century now remain. The church of **Sant Miquel del Port** on Plaça de la Barceloneta also dates from this time. Its interior layout and façade design are strongly influenced by the Italian Baroque. To the right of the façade stands the house in which the French diplomat Ferdinand de Lesseps, the driving force behind the Suez Canal in Egypt, lived during his tenure as consul in Barcelona (1842–48).

In the centre of the district is the lively **Plaça de la Font** with the new covered market, the Mercat de la Barceloneta. From the 1980s the seaward side of La Barceloneta was transformed. Manufacturing industry had to go, as did the beloved »chiringuitos«, in which fresh fish and seafood were prepared.

The simple fishing huts are symbolized by the **L'estel ferit** (»Injured Star«, 1992) a sculpture by the German artist Rebecca Horn that has become a landmark of the district. In front of the new beach promenade, fresh sand was trucked in. Smart establishments like Agua or the lounge Club CDLC liven up this section of beach until the small hours; despite its proximity to the harbour the water quality is good here.

** Barri Gòtic

✦ G 7

Location: northeast of the Rambles
Metro: Jaume I (L 4), Liceu (L 3)

The Barri Gòtic stretches from the harbour to the Cathedral and from the Rambles to the Via Laietana. It was from here that Barcelona was and is governed. The picturesque ensemble of narrow alleyways and romantic or grand squares took shape in the Gothic period, when Barcelona alongside Genoa and Venice was the most important trading centre in the Mediterranean.

Gothic quarter

The origins of this district, however, date back to Roman times. Parts of the old city wall, as well as other remains such as the pillars of a temple of Augustus, are still visible today. The Barri Gòtic has been the city's spiritual and worldly focus for the last two thousand years. The cathedral on Tabor Mountain, which at 12m/40ft is the highest point of the city centre, is surrounded by narrow medieval streets. The dukes of Barcelona and the kings of Catalonia and Aragón resided in the vicinity, the Catholic Monarchs received Christopher Columbus on his return from his first expedition here, and the city and provincial councils have been based here since the 14th and 15th centuries, respectively. Today, most of the Barri Gòtic is a car-free zone. High street shops like Zara, shoe shops and high-end fashion houses are ranged along Avinguda del Portal de'l Angel. Fashion boutiques can also be found in Canuda and Pontaferissa streets as well as more generally in the area between the cathedral and Plaça Catalunya. There are also a few long-established shops still surviving in the district, such as Manual Alpargatera, where alpargatas (espadrilles) are still made by hand. The area most worth seeing for its architectural monuments encompasses the Cathedral district, the former Jewish quarter and Plaça de Sant Jaume with its adjacent streets. The

---

! *Sardana* **Insider Tip**

Those visiting in July or between September and November should not miss the sardana dance spectacle on Sundays and holidays at noon. The square in front of the cathedral is turned into a dance floor for anyone who wants to join in the sardana circle dance, a symbol of Catalan identity.

Barri Gòtic

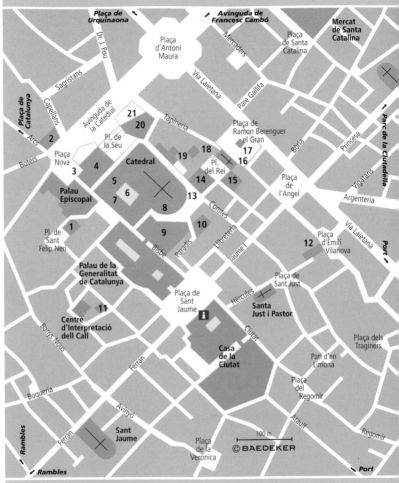

Plaça de
Urquinaona

Avinguda de
Francesc Cambó

Mercat
de Santa
Catalina

Dr. J. Pou

Plaça
d'Antoni
Maura

Mercaders

Plaça
de Santa
Catalina

Via Laietana

Sagristans

Pare Gallifa

Plaça de
Catalunya

Capellans

Avinguda de
la Catedral

Tapineria

Plaça de
Ramon Berenguer
el Gran

Parc de la Ciutadella

21
20

Arcs

2

Pl. de
la Seu

19

18

17

16

Bòria

Princesa

Boters

Plaça
Nova

3

4

Catedral

Pl.
del Rei

Vigatans

5

14

15

Plaça
de
l'Angel

Argenteria

Palau
Episcopal

7

6

13

Comtes

Via Laietana

8

Pl. de
Sant
Felip Neri

1

9

10

Bisbe

Paradís

Llibreteria

Jaume I

12

Plaça
d'Emili
Vilanova

Port

Palau de la
Generalitat
de Catalunya

11

Plaça de
Sant
Jaume

Hèrcules

Plaça de
Sant Just

Santa
Just i Pastor

Centre
d'Interpretació
dell Call

Banys Nous

Ciutat

Plaça dels
Traginers

Casa
de la
Ciutat

Pati d'en
Limona

Ferran

Plaça
del
Regomir

Boqueria

Avinyó

Ataúlf

Regomir

Rambles

Ferran

Sant
Jaume

Plaça
de la
Verònica

100 m

©BAEDEKER

Port

Rambles

1 Museu del Calçat
   (Footwear Museum)
2 Chamber of Architects
3 Roman city wall towers
4 Archdeacon's House
   (Institut Municipal d'Història)
5 Romanesque portal
6 Cloister
7 Porta de Santa Eulàlia
8 Porta de la Pietat
   (Access to the cloister)
9 Cannon's House
10 Columns of the Augustus Temple
   (inside the building)

11 Sinagoga Major
12 Galeria de Catalans Il·lustres
13 Portal de Sant Iu
14 Palau del Lloctinent
   (Archive of the Crown of Aragon)
15 Palau Clariana-Padellás
   (Museu d'Història de la
   Ciutat)
16 Capella de Santa Agata
17 Equestrian statue of Ramon
   Berenguer the Great
18 Saló de Tinell
19 Museu Frederic Marès
20 Casa Pia Almoina
21 Roman city walls

most beautiful squares in the district are the medieval Plaça del Rei, the utterly picturesque Plaça del Pi and Plaça de Sant Felip Neri as well as the the Plaça Reial with its uniform facades. In an easterly direction, i.e. towards the sea, something of the rough and dangerous side of Barcelona has been preserved in the dark and occasionally dingy streets. Here you can find kebab shops and kiosks as well as trendy pubs and restaurants.

TOUR

Plaça Sant Jaume

Starting point for this recommended tour is Plaça Sant Jaume, the historical and political centre of Barcelona. The spacious square is home to the Palau de la Generalitat (government palace) and the Casa de la Ciutat or Ayuntamento (town hall) opposite, both witnesses to the city's history.

> **! Insider Tip**
>
> *No hustle and bustle*
>
> **MARCO ⊕ POLO TIP**
>
> Just around the corner from Plaça Sant Jaume, in the courtyard of the Museum Frederic Marès (Plaça de Sant Iu 5), a simple garden café opens for the summer season. Café d'Estiu offers welcome respite from the bustling Barri Gòtic.

When it comes to official occasions, the Plaça is the place to go, particularly when events and festivals of national significance are involved. In Barcelona the word »national« is not used to refer to the whole of Spain, but to Catalonia, which isn't even officially a nation. Thus the opposing city and regional parliaments vie with each other for who can be the most Catalan.

When during the La Mercè festival the castellers make themselves into a towering column, on live camera in the background there are always likely to be activists belonging to the ERC, the Republican Left of Catalonia, with banners calling for the independence of the region. Even in Roman Barcino the forum was located on the site of the present-day square, where Spain's second republic was proclaimed in 1931. Of course in this centre of power the players of FC Barcelona also like to parade themselves before the jubilant crowd whenever they win the league title or another important trophy.

Casa de la Ciutat

Casa de la Ciutat dominates the southeastern side of Plaça de Sant Jaume. The magnificent building, dating originally from the 14th century, has kept its Gothic side façades, while the main façade was redesigned by Josep Mas in 1847, in contrasting neoclassical style. There is a beautiful external staircase in the remarkable courtyard. Inside the town hall is the large 14th century **Saló de Cent** (Council Hall) featuring tapestries in the Catalan heraldic colours of red and yellow. The **Saló de les Cròniques** (Hall of Chronicles) displays a mural by Joseph Maria Sert with highlights of Catalan history.

The former Palau de la Diputació, opposite Casa de la Ciutat, was built in the 15th century and once served as the seat of the principalities. Today, the Generalitat de Catalunya (autonomous government of Catalonia) can be found here. The magnificent Gothic courtyard is absolutely remarkable, as is the Gothic St George's Chapel on the first floor. The back section of the building features a charming patio with orange trees. To the north, the Palau is adjoined by the Audiencia, the former Court of Justice.

Palau de la Generalitat

On the corner of Carrer de Marlet and Carrer Sant Domènec del Call, in the tangle of streets west of Plaça Sant Jaume, once stood the main synagogue, erected in the 12th century and **probably the oldest Jewish house of worship in all of Spain**. The cellar rooms, which can still be visited, rest on Roman foundations. The actual synagogue is situated next to the reception room. The two windows on the left wall of the present-day entrance face the holy city of Jerusalem. Torah scrolls are kept in the shrine standing between the two windows.
❶ in summer: Mon–Fri 10.30am–6.30pm, Sat and Sun 10.30am–2.30pm, in winter Mon–Fri 11am–5.30pm, Sat and Sun 11am–3pm, www.calldebarcelona.org

Sinagoga Major

> **!** *Jewish Centre*   **Insider Tip**
>
> MARCO ⊕ POLO TIP
>
> The sites and history of the city's one-time Jewish quarter can be studied at the Centre d' Interpretació del Call on the Placeta de Manuel Ribé. The small visitors centre can be found to the southwest of the cathedral at the heart of the medieval Jewish quarter in the Barri Gòtic.
> Wed – Fri 11am – 2pm, Sat 10am to 7pm, Sun, holidays 10am – 8pm

Leading from Plaça de Sant Jaume to the ►Catedral is the picturesque Carrer del Bisbe Irurita which is spanned by a delicate »Gothic« bridge. However, as Gothic as the structure might look, it actually only dates from the 1920s. The Catalan prime minister uses it to get to the **Casa dels Canonges** (Canon's House), because that's where he lives rather than, as one might assume, in the government palace. Just past the Canon's House on the right you come to the cloister of the cathedral and straight on the Archdeacon's House.

Carrer del Bisbe Irurita

Founded in 1922, the Institut Municipal d'Història (City Historical Institute) is based in the beautiful Casa de l'Ardiaca (Archdeacon's House). Parts of the building date back to the 12th century, but most of its current appearance stems from the late Gothic period of the 15th century. The decorative figures, however, show the obvious influence of the Italian Renaissance. The interior of the building is only accessible to expert scientists, but the courtyard surrounded by an arcade with colourful ornate tiles and a Gothic fountain is well worth visiting.

Institut Municipal d' Història

The »Call« of Barcelona

A large Jewish community lived in Barcelona in medieval times, though their tracks have been obscured. Centuries after their violent expulsion, many Jews resettled in the Catalan metropolis.

About 4,000 Jews lived in Barcelona in the 13th century, 15 percent of the city's population at the time. The Jewish quarter **Call Major** was situated next to the cathedral, in the Barri Gótic. The smaller quarter **Call Menor**, founded in 1257, was located beyond the city walls between Carrer dels Tres Llits and Carrer de la Lleona, though it was torn down in the 19th century. Scientists are uncertain about the origin of the word »Call«. It was derived most likely from the Hebrew word »kahal«, meaning community. Today, the only reminders of the Call Major are the names of some alleys (e.g. Sant Domènec del Call, Carrer del Call), occasional Hebrew mural inscriptions, and a Hebrew inscription discovered in 1820 on Carrer de Marlet (on the corner of Carrer de l'Arc de Sant Ramon del Call) referring to a pious foundation of a rabbi named Samuel ha-Sardi. During the 15th century, when Jewish citizens were forced to leave their quarters in Barcelona and eventually Spain too, their residential and community buildings sank into oblivion. The Sinagoga Major was re-inaugurated as late as 2002, despite the fact that its original location had long since been discovered.

Red and Yellow Badge

The Barcelonian Jews were first mentioned in documents dating from the 9th century. During the Middle Ages, Jews formed an integral part of the economy, finance and science. They were merchants and craftsmen (jewellers, tailors, etc.), money lenders and changers, doctors, solicitors, translators and scholars. They worked for Catalan noblemen, and their services were greatly appreciated even by the royal court. However, Barcelona's Christian community was always suspicious of the Jews' foreign culture, their distinct sense for money and profound knowledge of medicine, which in the Middle Ages was deemed occult. In 1243, on the order of King James I of Aragon, all Jews living in the city were required to wear a red and yellow badge as a mark of distinction. During the night, the Call was locked.

Pogrom and Expulsion

In the 14th century, common people increasingly began to despise their Jewish neighbours. Many Christians felt cheated by the Jewish creditors. Other reasons for their accumulated hatred were envy and Christian fanaticism, as many Jews gained power through their economic potency. In 1391, a wave of pogroms broke out in the Andalusian town of Seville and swept through several cities in Spain. The same year, on July 5th, a Christian mob raided the Call of Barcelona, looting and murdering its residents. Several hundred Jews

Hebrew inscription in Carrer de Marlet, an alley in the Gothic Quarter

were killed. Ten years later, King Juan I had the Call closed, and the few families still remaining in Barcelona were forced to leave the city in 1424. In 1492, under the Catholic reign of Fernando and Isabel, all Jews still practicing their religion were expelled from Spain. Jews who converted to Christianity in order to prevent their expulsion soon faced the terror of the Inquisition. In 1992, almost exactly 500 years later, the Spanish king Juan Carlos I publicly apologized to the Jewish community for the expulsion of all Jews from Spain..

Spain's Largest Jewish Community

During the second half of the 19th century, as much as four centuries after the expulsion, Jews slowly began to resettle in Catalonia. In 1918, the Jews formed a new community in Barcelona. Before World War I (1914 – 1918), there were mainly Ashkenazi Jews originally from Austria and Germany. During the 1920s, the community was comprised of about 1,000 members. Although the dictator Franco was a friend of Germany the Regime never handed Jews over to Nazi Germany. In 1956, Morocco's declaration of independence instigated another wave of immigration, and Jewish tradesmen from the North African country found a new home in Barcelona and Southern Spain. The last wave of immigration took place in the 1970s. The Jews who settled in Barcelona originated from South America and were mostly intellectuals who no longer felt safe in their native countries, such as Argentina, Chile and Cuba, all ruled by dictators at the time. At present, between 4,000 and 5,000 Jews live in Barcelona, making it the largest Jewish community in Spain. The community has two functioning synagogues, one is Sefardic and more traditional, and the other is progressive and open to all Jews and people interested in the Jewish faith.

Palau
Episcopal
The Palau Episcopal (Episcopalian Palace) opposite the Institut Municipal d'Història was first mentioned in a document in 926. The oldest parts of the current building date back to the 12th and 13th centuries, and some also to the 15th century. The palace was renovated in 1883 and 1928. The two round towers of the Portal del Bisbe are remnants from the Roman Period. The inner courtyard with Romanesque arcades contains a modern statue of the Virgin Mary of ►Montserrat.

Plaça Sant
Felip Neri
Behind the Episcopalian Palace you come to the picturesque little Plaça de Sant Felip Neri with the ►Museu del Calçat (Shoe Museum).

Col.legi
d'Arquitectes
To the north on Plaça Nova the modern building of the **Architects' Association** (Col·legi d'Arquitectes) imposes itself on the cityscape. When the Catalan Architects' Association building was erected in 1962, it was one of the city's first high-rise structures. Today one might perceive the imposition of this grey tower block in the heart of the medieval Barri Gòtic as having being less than sensitive. Interesting, however, is the three-part sgrafitto on the façade, which bears the unmistakeable signature of Pablo Picasso, although the artist didn't actually carry out the work himself. The Catalonian capital is one of the most exciting cities in the fields of architecture and urban development. On the ground floor and in the basement of the chamber of architects there are regular exhibitions devoted to local and international themes. There is also an architectural bookshop.

❶ The Col·legi d'Arquitectes de Catalunya (CoAC) organises themed city tours for groups.

Plaça de la
Seu
The Plaça de la Seu (the square in front of the cathedral) is flanked to the north by the Casa Pia Almoina housing the Museu Diocesà (►Catedral). Passing along the long northeast side of the cathedral you'll arrive at the ►Museu Frederic Marès.

*Plaça
del Rei
Go left at the next turning to reach the Plaça del Rei (Royal Square), which shouldn't be confused with the ►Plaça Reial near the Rambles. It one of the most beautiful squares in the city and looks particularly striking in the evening light. Encircled by magnificent buildings from the 12th to 16th centuries, only the square's southern end opens up to the alleys of the old town, providing a spectacular backdrop for concerts or theatre performances, which often take place here on long summer evenings. Of course, it is also a popular meeting place for an evening cocktail.

Palau del
Lloctinent
In the southeast the attractive square is flanked by the ►Museu d'Història de la Ciutat. The west side is enclosed by Palau del Lloctinent del Rei (Palace of the Royal Governor), a plain-looking building

The Gothic Quarter is the centre of the old city of Barcelona

dating from the 16th century. Formerly the seat of the Governor of Barcelona, it now houses the Arxiu de la Corona d'Aragó (Crown of Aragón Archive). The emblem of the Generalitat is displayed several times on the building's façade.

The northern tract houses the Saló de Tinell (**Throne Room**), built in Romanesque style in 1370, also part of the Palau Reial, the former Royal Palace, with the tall watchtower standing adjacent. A visit to the Throne Room is not to be missed, regardless of whether you're interested in the temporary exhibitions that are held here. Apart from its historical importance, the enormous barrel-vaulted hall is itself mightily impressive. It's easy to imagine the significant occasions that have taken place here, including **Christopher Columbus** being received as a peer by the Spanish joint rulers Ferdinand II and Isabella I (Reyes Católicos = Catholic Monarchs) after his first expedition to the New World. Inquisitors also judged heretics in this room while down below on the square the stakes were prepared for the convicted.

Saló de Tinell

The eastern side is taken up by the Capella Santa Agata, a Gothic chapel built on the former Roman city wall, which once served as the royal palace chapel. It was built in the 14th century at the behest of

Capella Santa Agata

Jaime II and his wife Blanca de Anjou. The single-naved interior features a large altarpiece (1465) by Jaume Huguet, which is one of the most prominent works from the Catalan Gothic period. The stained glass windows in the choir feature coats of arms, including those of the Counts of Barcelona – reminiscent of the church's former significance. The sacristy contains the large iron wheelwork of a clock dating from 1576. In the chapel there is an entrance to the 16th century Torre del Rei Martí, named after the last count of the Barcelonan dynasty. From the square you can return to Plaça de Sant Jaume or continue to the metro station at Plaça de l'Angel.

Boqueria

✦ F 7

Location: Rambla de Sant Josep
Metro: Liceu (L 3)

Southwest of Rambla dels Flors, where the colourful flower market is held every morning, stands the grand Mercat de Sant Josep, the oldest, most significant and most attractive market hall in Barcelona. It is usually called simply La Boqueria, the »belly« of Barcelona.

»Belly of Barcelona«   Built between 1840 and 1914, a visit to this **market** is an absolute must! In the »stomach« of Barcelona you'll imagine this is what is meant by a culinary paradise. Chefs from the best restaurants in town come here to buy freshly caught fish and seafood, meat products, and fruit and vegetables from the Catalan coast or hinterland. The vendors compete with their aesthetic presentation of foods rather than ballyhooing their wares throughout the hall. The fruit displays resemble colour compositions of modern paintings. The overwhelming range of seafood – some of which is still alive – is sold in the round middle section and its diversity easily competes with the stock in some oceanography museums! The atmospheric hustle and bustle, the sounds, aromas and colours alone make an excursion to this market worthwhile, but you should definitely buy a little something while you're there such as the Catalan cream cheese called Mató, the spicy Xoriço sausage or simply some fresh fruit.

> **!** MARCO❂POLO TIP
>
> *Take a break at Pinotxo*   **Insider Tip**
>
> Those visiting the city will be glad to stop for a drink or snack at one of the stalls in the market hall. Stand number 67-68 (on the right when entering from the Ramblas) is home to the legendary Pinotxo Bar. This Barcelona institution is not to be missed; market traders take breakfast here before opening up their stalls.

The square in front of the market hall is called the Pla de l'Os (Bear Square – named after the travellers and their dancing bears that used to perform here), and is part of the Rambles. The street pavement here features a floor mosaic by Joan Miró from 1976. Opposite, take a look at the somewhat bizarre looking building of an umbrella shop with a large Chinese dragon mounted on the façade.

Pla de l'Os

Caixaforum

❋ **D 6**

Location: Av. Ferrer i Guàrdia 6–8
Metro: Plaça Espanya (L 1, L 3)
❶ daily 10am–8pm, Wed, July, Aug
till 10pm or 11pm

Admission free
**www.fundacio.
lacaixa.es**

At the foot of Montjuïc between the exhibition grounds and MNAC is the Caixaforum art and cultural centre, housed in the former Casaramoma textile factory.

The dedicated foundation of the La Caixa savings bank chose a very special building for their exhibition and cultural centre in Barcelona. The former Casa Ramona textile factory was built in 1911 by the Modernista architect Puig i Cadafalch. The brick building is an impressive example of Catalan industrial architecture. From 1940 right up until the 1990s, it served as the headquarters of the mounted police. The 12,000 sq m/129,000 sq ft exhibition centre was opened in 2002. With his gleaming white surfaces, the newly created entrance designed by Japanese architect Arata Isozaki stands in deliberate contrast to the ornamentation and the warmth of the brick building.
In addition to an auditorium for lectures and concerts and a media library, the Caixaforum regularly hosts special exhibitions.

Cultural centre

** Casa Batlló

❋ **G 6**

Location: Passeig de Gràcia 43
Metro: Passeig de Gràcia
(L 2, L 3, L 4)
❶ daily 9am–9pm (2pm when an

event is taking place)
Admission: €21.50
www.casabatllo.es

Casa Batlló, on the corner of Passeig de Gràcia and Carrer Aragó, was designed by Antoni Gaudí between 1904 and 1906 for the textile manufacturer Josep Batlló i Casanovas, and counts among the best-known Modernista monuments.

Casa Amatller and Casa Batlló, two gems on Eixample's Passeig de Gràcia boulevard

The exterior of the building contradicts almost all established rules of construction. This house is not just a house, but rather a monumental sculpture, with motifs from the legend of the dragon slayer St George (Sant Jordi). Gaudí's design is very naturalistic and everything seems organic and intertwined. Some of the free forms on the window façade of the first floor are reminiscent of plants, some of entrances to a cave. Above, the façade is covered with glazed ceramic tiles in shades of green, blue and ochre. The balcony railings made of hammered sheet steel look like skull bones, while the wavelike curved roof, with richly ornate chimneys, seems like the back of a dragon. Every bit as original as the façade is the interior: curved walls, ornate ceilings and beautiful woodwork.

*Casa Amatller Next to Casa Batlló, a further Modernista highlight awaits the visitor: Casa Amatller. Josep Puig i Cadafalch designed the building in 1898 for the chocolate manufacturer Antonio Amatller. The façade features motifs from Gothic secular architecture and is decorated with colourful ceramics. Through the porch with its rich azulejos decoration you will first pass the remarkable staircase. Based on a square ground plan and with its figuratively designed banister, it winds its way to the upper floors and is protected by a coloured glass roof. On the ground floor there's a shop and information area, where a film describes the history of the house's construction. Particularly worth seeing are the rooms on the first floor, where the Fundació Institut Amatller is based. It is the only part of the house that still has its original furnishings. Casa Amatller has been restored over the recent years.

❶ Only after registration by phone on tel. 934 670 466 260 or send an email to casessingulars@casessingulars.com

At the southern end of the same block (at the intersection of Carrer Consell de Cent) stands the Casa Lleó Morera (1905; interior closed to the public). This architectural work by Lluís Domènech i Montaner was built in pure Modernista style and adorned with flowery décor.

Casa Lleó Morera

✦✦ Casa Milà · La Pedrera

✦ G 5

Location: Passeig de Gràcia 92
Metro: Diagonal (L 3, L 5)
❶ daily 9am–8pm,
night visits 8.15pm

Admission: €20.50
www.www.lapedrera.com

Casa Milà, on the corner of Passeig de Gràcia and Carrer de Provença, is the final, and probably best-known, secular work by Antoni Gaudí.

Casa Milà, on the corner of Passeig de Gràcia and Carrer de Provença, is the final, and probably best-known, secular work by Antoni Gaudí. The monument, which today is a UNESCO World Heritage Site, looks more like a monstrous wax or clay creature than a residential building. Searching for straight lines is a futile endeavour: the entire façade with curvy, plant-looking balconies seems solidified in wavy movement. Even the numerous chimneys and ventilation shafts on the accessible, undulating roof are designed as bizarre sculptures. Gaudí ignored all common architectural principles with extraordinary consistency: the building's interior does not have a single load-bearing wall, but consists only of beams and pillars and the floor plan is different for every room. This house is so well known because its construction (1905–11) was not universally admired. Its design was often mocked and passionately rejected. Also, the lengthy construction period and Gaudí's frequent demands for changes provoked

Famous Gaudí creation

The ventilation towers on the rooftop of Casa Milà

hefty debates with the owner of the building, Milà i Camps-Segimon, which is why the villa soon earned its derogatory title **La Pedrera (the quarry)**. The entire building is grouped around two oval atria. The owner of the Casa Milà, the Obra Social Catalunya Caixa Art Foundation, has opened up the roof terrace, attic, the top and the first floors to visitors. The rest of the building is still occupied.

Tour The visitors' entrance is to be found on Carrer de Provença. From there, via a grotto-like staircase and lift, you will reach the Espai Gaudí. With the aid of information panels and models, here among the 270 parabolic brick arches of the attic you can familiarise yourself with Gaudí's architecture. A real honeypot is the roof terrace (La Azotea) directly above where visitors complete with chimneys that resemble figures. Jazz concerts (Nits d´Estiu a la Pedrera) regularly take place here from mid-June to the end of August. The tour then leads to the top residential floor, where some of the rooms are furnished in the Modernista style. Down on the first floor the Catalunya Caixa Art Foundation puts on exhibitions of art and culture, which can be visited free of charge.

Casa-Museu Verdaguer

✳ out-of-town

Location: Villa Joana (Vallvidrera)
Train (FGC): Baixador de Vallvidrera   **Admission:** free
❶ Sat and Sun 10am–2pm   **www.verdaguer.cat**

Villa Joana, today used as a museum dedicated to the Catalan poet Jacint Verdaguer, is located in the northern district of Vallvidrera, in the middle of a beautiful park.

To get there it's easiest to take the train (Ferrocarril de la Generalitat) from ▶Plaça de Catalunya in the direction of Sant Cugat to Baixador de Vallvidrera; from there it is only a five-minute walk southeastwards. The villa was originally a farmhouse, some parts of which date back to the Middle Ages. In 1920, the owner invited the sick Jacint Verdaguer i Santaló to live there. However, he died only a few weeks later, on 10 June, at the age of 57. In some of Verdaguer's virtually unchanged rooms, the museum exhibits original manuscripts as well as contemporary paintings and drawings. A large section is dedicated to his epic L´Atlàntida, for which the painter F. Vall produced a series of oil paintings.

Museum villa in a lovely park

After visiting the museum you can take a stroll through the 8 sq km/3 sq mi Parc de Collserola. With its various stalls and barbecues, this is a popular destination for Barcelonans, especially at weekends. Maps of the park are available at the Centre d'Information near Villa Joana.

Parc de Collserola

✳ Casa Vicens

✳ G 4

Location: Carrer Carolines 24
Metro: Lesseps (L 3)

Located in a narrow side street off Carrer Gran de Gràcia, Casa Vicens was built by Gaudí 1883–88 for the ceramics manufacturer Manuel Vicens i Montaner.

It is one of the architect's first completed projects. The still largely linear design reveals a strong influence from the Mudejar style, which developed during the Reconquista and combines Spanish and Arab elements. Characteristic is the decorative use of brick, which delicately embellishes the façade on the top floor in particular, as well as the lavish application of tiles. Noteworthy is the wrought iron railing, which features stylized palm tree fronds for decoration – trees that

Early Gaudí work

originally stood on the site and had to be felled for the Casa Vicens. Although, along with other Gaudí monuments, it has been declared a World Heritage Site, the Casa Vicens is closed to the public. In the basement are the utility rooms and kitchen, and the ground floor includes an ornamentally designed dining room and a smoking area in the oriental style, which is surmounted by a muqarnas dome. The Casa was extended by the architect Joan Serra de Martínez in 1925.

** **Catedral · La Seu**

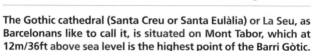

✦ G 7

Location: Plaça de la Seu
Metro: Jaume I (L 4), Liceu (L 3)
❶ daily 8am–12.45pm and 5.15pm –7.30pm free admission (without museum, choir and roof terrace),
1pm–5pm admission €6 (including museum etc.)
www.catedralbcn.org

The Gothic cathedral (Santa Creu or Santa Eulàlia) or La Seu, as Barcelonans like to call it, is situated on Mont Tabor, which at 12m/36ft above sea level is the highest point of the Barri Gòtic.

Symbol of the Barri Gòtic
Construction began in 1298 on the site of an old Romanesque monument, of which several stone reliefs can still be seen on the northeastern side portal. The cathedral was completed in 1448, except for its frontage and the dome tower, which were added in 1898 and 1913, respectively. The different phases of construction are clearly visible. The façade, with its spiky towers and filigree arches, is much more embellished than the high altar, and more than would be customary for a typical Catalan church. In some ways, it is reminiscent of monuments built further north, such as Cologne Cathedral in Germany. The layout of the cathedral is also somewhat unusual: the apse and the high altar are located in the southeast, while the main façade faces northwest.

Cloisters
From Plaça Sant Jaume, the beautiful cloister (claustre) can be entered via the Portal de Santa Eulàlia. Built between 1380 and 1451, it is lined with numerous chapels and altars dedicated to various saints, including the much-frequented Capella de Santa Llúcia (built in 1270). Magnolia, palm and orange trees create a charming contrast to old Gothic statuary. The mossy fountain in the middle of the cloister is crowned by a statue of St George and the Dragon (Sant Jordi). A tradition at Corpus Christi is to blow out an egg and let it spin on the fountain.

The cloister is inhabited by a small **flock of geese**, an old tradition whose origin has been explained in two ways: in the Middle Ages

Catedral Santa Eulàlia

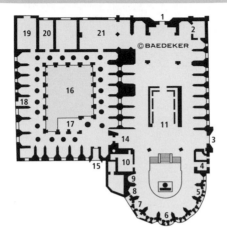

1 Main enttrance
2 Baptistery
3 Porta de Sant Iu
4 Capella de les Sants Innocents
5 Capella de l'Aparició
6 Capella de Sant Crist
7 Capella del Patrocini
8 Capella de Sant Miquel
9 Capella de Sant Antoni
10 Registry
11 Choir
12 Capella de Sant Climent
13 Capella de Sant Raimund de
   Penyafort
14 Porta de Sant Severi
15 Porta de la Pietat
16 Claustre (cloister)
17 Font de Sant Jordi
   (St. George Fountain)
18 Porta de Santa Eulàlia
19 Capella de Santa Llúcia
20 Sala Capitular (chapter room)
21 Capella del Santíssim Sagrament

they guarded the cathedral and its treasures – in the same manner as the Roman Capitol was guarded in the year 387 AD; and it has also been suggested that the white colour of the birds symbolizes the virginity of Saint Eulàlia.

The Museu de la Catedral in the former chapter house (Sala Capitular) features paintings by Spanish artists from the 15th and 16th centuries (especially Jaume Huguet), sculptures and liturgical items.

Cathedral Museum

The High Gothic interior (83m/272ft long, 37m/121ft wide, 25m/82ft high) comprises the usual nave and aisles, but the aisles are almost equal in height to the nave. They are lined by small galleries and chapels, mainly from the 16th and 17th centuries, with ornate Baroque altars underneath. The most impressive is the Capilla del Santíssim Sagrament, left of the high altar, which houses the 15th–16th-century alabaster tomb of the bishop St Olegarius († 1136), as well as the »Christ of Lepanto«, the alleged figurehead of the flagship of Don Juan d'Austria (►Museu Marítim), in which he won the sea battle against the Turks in 1571. The last chapel before the left transept displays a black Madonna, which resembles the famous image of the Virgin Mary of ►Montserrat.

Interior

Particularly worth mentioning is the spectacular **choir** in an unusual location right in the centre of the nave, separated off on three sides. The finely carved stalls (15th century) have royal emblems on their backs. The Knights of the Order of the Golden Fleece gathered here

13 white geese are kept in the cloister

in 1519. The **pulpit** (1403) is also an example of outstanding woodwork. Some of the magnificent stained glass dates back to the 15th century. A remarkable late-Gothic retable (16th-century) is displayed in the Capilla Major.

A staircase descending from the Capilla Major leads into the candle-lit **crypt**, where an alabaster sarcophagus made in Italy in around 1330 is thought to contain the remains of St Eulàlia, patron saint of both the city and the cathedral. In the sacristy you can view the cathedral **treasury** (Catalan: tresor), including a painting of the Madonna of the Rosary.

Roof terrace From the roof terrace (access from the interior of the church at the Porta de Sant Iu, admission €3) there are superb views of the city, its hinterland and the sea.

Museu Diocesà Right next door to the cathedral is the Museu Diocesà, the museum of the Diocese of Barcelona, housed in the **Casa Pia Almoina**, which was once the city's poor house. As such a building has stood on this site since the 11th century, but the oldest preserved remains date from the 15th century. The museum houses part of the diocesan archive and owns a collection of sacred art, mainly from the diocese, including various remarkable Romanesque works. The collection focuses on sculptures, paintings, ceramic and goldsmith art as well as liturgical garments from the early Middle Ages until recent times.

❶ Av. de la Catedral 4, Tue–Sat 10am–2pm and 5pm–8pm, Sun 11am–2pm, admission €6

Col·legi de les Teresianes

✳ F3

Location: Carrer Ganduxer 95–105
Train (FGC): Bonanova

The Col·legi de les Teresianes is the mother convent of the Teresian order, founded in 1876. Antoni Gaudí designed the building, which looks more like a fortress than a convent.

Antoni Gaudí was commissioned to complete the building in 1888, after work had already started. Compared to other works by the architect, the Col·legi de les Teresianes is of unusual sobriety – a concession to the rule of the order. The brick-built pointed arches of the façade, especially on the top floor, allude to Gothic models. The buildings house a school and can therefore only be visited as part of a guided tour (registration tel. 93 212 33 54).

Sobre design

✳ Colonia Güell

✳ out-of-town

Location: Santa Coloma del Cervelló (20km southwest)
Train (FGC): from Plaça d'España, lines S33, S8, S4
❶ Mon–Fri 10am–7pm, Sat & Sun 10am–5pm; Nov–April Mon–Fri until 5pm, Sat & Sun until 3pm
Admission: €7
www.gaudicoloniaguell.org

Antoni Gaudí was supposed to build a church for the planned workers' settlement of Colonia Güell in Santa Coloma del Cervello, just outside the city. Only the crypt was ever completed, but it is considered an architectural masterpiece.

Count Eusebi Güell, Antoni Gaudí's principal patron, had a small housing scheme built for the workers of his textile factory Santa Coloma del Cervelló, in 1898. Gaudí was commissioned to build a church for the settlement. His first drafts bear a striking resemblance to the ►Sagrada Família, but neither the church nor the housing scheme was ever completed. The foundations of the church, the crypt, were built between 1908 and 1916 on a flat hill covered in pines. Gaudí's orientation toward the Gothic style in terms of design is clearly visible, and yet he made use of his principle of »leaning columns«, allowing his interior to be seemingly unconstrained. The mosaics, especially the one above the entrance, as well as the coloured windowpanes, are particularly worth mentioning. Gaudí also designed the pews.

Crypt by Gaudí

Eixample

✦ E – J 5/6

Location: northwest of Plaça de Catalunya and the Rambles
Metro: Passeig de Gràcia (L 2, 3, 4)

Begun in the 19th century, this extension to the city with its grid layout of streets and square housing blocks now has the Barcelona's finest boutiques, restaurants and hotels. At its heart is the Quadrat d´Or, the »Golden Quadrant«, including some of the most remarkable Modernista buildings.

District with major works of Modernisme

L´Eixample means »extension«. Like a huge, regular grid, this planned part of the city covers a huge area, surrounding the Old City on three sides, extending as far as the foot of Mount Tibidabo and to the districts of Gràcia and Sant Gervasi, and from north to south all the way between Sants and Sant Martí (▶map, p. 176).

City expansion

At the beginning of the 19th century Barcelona's city limits were still clearly defined with the Old City forming the core area. During the course of 19th century, Catalonia experienced substantial economic growth and more and more people flocked to the emerging industrial city in search of work. The living conditions of the men, women and children who toiled in the factories were desperate. And the old-established population groups suffered from the unsanitary conditions and the narrow and crowded Old Town: Barcelona was bursting at the seams. In 1854, the government in Madrid finally allowed the walls to be torn down, and four years later the expansion of the urban area was approved by the authorities in distant Castile. The public competition was won by Antoni Rovira i Trias. According to his plans, the new districts around the Old Town were to spread out like a fan, interrupted by broad boulevards radiating from the centre. But Madrid turned down this scheme and instead approved the **draft by Ildefonso Cerdà**. His »plan around the city of Barcelona and its renovation and expansion project« provided for a grid-like expansion of the city. The square apartment blocks would each have bevelled corners and a side length of 113m/371ft. The blocks should be no more than five stories tall and have green courtyards. It soon became clear, however, that the ideal of a green and airy urban expansion would fall victim to reality: even at the start of the project the price of land increased faster than expected as the temptation to market green open spaces was just too great and speculation was rife.

**Quadrat d'Or

The development and construction of the Eixample ran parallel to Modernisme, the Catalan version of Art Nouveau. Especially in the so-called Quadrat d'Or, the golden square, which is located between

Casa Milà at the corner of Carrer de Provença, in the Eixample

Avinguda Diagonal, the Plaça de Catalunya and Aribau and Sant Joan streets, the wealthy bourgeoisie settled down and showed off their wealth in the shape of some extraordinary **Modernista buildings** (►MARCO POLO Insight p.180). Here you can find the architecturally remarkable houses of ►Casa Milà, ►Casa Batlló, ►Casa Calvet and Casa Amatller ►p.166). Through the centre of the Golden quadrangle runs Barcelona's most elegant street, the ►Passeig de Gràcia, with correspondingly smart boutiques and shops. The artistic highlight of the quarter is the ►Fundació Antoni Tàpies.

The L'Esquerra de l'Eixample, the left side of the Eixample, which continues towards the University, has been given the nickname **Gaixample** because of some gay-friendly bars.

L'Esquerra de l'Eixample

The Dreta de L'Eixample, the right side of the Eixample, is the location of the ►Sagrada Familia, the world famous landmark in Barcelona, which now hastens rapidly towards completion after more than a century of construction. A few blocks away there is another gem of Modernisme to admire at the ►Hospital de la Santa Creu i Sant Pau. In 1901 Domènech i Montaner was commissioned to build the hospital, which is now a UNESCO World Heritage Site.

Dreta de L'Eixample

Quadrat d'Or

1 Casa Victorià de la Riva
Carrer Ali Bei 1
Enric Sagnier i Villavecchia
2 Casa Modest Andreu
Carrer Ali Bei 3
Telm Fernàndez i Janot
3 Cases Joaquim i Antoni Marfà, Carrer Àli Bei 27-29
4 Casa Joaquim Cairó
Carrer Aribau 149 bis
Domènech Boada i Piera
5 Casa Conrad Roure
Carrer Aribau 155
Ferran Romeu i Cia
6 Casa Pascual i Cia
Carrer Aribau 175--177
Antoni Millàs i Figuerola

7/8 Casa Societat Torres Germans, Carrer Aribau 178
Jaume Torres i Grau
9/10 Cases Manuel Felip
Carrer Ausias Marc 22
Roc Cot i Cot
11 Casa Antonia Puget
Carrer Ausias Marc 22
Roc Cot i Cot
12 Cases Francesc Borés
Carrer Ausias Marc 30-32
Francesc Berenguer
i Mestres
13 Cases Antoni Roger
Carrer Ausias Marc 33-35
Eric Sagnier i
Villavecchia

14 Cases Tomas Roger
Carrer Ausias Marc 37--39
Eric Sagnier i
Villavecchia
15 Casa Antónia Borès
Carrer Ausias Marc 46
Juli Batllevell i Arús
16 Casa Francesc
de Paula Vallet
Carrer Bailén 36
Gabriel Borell i Cardona
17 Casa Jaume Sahis
Carrer Bailén 48
Josep Pérez i Terraza
18/19 Casa Rossend Capellades, Carrer Bailén 126
Jeroni Granell i Manresa

20/21, Cases Josep J. Bertrand
Carrer Balmes 44-50
Eric Sagnier i Villavecchia
22 Cases Antoni Miquel
Carrer Balmes 54
Jeroni Granell i Manresa
23 Cases Jeroni Granell
Carrer Balmes 65
Jeroni Granell i
Manresa
24 Cases Joan Pons
Carrer Balmes 81
Joan Ponts i Traball
25 Casa Jaume Larcegui
Carrer Balmes 83
Eduard Mercader i
Sacanell

▶

Finca Güell

 ✴ D 3

Location: Avinguda Pedralbes 7
Metro: Palau Reial, Maria Cristina (L 3)

Built as a country house for his patron the Duke of Güell between 1884–87, the Finca Güell today lies in the district of Pedralbes, one of the most desirable residential areas of the Catalan capital. The construction of this property marked the beginning of the long partnership between Gaudí and Güell.

Country estate The complex of the country estate consists of three main buildings: the single-storey porter's lodge to the left of the entrance, the large former stables and round riding hall. Stylistically the ensemble recalls the ▶Casa Vicens, but it also has echoes of the architecture of the Moorish era in Spain. The dome-shaped roofs of the porter's lodge and riding school support lanterns. The facades are clad in decorative tiles with only the window surrounds picked out in brick. Particularly worthy of note is the brick cornice surrounding the roof of the stables. The University of Barcelona acquired the property in the 1950s, and it was made a listed building in 1969. The Finca (not open to the public) is today the home of the **Real Càtedra Gaudí**, the Royal Gaudí Chair of the University of Barcelona.

Dragon Gate Particularly impressive is the 5m/17ft wide wrought iron entrance gate. It features a dragon with wide open mouth and spread wings; when you open the gate, the claws of the dragon move, which makes it look even more threatening. Gaudí was greatly inspired by the designs of Art Nouveau for this work.

* Fòrum

✦ L/M 7/8

Location: north end of Av. Diagonal
Tranvía: Fòrum T 5

It was on this extensive site at the northern end of Avenida Diagonal that the Universal Forum of Cultures was held in 2004. Since then it has continued to be developed within the framework of an ambitious urban renewal program, the El Fòrum quarter. Here you can see futuristic architecture, a marina and the Museu Blau.

Barelona's last major event after the Olympic Games of 1992 was the Universal Forum of Cultures in 2004. The event was intended to provide impetus for sustainable development and peace efforts worldwide. At the same time Barcelona once again revived the myth that it could keep on reinventing itself. The event involved not just the development of a large tract of land next to the sea. An entire district, the **Poblenou**, has been and continues to be demolished, renovated or rebuilt. New and expensive city flats have been built along the extended Avinguda Diagonal; tram, bike trails, the Parc Diagonal Mar and luxury hotels and shopping centres are all part of the district's new infrastructure.

A new district

The enforced structural change was named »**22@Barcelona**«. What sounds like an email address stands for the technology-oriented companies that the area is intended to attract and indeed have already set up shop in the area. The architectural beacons of the revamped old district are the **Torre Agbar**, which was completed in 2005, as well as the **Edifici Fòrum** which is situated at the far northern end of the Avinguda Diagonal. Right next to that on the expansive Parc del Fòrum a giant **solar sail** has become a kind of symbol of modern Barcelona. At the other side of the new marina, the animals from the zoo are to be provides with a new and larger home.

Since 2011 the Edifici Fòrum has had a new role. It houses the **collections of the geological and zoological museum**, which for decades languished in the Parc de la Ciutadella. Moving everything into the empty Edifici Blau, which was designed by the Swiss architects Herzog & De Meuron for the Universal Forum of cultures, benefits both the inventory of 3 million items as well as the Parc del Fòrum itself. Under the enormous skeleton of a whale that washed up on the shores of Barcelona 150 years ago, visitors ascend to the exhibition floor of the triangular building. The angled walls rendered in black plaster are ideal for the museum, which first devotes itself to the history of life on earth and evolution. Past the fossils you enter a

Edifici Fòrum / *Museu Blau

Modernisme in Barcelona

The industrial revolution and achievements like railways and electrical power brought Catalonia an economic upswing in the 19th cent., which in turn ushered in Catalonian Art nouveau, or Modernisme, around the turn of the 19th to the 20th cent. Truly representative structures were created especially in the Eixample quarter.

Collegi de les Teresianes

Palau Güell

Güell Pavillons

Straßenlaternen/Plaça Reial

Parc de la Ciutadella

Dragon at the fountain

Casa Vicens

Sagrada Família

Antoni Gaudí

* 25. June 1852 in Reus/Riudoms,
† 10. June 1926 in Barcelona
Catalan architect

Gran Hotel Internacional (torn down 1889)

Editorial Montaner i Simón

Castillo de los Tres Dragones

Lluís Domènech i Montaner

* 21. December 1850 in Barcelona, † 27. December 1923 there
Catalan architect und politician

Josep Puig i Cadafalch

* 17. October 1867 in Mataró, † 23. Dezember 1956 in Barcelo
katalanischer Architekt, Kunsthistoriker und Politiker

World exhibition: Exposició Universal de Barcelona | **1888** |

▶ **Political situation in Spain**

1873–74 | First republic

Kingdom of Spain

| 1850 | 1860 | 1870 | 1880 | 189 |

▶ **Selected epochs in architecture, art and literature**

HISTORISM

IMPRESSIONISM

ROMANTICISM NATURALISM

REALISM

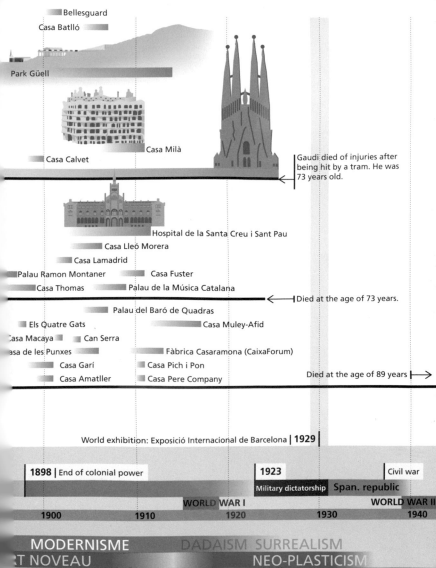

Bellesguard

Casa Batlló

Park Güell

Casa Milà

Casa Calvet

Gaudí died of injuries after being hit by a tram. He was 73 years old.

Hospital de la Santa Creu i Sant Pau

Casa Lleó Morera

Casa Lamadrid

Palau Ramon Montaner　　　Casa Fuster

Casa Thomas　　　Palau de la Música Catalana

← Died at the age of 73 years.

Palau del Baró de Quadras

Els Quatre Gats　　　Casa Muley-Afid

Casa Macaya　　Can Serra

Casa de les Punxes　　　Fàbrica Casaramona (CaixaForum)

Casa Garí　　Casa Pich i Pon

Casa Amatller　　Casa Pere Company

Died at the age of 89 years ↦

World exhibition: Exposició Internacional de Barcelona | 1929 |

1898 | End of colonial power

1923

Civil war

Military dictatorship　Span. republic

WORLD WAR I

WORLD WAR II

1900　　1910　　1920　　1930　　1940

MODERNISME　　DADAISM　SURREALISM

ART NOVEAU　　　NEO-PLASTICISM

CUBISM　　　ART DÉCO

CONSTRUCTIVISM

MODERNITY　NEW OBJECTIVITY

EXPRESSIONISM

The new landmark on the Barcelona skyline: Torre Agbar

spacious part of the building with rows of display cases containing stuffed animals. Less a multimedia experience, the Museu Blau is organised and structured along clear lines, which in the display cases with plants and minerals almost results in an artistic aesthetic.

As well as the usual museum shop with all kinds of Netoys and trinkets for children interested in natural history there is a media library that documents around 80 000 animal sounds and soundscapes.

❶ Tue–Fri 10am–7pm, Sat and Sun 10am–8pm; admission €6; Pl. Leonardo da Vinci 4-5, www.museuciencies.bcn.cat

Torre Agbar   From the Edifici Forum, Av. Diagonal leads to the Plaça de les Glòries Catalanes, near the 144m/472ft high Torre Agbar. This cigar-shaped tower, completed in 2005 according to designs by b Jean Nouvel, can be seen as the new symbol of the city. The blue and red light spectacular with which the tower adorns the Barcelona skyline every evening represents the club colours of FC Barcelona.

✳ Fundació Antoni Tàpies

✦ G 6

Location: Carrer Aragó 255
Metro: Passeig de Gràcia (L 2, L 3, L 4)
❶ Tue–Sun 10am–7pm
Admission: €7
www.fundaciotapies.org

The Antoni Tàpies Foundation has the most comprehensive collection of works by the Catalan artist. As well as the exhibition rooms a library has been installed in this, one of the earliest industrial Modernista buildings.

The Antoni Tàpies Foundation, which had been founded six years previously, opened its doors in the former Montaner i Simon publishing house in 1990. The brick building was erected in 1881–85 according to plans by Roser Amadó and Lluís Domènech. It was also the first building in the Eixample district to incorporate load-bearing steel. Most noticeable from the outside is Tàpies' surrealistic sculpture from 1990 called Cloud and Chair, placed on top of the building, even if, with its tangle of wire, not everyone immediately recognises it as a work of art. Most of the interior has been gutted in order to create more space for exhibitions. The foundation holds the **most comprehensive collection of Tàpies' works**, but also considers itself a research centre for contemporary art. The collection, which comprises several hundred works, includes drawings, paintings and sculptures from all phases, most of them donated by Teresa und Antoni Tàpies. Some of these works can be seen in the permanent exhibition. In addition, temporary exhibitions covering a variety of themes are laid on. The gallery around the interior »courtyard« is supported by slender, cast-iron pillars. Here, on old wooden shelving, a special library devoted mainly to 20th-century art and Asian cultures has been installed.

Fundació Francisco Godia

✦ F/G 6

Location: Diputació 250
Metro: Passeig de Gràcia (L 2, L 3, L 4)
❶ Mon, Wed–Sun 10am–8pm

Admission: €6.50
www.fundacionfgodia.org

Further enrichment to the museum landscape of Barcelona is provided by the Fundació Francisco Godia, which emerged from the private collection of the art expert and racing driver Francisco Godia Sales (1921–90).

Art from the 12th to the 20th centuries
Francisco Godia loved art and fast cars. The scion of a very wealthy family was not not just an entrepreneur but also, from 1950, a racing driver. The Maserati 250 F with which he was at times on the road has, unfortunately, disappeared from the collection. Some trophies and memorabilia from his sporting career can still be seen on the ground floor of the stately Casa Nogués. Since the last reorganization of the museum, which opened in 2001, the basement (mostly contemporary art) has been reserved for temporary exhibitions. The permanent collection is accessed via an elegant staircase, which is crowned by a dome of stained glass. The foundation, which was launched by his daughter Liliana Godia, manages a collection of 1500 works. The 15 cabinets can only show a small part of the collection, which focuses on the art of the Middle Ages, Modernisme and 20th century. On display are paintings by Spanish masters such as Berruguete and Zurbarán, Modernista painters like Santiago Rusiñol, Joaquim Mir and Joaquín Sorolla, ceramics and a walk-in sculpture by Cristina Iglesias on the outdoor terrace.

** Fundació Joan Miró

✦ E 7

Location: Parc de Montjuïc
Metro: Paral·lel (L 2, L 3), continuing by funicular
Bus: 150 (from Plaça Espanya)
❶ July–Sept Tue–Sat 10am–8pm
(otherwise till 7pm),
Thur till 9.30pm, Sun 10am–2.30pm
Admission: €11
www.fundaciomiro-bcn.org

One of the city's most beautiful museums is situated on the northern slopes of Montjuïc. Josep Lluís Sert designed the unusual building, which provides the perfect setting for the works of Joan Miró.

Artistic highlight
Joan Miró (1893 – 1983) established the foundation in 1971 and it moved into a stunning **cubist building made of snow-white exposed concrete**, which is a piece of art in itself, in 1988. The architects Josep Lluís Sert and Jaume Freixa, both friends of Miró, succeeded in creating a Mediterranean-looking monument that not only fits perfectly into the park landscape on the northern side of Montjuïc, but also successfully combines the interior and exterior with its light design, the alignment of different building sec-

! *All in one* **Insider Tip**

MARCO ⊕ POLO TIP

The Articket BCN secures access to the Museu Picasso, CCCB, MACBA, MNAC, the Fundació Joan Miró, Fundació Tapies and Gaudí's La Pedrera. It can be purchased for €30 at the tourist office or online at:
www.barcelonaturisme.com

The Fundació Joan Miró owns more than 150 sculptures

tions, and unobstructed inner courtyards. Visitors can enjoy a panoramic view of the city from here. The vast collection contains approx. 14,000 exhibits, including **paintings, prints, drawings, collage**, a number of large textile works and more than 150 sculptures. The museum provides a good overview of the artist's work and contains far more than just the famous – almost too often reproduced – idyllic-looking paintings, with their seemingly naïve shapes and bright contrasting colours. The rooms for temporary exhibitions of contemporary art can be found on the left side of the entrance level, while the permanent exhibition is housed on the right side of the ground floor and on the upper floor. Some sculptures are also displayed on the roof and in the park.

The individual halls bear the names of people who were important in Miró's life, such as his wife, friends and patrons. The artist's development is displayed chronologically, beginning with his first responses to Cubism and Fauvism and his orientation towards Surrealism; moving on to artistic inspirations gathered from other painters or from his journeys and, finally, displaying his very distinct **surrealist abstract style**. The paintings clearly show the great influence of Catalan landscapes on Miró's work, despite the fact that he spent his last years in exile on Mallorca. In the 1930s and 1940s, his work was mainly dominated by political events. During this period he produced a series of dark, nightmarish paintings, in which he dealt with the horrors of the Spanish Civil War and the Franco regime. The most prominent works in this exhibition include Snail Woman Flower Star (1934), Solar Bird, an enormous sculpture made of white Carrara marble (1968), and the lithographic series Barcelona (1939–44), which is considered Miró's bravest statement on the Civil War. The top floor also features various works by Miró's contemporaries (some Catalan artists, **Alexander Calder, Max Ernst, Henry Moore,** etc.), and also houses the library. The roof terrace, the light inner courtyard and the cafeteria provide idyllic corners to relax and savour the impressions of the exhibition.

Gràcia

 G/H 4/5

Location: north of the city centre
Metro: Fontana (L 3), Joanic (L 4)

Gràcia is a fascinating and lively district located next to Eixample, off the Avinguda Diagonal in the direction of Mount Tibidabo. Many artists feel at home in the alternative atmosphere of Gràcia.

Gràcia is a hot spot for lively nightlife

The small-town feel is reminiscent of the fact that it was once an au- **Artists'** tonomous village and only became a part of Barcelona in 1897. Dur- **district** ing the last third of the 19th century, Gràcia was known as a hotbed of radicalism. Its inhabitants once even declared it an independent republic. Although some constructional changes have been made since the 1980s, the quarter has not yet lost its rural charm. The houses are small, the streets are narrow, and pretty squares and quiet patios can be found everywhere; simple shops for everyday needs, craft enterprises, corner pubs, restaurants serving traditional food, and small lively markets – they all contribute to the **friendly and very un-metropolitan atmosphere**.

Numerous artists and students enjoy living among the unpretentious citizens of Gràcia. The alternative cultural movement began here during the 1970s. Now the centre of the avant-garde has shifted to Raval and Ribera, while Gràcia has kept its character as an artist›s village, with galleries and alternative shops. Mercè de Rodoreda's (▶Famous People) famous novel *The Time of the Doves* is set in this district.

Gràcia also has plenty of sights to offer besides ▶Parc Güell, one of **Sights** the most famous works of Antoni Gaudí, as well as his ▶Casa Vicens. Take a stroll along Carrer Gran de Gràcia (the narrower continuation of ▶Passeig de Gràcia) to **Casa Fuster**, directly behind the Avinguda Diagonal. It was built by Lluís Domènech i Montaner and his son Pere, and today houses a luxury hotel.

Carrer Gran de Gràcia also leads to the **Mercat de Llibertat**. This well-constructed Modernist market hall was built in 1893 by Gaudí's assistant Francesc Berenguer. Located on Plaça de Rius i Taulet is a 30m/100ft high **clock tower** from the 19th century, which is why the square is generally called Plaça del Rellotge. The tower was once a symbol of freedom; revolutionary demonstrations took place here on the square. If the tower is open, use this rare opportunity to climb up the beautiful spiral staircase leading to the observation deck.

The idyllic little squares of the district are ideal spots for a well-deserved break. With any luck, you might witness a spontaneous sardana dance or rehearsals for the district's one-week fair, the Festa Major de Gràcia, which takes place the week after 15 August.

Reasonably priced **bars and restaurants** can be found on every corner. Once Barcelona's first designer bar, the »Flash Flash« is a real institution and has maintained its 1960s style. The bar's speciality is the tortilla, served in all possible variations (Carrer de La Granada del Penedès). Gràcia is also worth venturing out to at night, especially around the slightly run-down **Plaça del Sol**, where there are numerous bars and clubs.

✳ Hospital de la Santa Creu i de Sant Pau

✳ J 4/5

Location: Carrer Sant Antoni Maria Claret
Metro: Hospital de Sant Pau (L 4)

This extensive hospital complex in the north of the Eixample district was designed by Lluís Domènech i Montaner in the Modernista style. With its 48 pavilions, it was opened in 1930.

Modernista-style hospital
The building of this hospital complex north of the Sagrada Família was made possible by a private donation. The architect Lluís Domènech i Montaner began work on the project in 1902. In the first building phase up to 1911 approximately a quarter of the building was completed. Unlike the way things were usually done at the time, the individual hospital departments are housed in independent pavilions and connected by underground passageways. Above ground the site is broken up by greenery. The façades of the buildings display the typical Modernista decorative style: fair-faced brickwork, colourful ceramics and natural stone. No longer used as a hospital, the building has been a UNESCO **World Heritage Site** since 1997. In the future, the UNU, the United Nations University, is set to move into the premises.

Jardi Botànic

✳ D 8

Location: Montjuïc
Metro: Paral·lel (L 3), further with the funicular and teleferic; autobus 50 (from Plaça Espanya)
❶ Nov–March, July and Aug daily

10am–6pm, otherwise till 8pm
Admission: €3.50
www.jardibotanic.bcn.es

Situated on the slopes of Montjuïc, the Botanical Garden is like a giant amphitheatre of plant life. The contemporary park layout of walkways and plantation spaces was conceived by a team working with the architect Carlos Ferrater.

Botanical Gardens
The garden opened in 1999. It incorporates about 70 small biotopes where plants from around the world that are adapted to the Mediterranean climate can thrive. Although the Mediterranean area accounts for only about 2% of the earth's landmass, about 20% of all the

world's plant species can be found here. The Barcelona-based Ferrater provided the site with a system of pathways, whose angled and seemingly arbitrary course both contrasts with and mimics the surrounding vegetation. The garden is divided into regions where the same or similar »dry-summer subtropical« climate prevails, such as California, parts of Australia, South Africa and Chile. A key task of the garden lies in the conservation of biodiversity.

Just to the north of the Botanical Garden, between the Olympic Stadium and the Museu Nacional d'Art de Catalunya, are the remains of an older botanical garden, the Jardi Botànic Històric, which was created in 1930. With the transformation of Montjuïc for the 1992 Olympic Games, parts of this garden were destroyed. In 2003 a truncated version of the historic garden was opened to the public.

Jardi Botànic Històric

Liceu

★ **F 7**

Location: Rambla dels Caputxins 65
Metro: Liceu (L 3)
❶ Guided tours daily 10am, viewing without tour 11.30am, noon, 12.30pm and 1pm,
www.liceubarcelona.cat

The magnificent Gran Teatre del Liceu was once the largest opera house in Spain.

Inaugurated in 1848, the building's plain façade concealed a spectacular auditorium, which was almost completely destroyed due to

Opera house

The Liceu's stunning auditorium

an electrical fault in January 1994 that caused a devastating fire.
Montserrat Caballé (▶MARCO POLO Insight, p.50), the famous
opera singer, lobbied for the opera's immediate reconstruction in her
hometown which, thanks to generous donations, was indeed made
possible.

The opera house was rebuilt according to the old plans, except with
better technology and improved acoustics and the interior design is
just as magnificent as that of its predecessor. Antoni Miró created the
opulent velvet curtain, while the avant-garde design of the ceiling is
by the Catalan artist Perejaume. The festive re-opening took place in
autumn 1999.

Llotja de Mar

✶ G 7/8

Location: Pla del Palau
Metro: Barceloneta (L 4)

**The Barcelona Stock Exchange (Catalan: Llotja) was founded
in the 14th century, when the city was experiencing a political
and economic heyday.**

Stock Exchange
The building, in which the Stock Exchange is still housed today, was
built between 1380–92, in the late Gothic style. It was finally remod-
elled in the neoclassical style after several expansions and modifica-
tions. The only section of the building that has never been modified
since it was first built is the elegant **Gothic Hall**, a room with vaulted
arches supported by slender pillars dividing it into three bays. Stock
exchange business still goes on here today. Also remarkable is the
staircase featuring allegories of industry and trade, as well as the
purely neoclassical rooms of the Junta de Comerç (Chamber of Com-
merce) on the upper floor.

Pla del Palau
The Pla del Palau, a square situated north of the stock exchange, is
also the maritime trade centre of Barcelona. It is surrounded by numerous trade, office and administrative buildings including the Gov-
ern Civil (civil administration).

Estació de França
A bit further north is the Estació de França (French Railway Station)
for train connections to the north. Spain's first train ran from here to
Mataró in 1848, but the present beautiful station building was only
built for the World Fair of 1929. Its two curving, 198m/650ft wide, iron
and glass sheds make it the biggest station in Spain and on its completion it was regarded as a pioneering achievement in platform shed construction.

✳ Monestir de Pedralbes

✦ **D 2**

Location: west of the centre
Bus: 75
❶ Tue–Sun 10am–5pm (Oct–March till 2pm),Sun 10am–3pm
Admission: €7

In the elegant district of Pedralbes lies the Monestir Santa Maria de Pedralbes. Founded in 1326, the monastery is a jewel of Catalan Gothic with a beautiful cloister.

The Poor Clare monastery, which was founded in the 14th century by Queen Elisenda de Montcada, is surrounded by a small park with cypress trees and native shrubs. In the verdant and almost rural surroundings the church and convent form an architecturally harmonious whole.
The name of the monastery is derived from the Latin petras albas (white stones). A white foundation stone is said to have been laid for the apse.

Poor Clare Monastery

The single-nave Gothic monastery church is entered through a door from the forecourt. The vast interior is flanked by chapels and divided by a rood screen. This grille separates the publicly accessible part of the church from that which is reserved solely for the monastic community. The 15th-century stained glass is well worth closer inspection, as is the alabaster tomb of Queen Elisend, the wife of King Jaume II, who died in 1364.

Monastery church

The courtyard, where a Renaissance fountain splashes under the palm and cypress trees, is filled with monastic silence.

Courtyard

The three-storey cloisters were laid out in grand proportions. On a tour you can see several of the so-called day cells, the small Capella de Sant Miquel (1346) as well as the adjoining refectory, kitchen and infirmary.

Cloisters

The **refectory** is a sober Gothic room whose walls are decorated with Latin bible quotes intended to inspire or warn the nuns. The **infirmary** consists of several small wards, each with 6–8 beds. Also worth seeing is the **kitchen** with its tiled walls, which was in use until 1983. A staircase leads down from the cloister to the utility and storage rooms. Items from the collection of the **monastery museum** are on display in the dormitorio.

Rooms

** Montjuïc

✦ C–E 7/8

Location: south of the city centre
Metro: Paral·lel (L 2, L 3); then funicular and Telefèric

On the south side of the city rises the 213m/699ft high Montjuïc, which is crowned by a castle and drops steeply to the sea. It is still sometimes called the »magic mountain«; in Celtiberian Roman times a temple of Jupiter stood here.

Popular recreation area

For Barcelonans Montjuïc can invoke mixed feelings, for the fortress strategically overlooking the entire city today recalls dark episodes in Barcelona's past. From here, the city's inhabitants were kept in check by the Castilian occupying forces during the War of the Spanish Succession. Later, during the Franco Regime, the fortification was a notorious prison, where political prisoners were executed on the eastern slope of the mountain and then thrown into the sea. Today, however, Montjuïc is the most extensive and popular recreational area of the city, with beautiful landscapes and lush parks.

The slow image change already began with the 1929 World Fair. Even in the 1960s, however, Montjuïc was strewn with shanty towns. The local mountain only became a recreation area with the Olympic Games of 1992, when the outdoor Teatre Grec and the Poble Espanyol, the Olympic sports facilities, as well as a number of museums as distinguished as the Miró Foundation were added to the existing exhibition halls and museums at the base of the mountain. The most recent developments are the modern botanical garden as well as the transformation of the fortress to a peace centre, which has not yet been completed. Thanks to its many attractions, beautiful gardens and amazing views, you can now easily spend a whole day on Montjuïc.

Getting there

Either take the cable car (**Transbordador Aeri**) that starts at the harbour and stops at Parc de Miramar. Or go to the Paral·lel metro station at Avinguda del Paral·lel where a **funicular** rides half-way up Montjuïc to Avinguda de Miramar. A cable car (**Telefèric**) continues directly to the front of the castle. Up on Montjuïc, a small diesel-powered tourist train (**Tren Turístic**) stops at all the interesting sights. It's also possible to reach most of the sights on Montjuïc by taking bus 50 from Plaça Espanya.

Transbordador Aeri: daily from 11am; single journey €11, return €16.50
Telefèric: from 10am, June–Sept till 9pm, spring/autumn till 7pm, winter till 6pm; single journey €7.50, return €10.80
Funicular: Mon–Fri 7.30am–8 pm, Sat & Sun 9am–9pm; single €2.15

View of Montjuïc

The entire summit area is occupied by the extensive fortifications of the Castell de Montjuïc, which is closely linked with the history of Barcelona. The fortress complex, constructed during the reign of King Felipe IV in 1640 and extended in the 18th century, gained particular notoriety during the Spanish Civil War. At that time, the mountain was used as a place of execution for undesirable opponents. During the Franco dictatorship, the facility served as a military prison.

Castell de Montjuïc

To do justice to the historical role of Montjuïc and to promote critical debate, the fortress is to be transformed into a place of remembrance and peace. In the rooms, which were previously occupied by the Museu Militar, it is planned to install an international peace centre, an information centre about Montjuïc and a visitor centre. The fortress, which provides magnificent views over the city and the port, remains open.

❶ daily 9am–9pm, Oct–March till 7pm

North of the castle, the road heading down into the city (Carrer Montjuïc) leads to the Mirador del Alcalde (excellent views of the city centre and the harbour) with its charming trick fountains. The pavement of the pedestrian zone is interesting, consisting of ornamental concrete pipes, bottle necks and bases, transmission chains and much more.

Mirador del Alcalde

Further south, the Cementiri de Montjuïc exudes a morbid charm. The vast necropolis was opened in 1883 and as well as memorials to the deceased also provides an art history of the cemetery, ranging

Cementiri de Montjuïc

from magnificent mausoleums to the simple urn wall. Amongst others, the architect of the Eixample district Ildefons Cerdà and the artist Joan Miró found their final resting place here.

Jardins de Mossèn Jacint Verdaguer   Stretching down the slopes to the northwest of the fortress, to Plaça Dante and the base station of the Telefèric, are the Jardins de Mossèn Jacint Verdaguer, which are named after the famous Catalan poet (1845–1902). The main focal point of the garden consists of the water terraces either side of the steps, in which various species of water lily grow. An inscription stone bears a poem by Verdaguer.

Plaça de l' Armada   Near the upper-most station of the harbour cable car is the Plaça de l'Armada, which offers a beautiful view of the harbour and the old town. The adjacent Jardins de Miramar contain a female sculpture by Josep Clarà.

Jardins de Mossèn Costa i Llobera   The steep slope of Montjuïc facing the sea is covered by the extensive Jardins de Mossèn Costa i Llobera (the poet Miquel Costa i Llobera was a contemporary of Verdaguer). They are reached via the Avinguda de Miramar from Plaça Dante. This finely landscaped park is famous for its great collection of succulents, cacti, and spurges. A bronze seated sculpture of a lace maker by Josep Viladomat sits on a platform.

Museums   Walking back to Plaça Dante and past the Fundació Joan Miró, the western part of Montjuïc is taken up by some of the sports facilities developed for the Olympics (►Anella Olímpica), the ►Museu d'Arqueologia, the ►Museu Etnològic, the ►Palau Nacional, the ►Jardi Botànic, the ►Pavelló Mies van der Rohe and the ►Poble Espanyol.

✷✷ Montserrat

✦ out-of-town

Location: 40 km/25 mi northwest of Barcelona
www.montserratvisita.com

The rocky massif of Montserrat rises around 40 km/25 mi northwest of Barcelona. It is famous in particular for the Benedictine abbey, whose foundation goes back to the 9th century. Montserrat was once mistakenly thought to be the Monsalvatsch in Wolfram von Eschenbach's medieval German tale that refers to a mountain called Monsalvat as the location of the Holy Grail. In all likelihood, however, this is to be found near the town of Salvatierra on the southern flanks of the Pyrenees.

Montserrat lies tucked into a spectacular mountain landscape

Getting there

It is best reached by driving southwest down the wide Avinguda Diagonal, past the Zona Universitària. Then take the motorway to Martorell. From there, a country road leads via Olesa to Monistrol. Shortly after Olesa is the base station of the teleferic (aeri) that leads directly up to the monastery.

There is also a direct railway connection to the teleferic, which leaves from the transport hub under Plaça Espanya. You can also take the train to the terminus station at Monistrol and there change to the Cremallera, a rack railway.

History

Legend has it that the monastery was founded in 880, in honour of a miracle-working image of the Virgin Mary. It was first mentioned in a document in 888. In 976 it was transferred to the Benedictine Order and, in 1025, was considerably expanded by monks from the Catalan towns of Ripoll and Vich. In 1409, under Pope Benedict XIII, it gained the status of an independent abbey and the monastery's printing press was established towards the end of the century. The monastery lost its enormous wealth during the Napoleonic Wars (from 1808), and the abbey was destroyed by the French in 1811. Further financial losses finally led to its closing during the Carlist Wars (1835–60). During the Civil War and the Franco regime, Montserrat was also a sanctuary for the politically persecuted. They composed leaflets, and the monks printed a newspaper critical of the regime.

Today, the monastery is mostly associated with the **School of Sacred Music**, which was founded in the 15th century. Its choirboys sing the Ave Maria (1pm) and at Vespers.

**Landscape Montserrat (serrated mountain), the Montsagrat (Holy Mountain) of the Catalans, is a forbidding and steep massif that rises from the plains above the right bank of the Riu Llobregat. Its fantastical, eroded rock formations make it look like a monstrous castle. The highest summit is Sant Jeroni, with a height of 1241 m/4071ft.

Monastery The monastery, with the basilica and the adjacent buildings, practically forms a village of its own. The access road terminates at the car park. The interior of the actual monastic complex can be accessed from Plaça de la Creu (Square of the Cross, after the cross sculpture from 1927, located on the left), which is flanked by a restaurant, souvenir shops, a post office and exchange booth. From there, you proceed to the broad and spacious Plaça de Santa Maria.

Museum To the right of the wide strip leading up to the basilica is the entrance to the **modern section** of the museum, located underneath the square. Only of regional significance, it contains works by Catalan painters from the 19th and 20th centuries. The **old section** is located on the left, in front of the main façade of the church, featuring a small Egyptian collection (several copies of known large sculptures, small terracotta items, cylinder seals, a human mummy and two sarcoph-

Montserrat

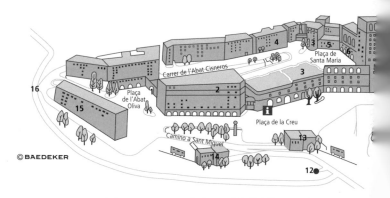

© BAEDEKER

1 Main entrance to monastery district
2 Audiovisual information panel
3 Museum (in two buildings)
4 Hotel
5 Gothic cloister
6 Archway
7 Basilica
8 Vocal school (Escolania)

agi), artefacts from the Neolithic Age, Roman and Byzantine ceramics and jewellery, coins, antique glass and various Jewish religious articles, including Torah scrolls. Running along the left of the square is the Abad Cisneros hotel.

❶ daily 10am–5.30pm, admission €6.50

At the top, the square is separated from the church precinct by an enormous gatehouse, built from 1942–68 and featuring five arches at the bottom and three arches at the top. The reliefs in the three upper arches depict (from left to right) St Benedict, the Assumption and St George, patron saint of Catalonia. With a bit of luck, you might see a group of Catalan pilgrims dancing the old Sardana folk dance here. Remains of the former 15th-century Gothic cloister can be found to the left of the façade. Between the gatehouse and the actual church, there is a very narrow inner courtyard, where the statue (1927) of St Benedict is located next to the monastery gate (not accessible). The entrance of the baptistery, adorned with modern reliefs, is also situated in the inner courtyard.

Basilica

The basilica, site of the highly revered image of the Virgin Mary, dates back to the 16th century. It was, however, considerably altered and refurbished in the 19th and 20th centuries. The façade is Renaissance in style but the figures of Christ and the Apostles were only placed there in around 1900.

The **Madonna of Montserrat**, called »Santa Imatge« in Catalan, is located above the high altar. It can be accessed via the stairs in the right transept, which are framed with chased silver fittings. The colourful wooden sculpture was created in the 12th or 13th century.

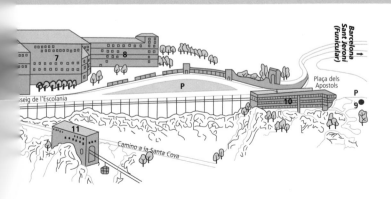

 9 Raimundus Lullus Monument
10 Restaurant
11 Top station of the funicular
12 Pau Casal Monument
13 Funicular to Cova Santa
14 Funicular to Sant Joan
15 Police (Guardia Civil)
16 Via Crucis (Way of the Cross)

Face and hands have blackened with age, which is why it is also called »La Moreneta« (the little dark-skinned one).

Legend has it that the image is the work of St Luke, who was brought to Spain by St Peter. The church is exited through the left transept. By the rock face outside, take a look at the numerous votive gifts (including wax limbs) and candles, and the holy fountain (Mistica Font de l'Aigua de la Vida) featuring a colourful majolica image of the Virgin Mary.

Way of the Cross
The Via Crucis (Way of the Cross) starts at the Plaça del Abat Oliba. Its 14 large statuary groups were created between 1904 and 1919 and renewed after the Civil War. A chapel (Virgen de la Soledad) can be found at the end. At the 14th station, a path leads up to the Ermita Sant Miquel (19th century); the previous building on the site already existed in the 10th century.

Cova Santa
A funicular leads up to the Cova Santa (sacred cave), where there is a chapel dating from the 17th century. It is said that the image of the Virgin of Montserrat was hidden inside the grotto during the Moorish Period, and was later rediscovered by shepherds.

Sant Joan
The station of the cable car leading up to Sant Joan is located at Plaça de la Creu; on the path there is a statue of the Catalan cellist Pau (Pablo) Casals (1876–1973). Sant Joan is one of thirteen former **hermitages** in the Montserrat region. A nice view of the monastery can be enjoyed from top station.

Sant Jeroni
Getting to the Capella de Sant Jeroni involves a steep, 20-minute climb. From there, it is another one-hour hike to the summit of Sant Jeroni, the highest peak of the Montserrat massif at 1241m/4071ft.

Museu Barbier-Mueller d' Art Precolombí

✴ G 7

Location: Carrer Montcada 12–14
Metro: Jaume I (L 4)
❶ Tue–Fri 11am–7pm, Sat and Sun

11am–8pm
Admission: €3.50
www.amigosprecolombino.es

Those interested in South American art should definitely visit the Museu d'Art Precolombí.

Museum of Precolumbian Art
The museum is housed in the medieval Palau Nadal. Exhibits include sculptures, ceramics, textiles, and ritual items of the Maya and Aztec

cultures, as well as the Olmecs and Incas, in other words Precolumbian art, i.e. from the period before the Spanish conquest. The exhibits form part of the Barbier-Mueller collection from Geneva.

Museu d' Arqueologia de Catalunya (MAC)

✦ D/E 7

Location: Passeig Santa Madrona 39–41
Metro: Espanya (L 1, L 3)
❶ Tue–Sat 9.30am–7pm,

Sun 10am–2.30pm
Admission €3
www.mac.cat

The Museu d'Arqueologia de Catalunya, the Archaeological Museum, is located near the southeastern perimeter of the exhibition grounds and at the foot of Montjuïc.

The impressive neoclassical circular brick construction was originally built as the Palau d'Arts Gràfiques for the 1929 World Fair, and expanded and assigned to its present-day function in 1932. The museum's exhibits date back to a collection founded in 1888. The museum focuses on the roots of Catalan history and one department is dedicated to the Balearic Islands. The exhibits date from the Iberian, Carthaginian, Greek and Roman periods; some even date back to the early Christian era and Visigoth culture. Worth mentioning are the finds from the famous Carthaginian necropolis by the mill hill in Ibiza Town (small terracotta items, busts, jewellery), as well as Attican and Etruscan vessels from the Greek city of Empúries around 50km (30mi) to the north on the Costa Brava.

Archaeological Museum

The extensive buildings of the former **Mercat de les Flors** (flower market) are situated across from the museum to the west. Today this is all a theatre complex with several stages. The Dance Theatre is especially renowned. In the narrow passage between the modern building and the old theatre there is a mural that fills an entire wall. It was done by the artist Miquel Barceló, who also designed the dome of the theatre.
❶ www.mercatflors.org

> **MARCO POLO TIP**
>
> **!** *Museums for Mondays*   Insider Tip
>
> Most museums are closed on Mondays. Where to go? The following houses are the exceptions which prove the rule: Casa Museu Gaudí, La Sagrada Família and Museum, Museu d'Art Contemporani (MACBA), Museu de Cera, Museu de l'Eròtica, Museu de Xocolata, Museu del Futbol Club Barcelona, Museu de la Música, Museu del Modernisme and the Museu Marítim.

* Museu d'Art Contemporani (MACBA)

✶ G 8

Location: Plaça dels Àngels 1
Metro: Universitat (L 1, L 2),
Catalunya (L 1, L 3)
❶ Mon, Wed–Fri 11am–7.30pm,

Sat 10am–9pm,
Sun 10am–3pm
Admission: €10
www.macba.es

The white building of the Museum of Contemporary Art with its glazed façade, designed by the American architect Richard Meier, provides a stark contrast to the atmosphere of the surrounding old buildings and the dark narrow alleys of ▶Raval.

Museum of Contemporary Art

The Museum of Contemporary Art was erected in the heart of the Old City district of Raval. It looks like a work of art itself, and the contrast between the elegant contemporary architecture and the shabby chic of the district is intended to provoke. The aim of the city planners to redevelop Raval through culture, or at least to lend it some impetus, appears to have worked.

Together with the FAD (Foment de les Arts i del Disseny) design centre and the Centre for Contemporary Culture (CCCB) just a few buildings further on, a kind of energy field has been created here, in which art galleries, design boutiques, trendy restaurants and bars have settled.

Behind the glass facade, the cylindrical entrance opens out into a spectacular hall, with ramps connecting the three floors given over to exhibitions. Here themed exhibitions of contemporary art are shown. The museum collection, which brings together 20th-century works produced from the 1940s onwards, focuses specifically on the art of Catalan conceptualism and more generally on Spanish art with works by Tàpies, Barceló, Chillida and Saura, as well as experimental 20th-century art by the likes of Öyvind Fahlström, Lucio Fontana and Marcel Broadhaers.

Plaça dels Àngels

The museum is located on Plaça dels Angels (not to be confused with Plaça de l'Angel), which is also the site of a former convent built around 1560, in very late Gothic style. Today, it is home to the central library for the municipal museums and the FAD.

Casa de Caritat

The Casa de Caritat is located directly next to the museum. Since the 13th century, the area belonged to the Augustinian canons; later a seminary was established here. The cloister received its present appearance in the mid-18th century according to Tuscan models. Today Casa de Caritat is enlarged by a modern extension and is used as

The American architect Richard Meier designed the museum

an art centre for architecture, design, fashion and photography: the
Centre de Cultura Contemporània de Barcelona (CCCB).
❶ Tue–Sun 11am–8pm, Thur till 10pm, admission €5, www.cccb.org

Museu de Cera

❖ G 9

Location: Passatge de la Banca 7
Metro: Drassanes (L 3)
❶ Mon–Fri 10am–1.30pm and
4pm–7.30pm, Sat and Sun
11am–2pm and 4.30pm–8.30pm,
in summer daily
10am–10pm
Admission:€15
www.museocerabcn.com

**The Museu de Cera (wax museum) is located in a 19th-century
building set back from the ▸Rambles. Its founder, Enrique
Alarcón, is a great cineaste, who created this eerily beautiful
attraction with interchanging groups of over 300 wax figures.**

Wax museum   However, the figures portrayed are easier to identify from their dress and surroundings than from familiar physiognomic features! The museum's main section is housed in a building that also provides a good insight into early Modernista architecture, as the interior has been left unchanged since it was decorated with wall and ceiling paintings. The tour starts on the **first floor** where various celebrities of the recent and remote past are displayed; for example, politicians, artists, scientists and two versions of Pope John Paul II. The **second floor** includes a group of film stars arranged on the swaying deck of an ocean liner. The **ground floor** leads to the »Viaje Ficción« (Fantastic Journey). A deep-sea diving bell and an underwater tunnel transport visitors to a fantastic world of stalactite caves, Stone Age people, space travel and science fiction monsters. The »Terror« section, including a display on various methods of execution, should not be shown to small children. The tour ends with the chamber of horrors featuring Frankenstein, Dracula and Dr Mabuse.

＊ Museu de la Ciència – CosmoCaixa

＊ F 2

Location: Carrer Roviralta 55
Train (FGC): Avinguda Tibidabo
❶ Tue–Sun 10am–8pm

Admission: €4
http://obrasocial.
lacaixa.es

Children and adults can have fun at this museum. Here you can join in, experiment, try out and get a clearer idea of so many secrets from the world of technology or the laws of nature.

Science museum   At the foot of Tibidabo, near the funicular valley station is the Science Museum, which is maintained by Foundation of the Caixa de Pensions de Catalunya foundation (Pension Fund of Catalonia). One significant part of the museum is the »Room of Matter«, which is split into four different sections. »Gases« illustrates the creation of the universe more than 13 billion years ago, the »big bang« and the development of matter, energy, time and space. The department of »Living Matter« demonstrates how life evolved on planet Earth 3–4 billion years ago. Finally, the period of »Intelligent Matter« deals with neutrons and illustrates how life reacts to changes in the environment. The room »Civilization« shows how human predecessors began to evolve into Homo Sapiens, who learnt to create for himself. There is also a 65m/210ft geological wall featuring all kinds of geo-

Children as well as adults can have fun in the science museum

logical formations. In the »Amazon Jungle« visitors find themselves in the midst of the typical flora and fauna of a tropical rainforest and physically experience humidity of 80 %.

Museu de la Música

✦ H 7

Location: C/Lepant 150
Metro: Glories (L 1, T 4 – 6);
Monumental (L 2); Marina (L 1, T 4)
🕐 Mon, Wed–Sat 10am–6pm,

Sun till 8pm
Admission: €4
**www.museumusica.
bcn.cat**

Founded in 1947, the Music Museum, with its collection of around 500 historic instruments, is to be found in the Auditorium adjacent to the ▶Teatre Nacional de Catalunya.

Music museum The string instruments include an extraordinary guitar collection dating back to the 17th century, which is one of the most comprehensive in Europe. Also noteworthy is the collection of bow instruments, including a peculiar-looking violin made of blue-painted porcelain, and another disguised as a walking stick. The museum also features wood and brass instruments, as well as keyboard instruments, particularly organs and harpsichords. Furthermore, the museum has original manuscripts and documents, as well as a collection of audio equipment from the last 100 years, a vinyl archive and a special library.

Museu del Calçat

✶ **G 7**

Location: Plaça de Sant Felip Neri 5   ❶ Tue–Sun 11am–2pm
Metro: Liceu (L 3), Jaume I (L 4)   **Admission:** €2.50

The Museu del Calçat (Shoe Museum) is housed in an attractive Renaissance building on the atmospheric Plaça de Sant Felip Neri, southwest of the Cathedral.

Shoe museum In the heart of the Jewish Quarter, El Call, the building used to be the seat of the city's shoemakers' guild. The museum documents the historical development of traditional Catalan shoemaking, as well as exhibiting a large number of shoes from various centuries. On display are also shoes that have been worn by celebrities, including Pau Casals, the clown Charlie Rivel and Carles Vallès, the first Catalan to conquer Mount Everest. One curious exhibit is a boot that was made for the statue atop the Columbus Monument; it is listed today in the Guinness Book of Records as the biggest shoe in the world.

Plaça de Sant Felip Neri Plaça de Sant Felip Neri is an idyllic little square to which Antoni Gaudí would go when working on the Sagrada Família. The name refers to the Italian Filippo Neri (1515–95), who founded the Congregation of the Oratory in 1575 and was canonised in 1622. The convent buildings on the square were erected in 1673 and modified in the 18th century. This typical work of the Counter Reformation exhibits Baroque features, something of a rarity in Barcelona. On the exterior facade you can still see bullet holes from the time of the Civil War (►MARCO POLO Insight, p.28), when several monks were shot here. The charming square served as location for Woody Allen's film *Vicky Cristina Barcelona* and also featured in the novel *The Shadow of the Wind* by Carlos Ruiz Zafón.

* Museum del Disseny de Barcelona

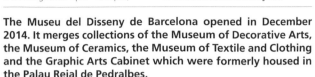

✦ J 6

Location: Pl. de les Glòries Catalanes, 37-38
Metro: Monumental (L2)
❶ Building: Mon 4pm – 8.30pm,

Tue – Sun
10am – 8.30pm
Admission: €5
www.museudeldisseny.cat

The Museu del Disseny de Barcelona opened in December 2014. It merges collections of the Museum of Decorative Arts, the Museum of Ceramics, the Museum of Textile and Clothing and the Graphic Arts Cabinet which were formerly housed in the Palau Reial de Pedralbes.

The new building, designed by MBM Arquitectes, is made up of two parts: one underground and another, shaped like a slanted parallelepiped, which emerges at 14.5m/47ft at the level of Plaça de les Glòries. In order not to reduce the space for public use it occupies a minimum footprint. Entrance to both parts is through a single vestibule with two points of access: one in Carrer d'Àvila and another in Plaça de les Glòries. The permanent exhibitions of all museums are presented in the overground building on four floors.

Disseny HUB Barcelona Building

The collection of the Ceramics Museum is made up of donations made to the city since the late 19th century, and the museum is not only aesthetically appealing, but also offers an excellent cultural historical overview. Items range from simple plates and bowls to gaudy dishes; from floor tiles and illustrated Frisians to avant-garde ceramic art. Prominent pieces include medieval pieces from the Almohade period, Mudejar productions from Aragon porcelain, dishes with a lustre finish from Manises in southern Spain, two 18th century tile plates that lavishly depict a bullfight and a feast and works by **Picasso, Miró and Miguel Barceló**. Visitors can also learn how single- or multi-coloured ceramics are produced and will also discover that the popular azulejos – such as the decorative tiles from 19th century Valencia – get their name from the Arabic »az-zuleycha« (mosaic stone) and not, as was commonly thought, from the Spanish word »azul« (blue). This is just one hint amongst many of the strong Arabic influence on Spanish ceramics.

*Museu de Ceràmica

The second museum in the Disseny Building is the **Museum of Decorative Arts**. On display is furniture and applied art from the Romanic period through to the present: artistically painted chests from the Gothic period; grand bureaus and secretaries from the Renais-

Museu de les Arts Decoratives

sance, with rich inlays in different coloured woods, mother-of-pearl and ivory; furniture from the Baroque, Empire, and Classic periods; furniture and accessories from Art Nouveau, Art Deco, and the Noucentisme periods, as well as from the 20th century. The latter exhibits demonstrate the growing influence of industrial design, but there are also extravagantly crafted pieces of furniture from the early 20th century as well as single items by leading Catalan designers such as Oscar Tusquets, Javier Mariscal and BKF from the 1980s.

Museu Tèxtil i d' Indumentària

The **Textile and Clothing Museum** shows how the image of the body has changed since the 16th century, both through fashion and with fashion. The presentation is similar to the kind of displays one encounters in contemporary fashion boutiques. The historical, sometimes precious exhibits are shown in display windows, with the period mannequins and settings designed to provide a critical look at the power of fashion and the image of beauty. So for anyone who is interested in fashion and not afraid of a critical examination of the subject, this museum is a must-see. Of the thousands of dresses, shoes and accessories from the collection only a few individual pieces can be displayed at any one time. In addition to historical clothes from earlier centuries (i.e. Coptic, Hispano-Arab, Gothic and Renaissance fabrics) the wonderfully light and elegant designs by Fortuny from the early 20th century and some creations by Cristóbal Balenciaga are exhibited. Younger Spanish designers such as Antonio Miró and Custo are also present. International famous fashion brands such as Pierre Cardin, Karl Lagerfeld and Dior are also represented and endow the exhibition with a fascinating survey of the development of the French Haute Couture. There is also a jewellery collection with about 500 pieces, a section on lacework and a collection of prints.

Gabinet de les Arts Gràfiques

The collections of the **Graphic Arts Cabinet** are for visitors with special interests. It shows samples of typography such as punches, matrices, tracing plates and of course prints.

Museu de l' Esport Melcior Colet

✦ F 5

Location: Carrer Buenos Aires 56–58
Bus: 6, 7, 14, 15, 27, 33, 34, 59, 66, 67, 68

❶ Mon–Fri 9am–4pm, closed Aug
Admission free

The Museu de l'Esport Dr. Melcior Colet (Sports Museum) is housed in a notable Modernista building designed by Puig i Cadafalch in 1911.

With its facade decoration and the steep, gabled roof with overhanging eaves, Cadafalch's town house resembles alpine style more than Modernisme. In 1982 the doctor Melcior Colet transferred his former practice and private clinic to a foundation that bears his name. Its goal is to nurture sport and its cultural significance. As is so often case in Barcelona the goals and ideals of the foundation are mixed with a good dose of patriotism. Most of the approximately 900 exhibits relate to Catalan athletes and their successes. So, for example, you can see the ice axe with which the Catalan Carles Vallès climbed Mount Everest in 1985.

Sports museum

★ Museu del Futbol Club Barcelona

★ C 4

Location: Carrer Aristides Maillol
Metro: Collblanc (L 5), Palau
Reial (L 3)
❶ mid-April–mid-Oct daily
9.30am–7.30pm, mid-Oct–mid April

Mon–Sat 10am–6.30pm, Sun
10am–2.30pm
Camp Nou Experience: €23
www.fcbarcelona.cat

Barça – FC Barcelona – is not just a football club but an institution. The tour of the Camp Nou stadium and visit to the club museum are among the city's most popular attractions.

The club's stadium, the **Camp Nou,** lies to the southeast of the Zona Universitària on a site that was transformed to house facilities for the Olympic games. Able to accommodate almost 100,000 spectators it is one of the world's largest football stadiums.

Museum of FC Barcelona

The club, which has been national champion and European cup winner several times during the course of its eventful history, also operates its own museum here. The **Camp Nou Experience** includes entrance to the museum and the tour of the stadium. The latter leads through the visitors' changing rooms to the pitch, the VIP stand, the press boxes and VIP rooms before entering the **Museum**. After the recent renovations nothing now remains of the somewhat antiquated look of what has become the most visited muse-

> **!** *FC Barcelona live*   Insider Tip
>
> Those hoping to see FC Barcelona in action are highly advised to buy match tickets before travelling. They can be best purchased on the club's website www.fcbarcelona.cat. Ticket prices start at €39 (behind the goals; depending on the quality of the visiting team) and will be sent by email to be printed at home.

FC Barcelona

20 teams play in the Spanish premier league, the Primera División, but only two teams actually compete for the title: since its first season in 1928/29 the champion has been Real Madrid 32 times, and FC Barcelona 22 times.

Goal difference of the official Clásicos

Founded	29. November 1899
Members	169,000
Stadium	Nou Camp (99,354)
Titles (international and national)	89
Sales (season 2013/2014)	€530 mil.
Debts	€331 mil.

▶ **Number of wins in selected competitions**

■ FC Barcelona
□ Real Madrid

www.fcbarcelona.cat

Home   **Away**

30

25

20

15

10

Spanish Championship	Copa Del Rey	Champions League	European Supercup	FIFA World Cup

▶ **British players and coach**

FC Barcelona

Gary Lineker, S
1986 – 1989

Mark Hughes, S
1986 – 1987

Steve Archibald, S
1984 – 1987

G = Goal
D = Defence
MF = Midfield
S = Striker
C = Coach

▶ **FC Barcelona – famous players**

- Neymar, S, since 2014
- Thierry Henry, S, 2007 – 2010
- Lionel Messi, S, since 2004
- Ronaldinho, MF/S, 2003 – 2008
- Ronaldo, S, 2002 – 2007
- Frank de Boer, D, 1999 – 2003
- Luís Figo, MF, 1995 – 2000
- Xavi, MF, since 1991
- Andoni Zubizarreta, G, 1986 – 1994
- Diego Maradona, MF, 1982 – 1984
- Johan Cruyff, MF, 1973 – 1978

Coaches

- Luis Enrique
  since 2014
- Tito Vilanova
  2012– 2014
- Pep Guardiola
  2008 – 2012
- Frank Rijkaard
  2003 – 2008
- Radomir Antić
  2003

▶ **El Clásico matches**

229 matches

(without friendly games; in October 2014)

These players scored for both teams ▼

LUIS ENRIQUE RONAL

Real Madrid

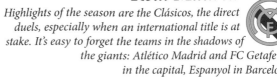

Highlights of the season are the Clásicos, the direct duels, especially when an international title is at stake. It's easy to forget the teams in the shadows of the giants: Atlético Madrid and FC Getafe in the capital, Espanyol in Barcelona.

Founded	6. March 1902
Members	85,000
Stadium	Santiago Bernabéu (80,354)
Titles (international and national)	84
Sales (season 2013/2014)	€604 mil.
Debts	€602 mil.

Home   Away

www.realmadrid.com

Real Madrid

Gareth Bale, MF, 2013 –
David Beckham, MF 2003 – 2007
Michael Owen, MF 2004 – 2005
Steve McManaman, MF 1999 – 2003
John Toshack, C 1989 – 1990, 1999
Laurie Cunningham, S 1979 – 1983

©BAEDEKER

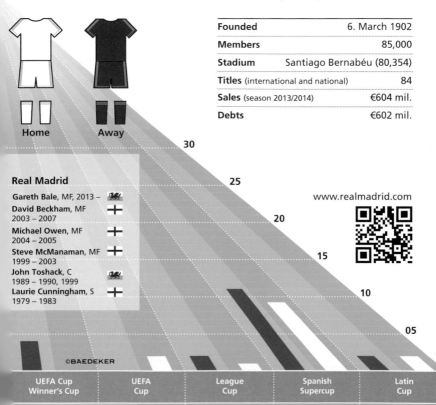

30
25
20
15
10
05

UEFA Cup Winner's Cup | UEFA Cup | League Cup | Spanish Supercup | Latin Cup

89 Wins Barca

92 Wins Real

48 Undecided

S FIGO   JOSEP SAMITIER

▶ **Real Madrid – famous players**

Toni Kroos, MF, since 2014
Ronaldo, S, 2002 – 2007
Zinédine Zidane, MF, 2001 – 2006
Luís Figo, MF, 2000 – 2005
Roberto Carlos, D, 1996 – 2007
Raúl Blanco, S, 1994 – 2010
Iker Casillas, G since 1989
Fernando Hierro, D, 1989 – 2003
Günter Netzer, MF, 1973 – 1976
Ferenc Puskás, S 1958 – 1966
Alfredo Di Stéfano, S, 1953 – 1964

Coaches

Carlo Ancelotti since 2013
José Mourinho 2010 – 2013
Manuel Pellegrini 2009 – 2010
Juan de Ramos 2008 – 2009
Bernd Schuster 2007 – 2008

FC Barcelona's museum of is one of Catalonia's most visited museums

um in Barcelona. With the help of design and technology the club's history and players come alive, and you can relive some of the most magic moments on touchscreen consoles. The tour ends at the enormous fan shop, where they have everything the fan's heart could possibly desire, from the latest club strip to the club tie to babies' bibs in the club colours.

Museu del Modernisme Català

✦ F 6

Location: Carrer Balmes 48
Metro: Passeig de Gràcia (L 2, L 3, L 4), Universidad (L 1, L 2)
❶ Mon–Sat 10am–8pm,

Sun 10am–2pm
Admission: €10
www.mmcat.cat

One of the newest museums of the city is dedicated to the art of Modernisme. On display in the rooms of a former textile warehouse are furniture, paintings and sculptures.

Since 2010 the Museu del Modernisme, housed in a building in the Eixample district designed by Enric Sagnier, has been exhibiting works of the Catalan version of Art Nouveau. The approximately 350 exhibits include furniture, paintings, and a number of sculptures produced by Joan Busquets, Ramón Casas, Antoni Gaudí, Gaspar Homar, Josep Llimona, Joaquim Mir and Puig i Cadafalch, amongst others. The presentation of the private collections of two antique dealers is a bit unimaginative and makes the ground floor look more like a furniture shop than a museum. There is more atmosphere in the basement, where as well as sculptures and paintings there is stained glass to be seen.

Museum of Modernisme

✶ Museu d'Història de Barcelona (MUHBA)

G 7

Location: Plaça del Rei
Metro: Catalunya (L 1, L 3), Liceu (L 3), Urquinaona und Jaume I (L 4)
🛈 Tue–Sat 10am–5pm (April–Oct till 7pm), Sun 10am–8pm
Admission: €7
www.museuhistoria.bcn.cat

The history of Barcelona is told in a late Gothic city palace. As well as the remains of the Roman settlement of Barcino in the basement you can also admire the throne room of the royal palace.

The 15th-century palace that now houses the city's historical museum originally stood at another spot but was transferred piece by piece to ▶Plaça del Rei in 1931. During excavation work for the foundations at the new location, the contractors unearthed foundations that turned out to be the remains of a once sizeable Roman town. The museum's entrance ticket is also valid for other attractions on Plaça del Rei: the raised royal chapel Santa Agata with an altarpiece by Jaume Huguet and the large 14th-century Saló de Tinell, a hall in the former Royal Palace (▶Museu Frederic Marès). It was here that Christopher Columbus was first received by the Catholic Monarchs upon his return from his first journey to the Americas (▶Barri Gòtic).

Museum of the History of Barcelona

The exhibits in the museum are explained in great detail and also in an easily understandable way, which makes most of it eminently suitable for children. The exhibits largely document the historical development of the city since the Middle Ages. Most fascinating, however, are the excavated **remains of the Roman town** in the museum's basement, as well as replicas from the excavations, including parts of

Museu d'Història de la Ciutat/Plaça del Rei

Plaça de Ramon Berenguer el Gran

Avant-cambra

Capella Santa Agata

Museu d'Història de la Ciuta

Plaça del Rei

Saló de Tinell

Gardens of Palau Reial

Palau del Lloctinent

(Archive of the crown of Aragón)

Baixada de Santa Clara

Placeta de Sant Iu

Carrer dels Comtes

©BAEDEKER

the thermal baths, floor mosaics, remains of the city walls and the water and sewer systems. Even an oil press with large bulbous storage vessels is displayed in the place where it was originally found. From the basement of the museum, visitors can enter a narrow shaft built vertically into the city wall which clearly shows Roman spoils built into the medieval walls (column drums, etc.). Before leaving the museum, enjoy the view of the Plaça del Rei from the small terrace on the second floor.

Museu Egipci

✦ G 6

Location: Carrer València 284
Metro: Passeig de Gràcia (L 2, L 3, L 4)
❶ Mon–Sat 10am–8pm,

Sun 10am–2pm
Admission: €11
www.museuegipci.com

The sophisticated but readily comprehensible collection of the Egyptian Museum was endowed by entrepreneur and patron Jordi Clos. On display are finds from all periods of Egyptian civilization.

This not very large museum in the Eixample district is divided into subject areas such as pharaohs, jewellery, ceramics, Egyptian deities and cults of the dead. The 600 or so exhibits in the collection are displayed on two levels, with special exhibitions being held in the basement. On the secluded roof terrace there is a pleasant café, which however only has irregular opening times. The Fundació Arqueológica Clos was founded by Jordi Clos, the president of the Derby hotel group, in 1993.

Egyptian Museum

Museu Etnogràfic Andino-Amazònic

✳ **D 3**

Location: Carrer Cardenal Vives i Tutó 2–16
Metro: Espanya (L 1, L 3)

❶ opening times by arrangement
Tel. 9 32 04 34 58

A small museum, but one which definitely has its own charm, is the Museu Etnogràfic Andino-amazonic, the Ethnographic Museum of the Andean and Amazonian world.

It is run by the **Capuchin Order** (Caputxins de Sarria) and is also housed in the monastery's facilities. The collection, which is not very comprehensive but outstandingly maintained and presented, specializes in the cultures of the order's Latin American area of missionary activity. The exhibits on display were collected by monks from the second half of the 19th century onwards in the Amazon basin as well Columbia, Brasil and Peru; they include artefacts, weaponry, stuffed animals and a collection of insects.

Museum of the Andes and Amazon

Museu Etnològic

✳ **D/E 7**

Location: Passeig de Santa Madrona
Metro: Espanya (L 1, L 3)
❶ closed for renovation work

www.museu
etnologic.bcn.es

The Museu Etnològic (Museum of Anthropology) is situated on the Passeig de Santa Madrona, which winds its way up Montjuïc.

The layout of the building, which was purpose built as a museum in 1973, consists of several joined hexagons. Generously proportioned

Ethnological Museum

windows make for a well-lit exhibition space. The collections, which comprise a total of more than 20,000 exhibits, focus on **Asian, African, American and Oceanic cultures**, and cover biological, ethnographical, cultural and social aspects. The museum's rich inventory is selectively used for temporary exhibitions on specific subjects. Currently, the museum is closed for major renovation works, with the reopening date to be confirmed.

✶ Museu Frederic Marès

✳ G 7

Location: Plaça Sant Iu 5–6
Metro: Jaume I (L 4)
❶ Tue–Sat 10am–7pm,
Sun 11am–8pm

Admission: €4.20
www.museu
mares.bcn.cat

A complex of buildings that belongs to the former royal palace now houses the extensive collection of the sculptor Frederic Marès (1893–1991). Whether it was Romanesque art, Roman reliefs or early bicycles, Marès' passion for collecting knew no bounds.

Museum of a collector Marès was an almost obsessive, yet absolutely chaotic collector. During the course of his long life, he amassed a huge amount of the most varied of items from every period, including precious works of art as well as multiple samples of ordinary everyday objects. In 1944 Marès donated his collection to the city of Barcelona. Two years later the museum was opened in a part of the building that belonged to the palace of the Royal House of Aragón-Catalonia (►Barri Gòtic). In 1952 the artist and collector moved into the property himself, having a flat installed on the third floor. The museum is entered through a picturesque courtyard garden (with a pleasant café) and you're immediately impressed by the sheer number of exhibits, then exhausted by their scope and finally touched because you're always trying to get into the mind of this passionate collector. Then you will be torn between outstanding ecclesiastical art works – including as one of the highlights

MARCO ⊕ POLO TIP

! *City of art* **Insider Tip**

Barcelona is a city of art foundations. A recent addition is the Fundació Alorda Derksen. Contemporary art by the likes of Jaume Plensa, Anish Kapoor and Damien Hirst can be admired in the galleries (Calle Aragó 314, Wed – Fri 10am – 1pm, 4pm – 7pm, Sat 10am – 2pm, 4pm – 8pm). Guided tours for groups (€5) must be arranged in advance, tel. 93 272 62 50 (www.fundacionad.com)

Museu Frederic Marès

Second Floor

Library of Frederic Marès

WC

»Sentimental« Department
- 1-2 Iron work
- 3 Montserrat
- 4 Arms
- 5 Ladies' culture
- 6 Smoker's utensils
- 7 Vases
- 8 Photography
- 9 Watches and chronometers
- 10-14 Ceramics und glass
- 15 Religious art
- 16 Gentlemen's cultures

First Floor

WC

Lift

Sculptures
- 14,15,17 Gothic, 15th cent.
- 16 Textiles and clothes
- 18-24 Renaissance, 16th cent.
- 25-27 Baroque, 17th-18th cent.
- 28 Catalan Art

Main Floor

Carrer de la Tapineria

Café

Baixada de la Canonja

WC

Atrium

Special Exhibitions

© BAEDEKER

Carrer dels Comtes

Plaça de Sant Iu
← **Entrance**

Sculptures
- 1 Antiquity, 400 BC-AD 300
- 2-5 Romanesque, 11th-14 th cent.
- 6-13 Gothic, 13th-14th cent.

Basement

Sculptures
- 12 Stone sculptures, 4th-16th cent.

Jaume Juguet's Christ on his way to Golgotha – and Roman finds on the ground floor, and other sacred objects and chests, coins and dolls on the first floor. The not very serious »Col·lecció Sentimental«, the curious Sentimental Department on the second floor, presents a collection of Baroque objets d'art, advertising images, dried flower bouquets, ashtrays, old photo cameras, and much more, all united under one roof.

** Museu Marítim

✦ F 8

Location: Av. de les Drassanes
Metro: Drassanes (L 3)
❶ daily 10am–8pm

Admission: €5 (free
Sun from 3pm on)
www.mmb.cat

Near the harbour, to the west of the Columbus Memorial, lie the Drassanes, the halls of the former royal dockyards. Since 1929 they have been home to the Museu Marítim (▶MARCO POLO insight, p. 218), which with its exhibits is one of the most important museums in Catalonia.

Maritime Museum

The medieval shipyards are an attraction in their own right. They were erected in the 13th and 14th centuries and warships and trading vessels were constructed here until well into the 18th century; up to 30 ships could be in production at the same time.

The Maritime Museum offers an abundance of artefacts from the history of sea travel up to the present. There are ships and ship's models, nautical equipment, tools and weapons, as well as information about the harbour and the royal shipyards of Barcelona. The museum's highlight is the replica of the **Royal Galley,** the flagship of the Venetain-Spanish fleet commanded by Juan de Austria, which defeated the Ottomans near Lepanto in 1571. Those interested in sailing will be fascinated by the Flying Dutchman-class dingy with which Spain won Olympic Gold in 1992.

The triple-masted wooden **schooner Santa Eulàlia** is also part of the museum and can be visited at its berth at the Moll de la Fusta – if it's not out on the high seas.

Santa Eulália: April–Oct Tue–Fri, Sun 10am– 20.30pm, Sat 2pm–8.30pm; Nov–March Tue–Fri, Sun 10am– 5.30pm, Sat 2pm–5.30pm; admission €1

★★ Museu Nacional d'Art de Catalunya (MNAC)

✦ **D 7**

Location: Mirador del Palau Nacional
Metro: Espanya (L 1, L 3
❶ May–Sep Tue–Sat 10am–8pm

(Oct–April till 6pm) ,
Sun till 3pm
Admission: €12
www.mnac.es

With its superb collections from all periods of Catalan art history, the Museu Nacional d' Art de Catalunya (MNAC; Museum of Catalan Art) in the Palau Nacional is among the most important attractions in Barcelona.

Crowned by a dome, the Palau Nacional (National Palace) stands at the top of a broad flight of steps. The Neo-Baroque palace was originally built for the World Fair in 1929 and it has housed the Museu Nacional d'Art de Catalunya since 1934. In the 1990s the interior was completely redone by the Italian architect Gae Aulenti and since then has provided the perfect setting for the exhibits of this world-class museum.

Palau Nacional

The Department of Romanesque Art (11th–13th centuries) is particularly fascinating, as it is considered the most comprehensive collection of its kind in the world. Splendid frescoes of numerous churches from the region of the Catalan Pyrenees are exhibited here. The impact of these unique exhibits is further intensified by their sophisticated presentation: the original vaults and apses have been precisely reconstructed in the museum, even including the original frescoes. Meanwhile the churches have had copies true to the originals installed. Photographs, layouts and plans of the churches provide proof of the paintings' original locations. Highlights of the collection are the colourful **frescoes from the apses of the Sant Climent and Santa Maria churches in Tahul**, featuring an image of Christ with the inscription »Ego sum lux mundi« (I am the light of the world) and a display of the Last Judgement and the sinners in hell. There are also altar panels, capitals, figures and more.

Romanesque

Some sections in the Department of Gothic Art (14th and 15th centuries) are not arranged chronologically, but systematically. The collections are not merely restricted to Catalonia, but also include works from other Spanish regions, as well as Flemish and Italian artists. Wooden and stone sculptures, panels and altar panels are exhibited. A number of colourful murals illustrate Catalonia's occupation of Mallorca in 1229.

Gothic

** *Barcelona's Shipyards*

The shipyard (drassanes reials = royal docks) was built in the 13th century and continually expanded until the 18th century. The buildings themselves are an extraordinary expression of Western Gothic architecture, while their spaciousness, high arches, vaults and niches remind of Gothic churches. Here, the galleys and caravels of the Aragonese Crown were built, serviced and repaired. With the discovery of the Americas and the navy's interests shifting towards the Atlantic, the significance of the shipyard faded until the buildings were only used as warehouses. In 1936, it was decided to turn the complex into a museum. Since 1976 it has been a site of historic interest.

❶ »Real« Galley

The large hall is dominated by the excellent replica (1:1 scale) of the »Real« galley. It was built in honour of the 400th anniversary of a crucial event in Spain: the »Real« was the flagship of the fleet which defeated the Turks under the command of Don Juan d'Austria on 7 October 1571, near Lepanto (on the Peloponnese Island of Greece) and gained Spain's supremacy over the Mediterranean. 236 oarsmen had to propel the 60m/197ft galley. The replica, with its rich gold ornamentation and the delicately carved

The exhibition rooms resemble the interior of Gothic churches

figurehead (Neptune, god of the sea, riding on a dolphin), does not look much like a battleship.

❷ Figureheads

The exhibition of figureheads from the 18th and 19th centuries on the upper floor is well worth seeing.

❸ Steam navigation

This section features the replica of parts of a ocean-going steamer from around 1900, reflecting the social contrast between the pleasure travellers in the salon and the immigrants in steerage. There is also a replica of Narcis Monturiol's submarine. Here, visitors see the underwater world the way the inventor must have experienced it on his dives.

❹ Documentation centre

Maritime documentation centre (Centre de Documentació Marítima) and educational centre specially aimed at schoolchildren.

❺ Cafeteria and museum shop

The many impressions need to be digested – why not at the cafeteria... Those looking for unique souvenirs are sure to find some in the museum's shop.

The Museu Picasso is one of the most visited museums of Barcelona

1957 paraphrase of Diego Velázquez' work of the same name, stand apart from the chronological sequence, and an entire room is dedicated to Picasso's examination of this topic. Additional sections, shown individually, include graphic works from 1962 to 1972, and ceramics from the years 1947–65. A cafeteria is located on the ground floor of the museum.

Palau Dalmases

A few steps further along Carrer Montcada at No. 20 stands the Palau Dalmases, in which the »Omnium Cultural« organisation, which promotes and preserves the Catalan culture, has been housed since 1962. The 17th-century (originally 15th-century) palace has a lovely courtyard complete with Renaissance staircase.

✳ Palau de la Música Catalana

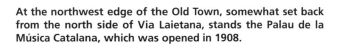

✴ **G 7**

Location: Carrer Sant Pere Més Alt
Metro: Urquinaona (L 1, L 4
❶ Tours daily every 30 min
10am–3.30pm,

Easter & July till 6pm,
Aug 9am–8pm.
Admission: €18
www.palaumusica.org

At the northwest edge of the Old Town, somewhat set back from the north side of Via Laietana, stands the Palau de la Música Catalana, which was opened in 1908.

The concert hall, the boldest and most modern work of the architect **Lluís Domènech i Montaner**, was built between 1905 and 1908, as an »Ode to Catalonia«. It was commissioned by the Catalan National Choir, which still owns the building today. Countless numbers of concerts have taken place here, primarily with choral music, but also chamber music and symphony music. Many famous composers, soloists, and ensembles have and still do perform here. The building sums up the whole **magnificence of Modernisme**, representing the attitude to life, the tastes and the affluence of the Catalan bourgeoisie. Some observers might consider it overdone and even outlandish, but no one can deny its impact; in 1997 UNESCO declared it a World Heritage Site.

Magnificent work of Modernisme

The colourful façade can be read like a picture book: mosaic columns support busts of Bach, Beethoven, Wagner and others; allegorical mosaics with musical and local themes embellish the upper floor. Everything is richly decorated. A pair of binoculars would be useful to better make out the fine details of the domed roof and the stained glass windows.

The building's interior, which you can visit on a guided tour (or of course if you are seeing a concert), is equally overwhelming. The entrance, lobby and entrance staircase to the large **concert hall** are festooned with floral ornamentation. Vines, roses, lilies and other flowers cover the columns, walls, and ceiling. The staircase is lined with candelabras. The large and splendidly colourful concert hall (approx. 1700 seats) entered from the upper floor forms the climax of the tour. Tall, stained-glass windows frame the organ. The grand central **skylight** of blue and golden glass is surrounded by women's faces forming a choir, and descends from the coffered ceiling into the hall like an enchanting drop of glass. Marble statues stand on both sides of the stage, including Wagner's Valkyrie and a bust of Beethoven. The back of the stage is decorated with mosaic figures with terracotta heads.

Interior

The modernistic Palau de la Música is a splendid venue for concerts

Those lucky enough to experience a concert here will be given both an aural and a visual treat. The concert hall has its own chamber orchestra. Performances range from classical to contemporary and experimental music, jazz and pop.

✴ Palau Güell

✴ F 7

Location: Carrer Nou de la Rambla 3–5
Metro: Drassanes, Liceu (L 3)
❶ Tue–Sun 10am–8pm (Oct–March

till 5.30pm)
Admission: €12
www.palauguell.cat

In 1886, architect Antoni Gaudí received a commission from Eusebi Güell to build a residential house in Bourgeois style on an ancient narrow city street, a seemingly impossible task for an uneven piece of land 18 x 22m/59 x 72ft. However, Gaudí approached the challenge with confidence and created a masterpiece, which has been a UNESCO World Heritage Site since 1984.

The house has a stern and cold façade. The narrow Gothic windows, the portcullis-like gates, and the doors protected by metal grates are not reminiscent of a castle by mere coincidence; they also offered protection from the not-so-bourgeois neighbourhood. The two entrance portals bear the initials E and G, formed of wrought iron. The floor of the inner **courtyard** appears to be tiled, but it's actually made of wood in order to dampen the sound of horses' hooves.

Another Gaudí building

Because space inside is limited, access is restricted to a maximum of 22 people every 15 minutes. Tickets sell fast and it's best to go in the morning to reserve a ticket for later. Despite the small interior Gaudí managed to create the feeling of spaciousness. The salon at the core of the building was intended for poetry readings and in-house concerts – Eusebi Güell was a big fan of the arts. It reaches from the first floor to the roof crowned by a parabolic dome. In this way, Gaudí was able to substitute width with height. The living spaces are arranged around this domed space; stables were located on the ground floor. Mock windows (indirectly lit sheets of glass) imitate various nonexistent views. The interior – mainly designed by Gaudí himself – is extravagantly decorated using the finest materials. It demonstrates not only the taste and wealth of the builder, but also the inventiveness of Gaudí and the Modernisme style in general, which can today seem somewhat bizarre.

Interior

Not even the roof was spared its share of »structural artwork«. The dome and the chimneys – similar to "Casa Milà – became decorative sculptural elements. On top of that, the roof has fantastic views of Raval and the harbour.

Parc de la Ciutadella

✳ H 7/8

Location: Passeig Picasso / Passeig de Pujades
Metro: Barceloneta, Ciutadella (L 4)

The Parc de la Ciutadella (Citadel Park) is a spacious park at the northeastern edge of the historic Old City. It was laid out on the site of the razed citadel, which had been built in the 18th century by Philipp V, in order to suppress the rebellious city population and to secure the area surrounding the harbour.

Most of the military buildings were torn down in the middle of the 19th century and a park was laid out on the grounds. It was subsequently the site for the 1888 World Fair, since which time the Moorish-style triumphal arch has marked the northern entrance to the park. Today visitors can walk the promenades and take a peaceful

Citadel

break among the shrubs, trees, lawns and fountains. Besides the zoo and some interesting Modernista buildings, the Parlament de Catalunya, the parliament of the autonomous region of Catalonia is located here.

Castell dels Tres Dragons
At the western end of the park is the so-called Castell dels Tres Dragons. The »Castle of the Three Dragons« was designed by Lluis Domènech i Montaner for the World Fair of 1888. The building long housed the Zoological Museum, which has been closed since it moved to the ▶Museu Blau.

Hivernacle
Adjacent to the Castell dels Tres Dragons is the L'Hivernacle. This conservatory is an impressive iron and glass construction so typical of the late-19th century. Occasionally concerts are performed within. It borders a small garden, which is in turn flanked by the former Geological Museum. The latter was built in 1882 by Antoni Rovira in neoclassical style. Today the museum's collections also belong to the "Museu Blau.

Umbracle
Also interesting is the Umbracle, a construction of brick and wood, which was built during the course of the 1888 World Fair. Tropical plants grow beneath the open roof.

Cascade
In the northern part of the park you come to a lake where it's possible to rent out a rowing boat. Just a short distance away towards Passeig de Pujades is a small pond. It is dominated by a bombastic cascade with numerous allegorical figures, flanked by water-spouting griffins. The grotto in the middle part is one of Gaudí's early works. In front of the cascade is a bandstand and a simple garden restaurant. In the eastern part of the park, in the direction of La Barceloneta, you will reach the site of the ▶ oo.

Parc de l' Espanya Industrial

✦ D 5

Location: Carrer del Rector Triado
Metro: Sants-Estació (L 3, L 5)

With its post-modern countenance, the Parc de l'Espanya Industrial is by no means uncontroversial. Some consider it to be a successful composition of modern architecture, contemporary art, and leisurely fun. Others find it cold and subdued.

Nevertheless, the park is well used as the area lacks suitable alternatives for leisure activities. Constructed in 1985, it was designed by Basque architect Luis Pena Ganchegui as a modern version of a Roman bath. It is slightly reminiscent of a movie set for some futuristic Hollywood film, with the towers, staircases and cypress trees reflected in the water of the lake. The park is spread over two levels. The ten »**lighthouses**« on the upper level serve as lookout towers. Next to a number of water fountains, the large metal sculpture of the Dragon of St George by Andreas Nagel is especially enjoyed by children, who use it as a water slide. Multilevel, extended seating benches of light natural stone lead to a small lake and canal; boats are available for rent. The park's squash and basketball courts provide for good recreational activity.

A modern Roman bath

The nearby Plaça Països Catalans in the vicinity of Barcelona-Sants railway station has a rather unfortunate modern design and is derogatorily referred to by Barcelonans as the »Gasolinera« (petrol station), because of its large, free-standing metal roof.

Plaça Països Catalans

✳ Parc del Laberint

✦ J 1

Location: north of the Passeig de la Vall d'Hebron
Metro: Mundet (L 3)
❶ daily from 10am on
Admission: €2.17, free Wed and Sun

The modern residential areas of Montbau and Vall d'Hebron stretch out in the far northwestern corner of the city. The nearby picturesque Parc del Laberint, the oldest and most atmospheric park in the city, forms an complete contrast.

In 1791, Count Antoni Desvalls began to build a classic, early romantic park on his property, a piece of land that was, at that time, still far away from the city. The park was developed around an old fortified tower that had already existed on that spot since the 14th century. No less than four landscape architects were involved in the planning: one from Italy, one from France, and two from Catalonia. The park immediately fascinates all visitors. The thick, lavish vegetation, the abundance of ponds, canals, cascades and goldfish ponds create a dreamlike, romantic atmosphere. Again and again you encounter statues of characters from Greek mythology or a small marble temple. The park also features a classical fountain pavilion, and even a »fake« cemetery, constructed solely for decorative purposes. The true highlight of the park, however, is the **labyrinth**, to which the park

Enchanted park

The Parc del Laberint is ideal for playing hide and seek

owes its name. The maze of cypress trees is fun to get lost in. Because the number of visitors allowed in the park at any one time is limited, you may need to wait to get in. Classical music concerts take place in the early summer months (June–July).

** Parc Güell

✶ H 3

Location: Carrer Olot
Metro: Lesseps (L 3)
🕐 daily 8am–9pm

Admission: €7
www.parkguell.es

»At around midnight, we went down to the festival at Park Güell. ...I had instinctively expected something completely preposterous. That was lucky, because I think those who come unprepared to the park at night might be shocked for life«. Those were the comments of author Meier-Graefe in 1910, after a night-time visit to Parc Güell. The park shouldn›t be quite as confusing to visitors today, yet it leaves an unforgettable impression on everyone.

A park by Gaudí
In the Vallcarca district, which lies between Eixample and Mount Tibidabo, the park is laid out over the southern flank of Mount Carmel. Antoni Gaudí constructed it between 1900 and 1914 on a piece of completely inhospitable land. The original plan was for a small garden community with 60 small houses, a market square and a forum. However, this was rejected by the wealthy residents and therefore never carried out. Only a very small number of buildings emerged, one of them being the house in which the architect himself resided. Today it is home to the Museu Gaudí. The park itself re-

mained intact, and although it was neglected and had deteriorated during the Franco era, Barcelona remembered this cultural treasure in the 1980s and restored it to its original splendour. It has been a **UNESCO World Heritage Site** since 1984. The cumbersome walk to the top can be avoided by taking the escalator, which starts on Avinguda de l'Hospital between Lesseps and Vallcarca metro stations. The southeastern perimeter wall of the park (Carrer Olot) features colourful majolica medallions, which display the name of the park in a repeating pattern. The park has several entrances, though seven were originally planned (after the ancient city of Thebes). The **main entrance** on Carrer d'Olot is bordered by two small fairytale-looking buildings with flowing lines: one is reminiscent of an elephant raising its trunk, the other of a mushroom.

The park itself is divided into various zones, one structurally designed part in the southeast and a natural park in the northwest. Just beyond the main entrance, a double flight of steps leads up to the Sala Hipóstila, a **hall of columns**, the roof of which creates the forum above. The most distinguishing feature of the steps is the colourful dragon that represents Python, »guardian of the subterranean waters«, according to Greek myth. The hall of columns was originally intended as the market square of the garden community and even empty it is overwhelmingly impressive. 86 Doric columns hold up the mighty roof, while the outer rows of columns lean strongly inward to absorb the strain of the arches. The hall is decorated with an abundance of symbols – suns representing the seasons, circles representing the phases of the moon, Christian symbols, Sanskrit writing and Egyptian symbols. Figures from Greek mythology find themselves standing next to Old Testament characters. The steps lead up to the expansive **forum square** and to a higher terrace at its northern end, the aspect of which was specifically designed to provide shade in the summer and sun in the winter. The terrace offers a view of the lively proceedings on the forum, which was actually intended for assemblies and theatre and now serves as a gathering place for visitors from around the world. The wall surrounding the forum is designed as a **single, long wavy bench**. Particularly at the southern end overlooking the city, the pronounced wavy shapes create separate, almost closed-off compartments. Take the time to examine the original decorative ceramic fragments in all colours of the rainbow that completely cover the bench. The ergonomically shaped seats were designed to drain off rainwater, demonstrating that Gaudí was

? MARCO ⊕ POLO INSIGHT

Made of rubbish

The colourful mosaics between the capitals of the archaic-looking columns in Parc Güell are constructed of rubbish, using pieces of tile, broken bottles, stones and even pieces of ashtrays and porcelain dolls.

The endless bench at Parc Güell with its famous mosaic

also a practical thinker. He is said to have had a worker sit naked on soft plaster in order to create a true-to-life mould. The terrace offers a magnificent view of the city and the ocean, but it is well worth taking the time to see other parts of the park, with its colonnades, viaducts, grottoes and lavish vegetation. Often it is difficult to tell the difference between the natural and the man-made features amongst the trees, bushes, cacti and climbing vines – a perfect harmony of nature and human design.

Museu Gaudí The house situated in the middle of the park and constructed by Francesc Berenguer in 1904, was Antoni Gaudí's home from 1906 to 1926. It has been converted to a museum exhibiting original sketches, items from the estate and countless pieces of Modernista furniture, many acquired from "Casa Milà and "Casa Batlló.

❶ June–Sep daily 9am–8pm, April and May 10am–8pm, Oct–March 10am–6pm; admission €5.50; www.casamuseugaudi.org/

Parc Joan Miró

✳ E 6

Location: Carrer de Tarragona
Metro: Plaça d' Espanya (L 1, L 3), Tarragona (L 3)

Close to Plaça Espanya is the Parc Joan Miró with its palm trees. Visible form afar is the 22m/72ft high sculpture »Woman with Bird« by Joan Miró.

The park was created shortly after the first free elections were held in Barcelona, after the end of the Franco regime. It takes up the area of four manzanas, those uniform blocks of Ildefons Cerdà's Eixample scheme. Originally the plot was occupied by the municipal abattoir. Parc Joan Miró can be entered from any side. It is divided into two levels. The larger is deeper and is shaded by a dense palm grove. Also, some holm oaks and pine trees grow on the site. Boule courts and sports fields have also been created in the lower part, and they are very popular – particularly at weekends. On the upper level there are lawns and a large, shallow pool, out of which rises the famous phallic sculpture by Joan Miró: the work entitled Dona o Ocell (Woman and Bird, 1983) was a gift from the artist to his hometown.

Park with palm trees

* Passeig de Gràcia

✳ G 6/7

Location: from Plaça de Catalunya to Plaça Joan Carles I
Metro: Passeig de Gràcia (L3, L4), Diagonal (L3)

The Passeig de Gràcia is without doubt Barcelona's most elegant and impressive grand boulevard. It forms the main axis of the Quadrat d'Or (Golden Square) in the ▶Eixample district, so named because of its large concentration of Modernista buildings.

It connects Plaça de Catalunya at the edge of the Old City with the former suburb and now district of Gràcia that borders Eixample to the northwest, where the Passeig continues as the considerably narrower Carrer Gran de Gràcia. Along the broad tree-lined avenue are bank buildings, exclusive fashion and jewellery shops, luxury hotels and tapas restaurants.

Grand boulevard

Between the transverse streets of Consell de Cent and Arago is the so-called **Manzana de la Discordia**. However, the »apple of discord« does not here refer to the dispute between Pallas Athena, Hera and Aphrodite, and the question of who deserved the Golden Apple, but

MARCO ⊕ POLO TIP

! *In the world of fragrances* **Insider Tip**

39, a perfume company with a branch on Passeig de Gràcia, hosts a small specialised museum (Museu del Perfum) offering an interesting glance into the history of fragrances; exhibits include highly artistic vessels, vials, etc. from Antiquity to the present, via Baroque (17th/18th century).

to which is the most beautiful Modernista building. In Spanish, manzana not only means apple but also block. Standing cheek by jowl are the ▶Casa Batlló by Gaudí, the Casa Amatller by Puig i Cadafalch, followed by the Casa Lleó Morera by Domènech i Montaner. A little further up is Gaudí's ▶Casa Milà, better known as La Pedrera. Also well worth a visit is the **Palau Robert**, a neoclassical palace at the top of the Passeig where in addition to the secluded garden regular exhibitions are mounted and a tourist information office is housed.

The greenish-grey, textured hexagonal tiles of the pavements were designed by Antoni Gaudí (▶Famous People). The Catalan capital's coat-of-arms also appears repeatedly on the many decorative wrought-iron lampposts.

✳ Pavelló Mies van der Rohe

✳ **D 7**

Location: Francesc Ferrer i Guàrdia 7
Metro: Plaça d' Espanya (L 1, L 3)
Admission: €5
❶ daily 10am–8pm
www.miesbcn.com

In the vicinity of the Palau Nacional and the neoclassical trade fair halls, the German Pavilion for the 1929 World Fair appears like it's from another time. With this building, Mies van der Rohe succeeded in creating a masterpiece on modern architecture.

German pavilion for the World Fair

Born in 1886, the architect **Ludwig Mies van der Rohe** was the last director of the famous Bauhaus in Dessau, Germany, and it was he who was chosen to design the German pavilion for the 1929 World Fair in Barcelona. This replica of the original was inaugurated in 1986 on what would have been his 100th birthday. The Pavelló Mies van der Rohe is impressive for its strict and clear lines as well as for the aesthetic effect of its materials of glass, steel, and polished natural stone. In the atrium stands a bronze copy of a statue by Georg Kolbe. The upholstered chairs in the interior of the pavilion were designed for the World Fair and specially named »Barcelona«. Their timeless elegance is still captivating today. An affiliated documentation centre works closely together with the Mies van der Rohe Archive of the Museum of Modern Art in New York City.

The Barcelona Pavilion, designed by Ludwig Mies van der Rohe, was the German Pavilion for the 1929 International Exposition

Plaça de Catalunya

G 6

Location: Stadtzentrum
Metro: Catalunya (L 1, L 3)

Plaça de Catalunya forms the northwest end of the city centre's historic Rambles. It is also the geographical centre of Barcelona and an important traffic junction.

Redesigned several times since its construction in the middle of the 19th century, the square offers leafy areas, a fountain and a pool, as well as numerous sculptures and memorials, yet it presents something of a disjointed impression, perhaps due to the many changes it has undergone. It is framed by large banks, office buildings and businesses, including the Banco Español de Crédito on the northwestern side and the towering Telefónica building on the eastern side. Even the traditional **Café Zurich** has been moved to a nondescript block after its former home was torn down, though much of its former atmosphere has been preserved by keeping the original interior design. The open space in the middle of the square is host to many events and political demonstrations. There are always a lot of people here, as well

Disjointed impression

> **!** *Rest with a view* **Insider Tip**
>
> The ninth floor of the Corte Inglés offers a large self-service restaurant with a viewing terrace, which is recommended for a pleasant break during a tour of the city, as well as for the great view of central Barcelona.

as pigeons, which have been known to attack pedestrians with the flapping of their wings. Underneath the square is the most important **metro junction in the city**, which is accessible from several sides. Suburban trains going to ▶Tibidabo and Pedralbes also start from here. The large **tourist information office** is also located underground.

El Corte Inglés　At the north side of the square stands the El Corte Inglés department store, which is certainly worth a visit, not least for its extensive selection of regional items. An interpreter service is available via in-house telephone, where foreign customers can receive shopping assistance in their native language.

Casa Calvet　Just north of the Plaça de Catalunya is the Casa Calvet (Carrer Casp 48). Built in 1898–1900, this is another work by Antoni Gaudí. Compared to his other designs, with its minimalist façade the building appears almost spartan. The architect received the Architectural Prize of the City of Barcelona for Casa Calvet. The same applies to Gaudí's furniture designs, some of which can be found at the Gaudí Museum (▶Parc Güell). Casa Calvet is privately owned and the interior is therefore not open to visitors.

Plaça Espanya

✳ D/E 6

Location: southwest of the city centre
Metro: Espanya (L 1, L 3)

> **!** *Cocktails and cuisine* **Insider Tip**
>
> Just five minutes from the Plaça Espanya, star chef Ferrán Adria has opened a tapas and cocktail bar. The creative little delicacies at »Tickets Vida y Tapa« (Avinguda Parallel 164) are much sought after. Advance booking is essential. This can only be done online: www.ticketsbar.es
> ▶Enjoy Barcelona, Food and Drink

The circular Plaça Espanya serves as the most important traffic hub on the west side of the city.

This is where the wide Gran Via de les Corts Catalanes (usually nicknamed Gran Via), which cuts through the entire city in a straight line, intersects with the Avinguda de la Paral·lel. »España Ofrecida a Dios« (Spain dedicated to God), an elaborate memorial fountain, rises in the middle of the square. Two towers on the southeastern side, modelled on St Mark›s in Venice, form the entrance to the grounds of the exhibition grounds. On the northern side is the former **bullring** (►Plaça de Toros), erected in 1900 in Neomudejar style with approx. 15,000 seats. The last corrida to be contested here was in 1977. The facility was completely gutted and converted into a shopping mall with cinemas and restaurants, which opened in 2011. Responsible for the scheme was the British architect Richard Rogers. The rooftop terrace offers a good view of the Plaça Espanya and the city.

Plaça de Toros

— ✴ **E 6, H 6, K 7**

Location: Gran Via de les Corts Catalanes 385 and 747
Metro: Espanya (L 3) respectively Monumental (L 2)

Until a few years ago, Barcelona had two bullrings, the Plaças de Toros or Plaças de Braus. The bullring right on ►Plaça Espanya has now been converted into a large shopping mall. Neither do corridas any longer take place at the second arena, La Monumental, situated near the northeastern end of the Gran Via (No 747). Bullfighting has been outlawed in Catalonia since 2012.

The last bullfight at La Monumental took place on 2. September 2011. **La** The arena, which could hold up to 20,000 spectators, is well worth see- **Monumental** ing even without the bloody spectacle. It was completed in 1914 and evinces a lavish combination of Mujedar and Byzantine style elements.

In the complex is a small bullfighting museum, in which weapons, **Museu Taurí** stuffed heads of famous fighting bulls and some of the dazzling Trajes de Luz, the working costume of the torreros, can be seen.
❶ Mon–Sat 11am–2pm and 4pm–8pm, Sun 11am–1pm; admission: €4

✳ Plaça Reial

— ✴ **F 7**

Location: Rambla
Metro: Drassanes, Liceu (L 3)

The Plaça Reial (not to be confused with Plaça del Rei in the ►Barri Gòtic) is connected to the Rambla dels Caputxins via the ultra short Carrer Colom.

Atmospheric square The pretty, enclosed square is surrounded by classical buildings that open up on the ground floor forming arcades of shops and restaurants. It was created around the middle of the 19th century on the site of a former Capuchin monastery. It mirrors the Napoleonic style of city squares, but its unique lively flair is more reminiscent of an Italian piazza. In the middle of the square, the fountain of The Three Graces features lampposts and benches designed by Antoni Gaudí, and is surrounded by tall palm trees.

Back to former glory In the 1970s, the square was a dilapidated place with dubious bars and hotels renting rooms by the hour. Drug dealers, prostitutes and the homeless dominated the scene, but Plaça Reial was restored to its former glory and has now long been an attractive meeting place once again. During the day, people come here to relax or just watch chil-

The wonderful Plaça Reial is nearly always busy, whether during the day or late at night

dren play, in the evening to dine well at one of the terrace restaurants, simply stroll across the square or go to a nightclub of jazz bar. Drug dealing has not completely disappeared however, which is why the police continue to maintain their demonstrative presence here.

MARCO ⊕ POLO TIP

! **Refugi 307** Insider Tip

Hundreds of shelters were built during the Spanish Civil War. Refugi 307 is one of them. Over 400 yards of tunnels can be explored on Sundays at 10.30am and 11.30am (Spanish) and at 12.30pm (Catalan). Entrance: Nou de Rambla 169 (west of Plaça Reial).

✳ **Poble Espanyol**

✦ **D–E 8**

Location: Avinguda Marquès de Comillas
Metro: Espanya (L 1, L 3)
⊙ daily from 9am, Mon till 8pm, Tue–Wed,Thur–Sun till midnight, Fri till 3am, Sat till 4am
Admission: €12
www.poble-espanyol.com

The Poble Espanyol (Spanish Village) on ▶Montjuïc is, like so much else in Barcelona, a remnant of the World Fair of 1929. It was intended to provide visitors with a realistic impression of the various regions of Spain and of their characteristic building styles.

There are **more than one hundred buildings and palaces recreated** true to their original examples. Many well-known artists contributed to the selection and compilation of designs. The houses are arranged around Plaça Major, the main square near the entrance. From here, visitors can stroll through picturesque streets and small alleys, which also provide many a view into lovely courtyards. A sculpture garden depicts 36 works of contemporary Spanish sculptures and a special exhibition is dedicated to sculptor Josep Guinovart (1927-2007).

Spain in miniature

The Poble Espanyol is very popular among tourists, especially due to the large number of businesses producing and selling **high-quality handicrafts and artwork** in many of its buildings. There is a vast selection of glass, ceramics, enamels, prints, textiles, and leather goods. Food and drink are also here in abundance; on a stroll through the village it is difficult to choose from the many eateries and pubs, which offer specialities from all parts of Spain. There are also good nightclubs and a well-known flamenco bar that is even appreciated by locals. An information centre is located at the entrance area, between the book and souvenir shops. In the low season not all shops and restaurants in this open-air museum are open and sometimes it might seem like a Sunday afternoon somewhere out in the Spanish provinces.

Fundació Fran Daurel	Definitely worth seeing is the Fundació Fran Daurel. This Private Collection brings together mainly Catalan artists such as Cuixart, Tàpies and Barceló. Works by Dalí and Picasso can also be seen. ❶ daily 10am–7pm

Port

✳ A–H 8–10

Location: eastern part of the city
Metro: Drassanes (L 3), Barceloneta (L 4)

The harbour (Port Franc de Barcelona) takes up the entire coastline between the district of Barceloneta and the southern flanks of Montjuïc.

Major port	Before Spain turned to the Atlantic and its domains and South America during the 17th century, Barcelona had one of the most significant ports in the Mediterranean region. To this day, it is the second-most important port in the country after Valencia. The northern part of the harbour area and the coastal strip on the other side of Barceloneta were extensively remodelled and expanded in 1992. The commercial port extends along the base of Montjuïc, from which it is separated by the wide Cinturó del Litoral. Much the most interesting area for tourists is the attractively redesigned northeastern section of the harbour. The **Moll de Barcelona**, which borders the southern end of this section, is the landing stage for ferries and passenger ships servicing the Balearic Islands of Mallorca, Menorca and Ibiza.
Mirador de Colom	A stroll through the harbour area may well start at the Columbus Monument (Monument a Colom or Mirador de Colom), rising 60m/196ft above Plaça del Portal de la Pau. Erected for the 1888 World Fair, the iron pillar weighs 205 tons. Its base is adorned by al-

MARCO POLO TIP

❗ *Harbour trip on a swallow* **Insider Tip**

Located near the Columbus Monument is the landing stage for the golondrinas (swallows), 20m/65ft long boats offering tours through the harbour (approx. 30 minutes). The same landing stage is also used for two modern catamarans and a large catamaran for sailing.

A Man of Dreams and Inventions

*Narcis Monturiol dreamt of a better world and created the first fully
operational submarine. His second, technically more sophisticated
model, however, had to be scrapped.*

The name of the Avinguda D'Icària
is a reference to the book »Journey
to Icaria« from 1839, by the French
utopian socialist Étienne Cabet
(1788 to 1856). The author's dream
was to create a new and equal society, and this was particularly supported in Barcelona. Among his
admirers was also Narcis Monturiol
(1819 – 1885). Born in Figueres, he
was the publisher of the Barcelonian weekly newspaper »Vamos a
Icaria« (Lets go to Icaria). Later,
Monturiol became known as the
ingenious inventor of the first operational submarine.

Success and Failure

The idea of building a submarine
came to Monturiol when he was
forced to witness a coral harvester
drown at the coast of Cadaqués.
Initially he tried to develop a diving boat that would allow coral
harvesters to get to the ocean
floor near the shores. At that time,
corals were a rather lucrative
source of income. His »Ictíneo« was
a 13.5m/44ft wood submarine
powered by men. His first two
2-hour dives in 1859, in the harbours of Barcelona and Alicante,
were both successful. Fifty more
dives followed between 1859 and
1862. The problem of oxygen supply was solved by using a mix of
zinc, manganese peroxide and po-
tassium chlorate, which reacted
and produced large amounts of

oxygen gas. The submerging and
surfacing of the submarine was already regulated by flooding or
pumping out the ballast tank.

In 1862, when the Spanish government showed interest in the submarine project, Narcis Monturiol
built the »Ictíneo II«. The 17m/56ft
submarine was supposed to be op-
erated with a 6hp steam engine.
By then, however, the ingenious
inventor was financially ruined. In
order to pay his debts he was
forced to sell his »Ictíneo II« to a
scrap dealer.

After that, Monturiol only fo-
cussed on his political career as a
parliamentary member of the First
Spanish Republic and author of dis-
courses on social utopias.

legorical figures, while the pedestal features several sculptures illustrating the important stages in Columbus' life and his expeditions. The monument is crowned by an 8m/26ft Columbus statue facing the sea due east instead of due west to the New World. This could be seen as a concession to the city of Barcelona, which was excluded from trade with America for centuries, and lost its supremacy at sea for a long time because of Columbus. A lift takes visitors up the pillar and into the ball on which Columbus stands, providing an excellent view of the old harbour and the city.

❶ June–Sept daily 9am–8.30pm, Oct–May daily 10am–6pm

Moll de la Fusta The stretch of harbour between the Portal de la Pau and Plaça d'Antoni Lòpez is called Moll de la Fusta. The parallel-running Moll de Bosch i Alsina is connected to it via two drawbridges and was designed as a spacious beach promenade with benches, restaurants, and an underground car park.

World Trade Center The World Trade Centre, an almost circular shaped, eye-catching building at the end of the southern Moll de Barcelona, was designed by the renowned architect group of Pei, Cobb, Freed & Partners, who also built Canada Square at Canary Wharf in London. The centre has become one of the most important gateways for southern European markets. It comprises an auditorium, more than thirty conference rooms equipped with state-of-the-art media technology, several gourmet restaurants and the luxurious Gran Marina Hotel with 290 rooms.

Moll d'Espanya Not far from the Columbus Monument and the harbour administration building, the Rambla del Mar is a wide pontoon pedestrian bridge, which leads across to the Moll d'Espanya and closes off the basin of the Old Harbour. Numerous new buildings have transformed the Moll d'Espanya into an enormous recreational centre with a large underground car park.

Maremàgnum The Maremàgnum, a stunning-looking building made of dark glass, metal and concrete, attracts many shoppers and visitors. It brings under one roof a great number of cafés and restaurants, shops that stay open all day and boutiques and art galleries, as well as a large amusement centre called »Big Fun«.
A massive cinema complex (Cines Maremàgnum) built on the pier offers entertainment galore: visitors can choose between eight cinemas and one Imax theatre.

*Aquàrium The main attraction on the Moll d' Espanya is the Aquárium, which is said to be the largest of its kind in Europe. A great number of nearly ceiling-high saltwater tanks are home to flora and fauna from

The Old Port

every ocean of the world. The absolute highlight is the gigantic underwater landscape with sharks, moray eels, headfish and other smaller and larger sea animals. A sunken ship demonstrates the working methods of underwater archaeology. Visitors cross the large tank on walkways through two underwater glass tunnels, which create the feeling of diving among and of being in close contact with the fish. A staircase leads from the aquarium up to the rotunda, with an informative and well-prepared exhibition on »The Sea – Route of Trade and Culture«, including a timeline (starting with the 2nd/1st centuries AD), presentation boards and video sequences.

➊ daily 9.30am–9pm, Sat and Sun till 9.30pm, Aug till 11pm; admission €18
www.aquariumbcn.com

Not far from the northern end of the old harbour basin is a replica of an early wooden submarine. The original, the Ictíneo II, built by Narcís Monturiol (▶MARCO POLO Insight, p.239) was launched in Barcelona in 1859. It completed 54 dives down to a depth of 20m/65ft. The replica was built in 1993 for the film Monturiol, Senyor del Mar.

Ictíneo II

The **Palau de Mar**, a former warehouse building, forms the northern end of the harbour area and is home to the Museu d'Història de Catalunya and other cultural institutions. The museum takes visitors on an interactive tour of the history of Catalonia, from its pre-history to the present. Its main focus is on the development of Catalonia as a dominant Mediterranean power, the end of the Spanish colonial pe-

Museu d'Història de Catalunya

Barcelona's Harbours

Barcelona's old harbour Port Vell has become a leisure area long since. From there you can see the commercial port which is the second largest in Spain after Valencia and the largest cruiseship harbour in Europe by passenger numbers.

▶ **Barcelona**

Barcelona city centre

Port Vell

Port

5km/3mi

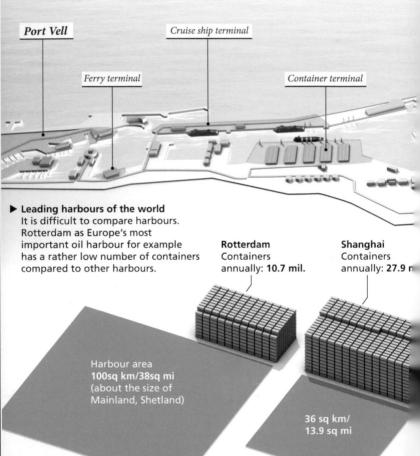

Port Vell

Ferry terminal

Cruise ship terminal

Container terminal

▶ **Leading harbours of the world**
It is difficult to compare harbours. Rotterdam as Europe's most important oil harbour for example has a rather low number of containers compared to other harbours.

Rotterdam
Containers annually: **10.7 mil.**

Shanghai
Containers annually: **27.9 n**

Harbour area **100sq km/38sq mi** (about the size of Mainland, Shetland)

36 sq km/ 13.9 sq mi

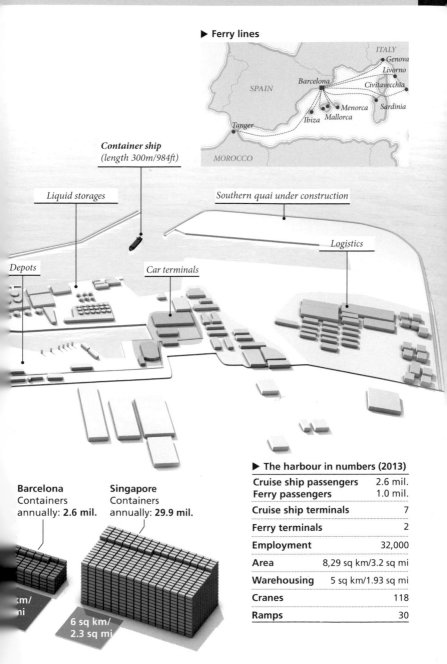

▶ Ferry lines

ITALY
Genova
Livorno
Barcelona
Civitavecchia
SPAIN
Sardinia
Menorca
Ibiza *Mallorca*
Tanger
MOROCCO

Container ship
(length 300m/984ft)

Liquid storages

Southern quai under construction

Logistics

Depots

Car terminals

Barcelona
Containers
annually: **2.6 mil.**

Singapore
Containers
annually: **29.9 mil.**

km/
ni

6 sq km/
2.3 sq mi

▶ The harbour in numbers (2013)	
Cruise ship passengers	2.6 mil.
Ferry passengers	1.0 mil.
Cruise ship terminals	7
Ferry terminals	2
Employment	32,000
Area	8,29 sq km/3.2 sq mi
Warehousing	5 sq km/1.93 sq mi
Cranes	118
Ramps	30

riod, the Industrial Revolution, and the re-establishment of Catalonia's autonomy.

❶ Tue–Sat 10am–7pm, Wed till 8pm, Sun 10am–2.30pm, admission €4. www.mhcat.net

** Transbordador Aeri A real treat for those who are not afraid of heights is a ride over the harbour basin in the cable car, the Transbordador Aeri dating from 1931. The view of the port facilities and the broad Passeig de Colom is quite spectacular. The cable car terminates at Moll Nou by Torre de Sant Sebastià at the southern end of Barceloneta, a 96m/314ft high steel grid mast. An intermediate station is the 158m/518ft high Torre de Jaume I, by the Moll de Barcelona, in front of the World Trade Centre. The route ends on the northeastern side of Montjuïc, near the Jardins Mossèn Costa i Llobera (cactus garden).

❶ daily from 11am; single journey €11, return €16.50

Port Olímpic

✳ H/J 8

Location: north of Barceloneta
Metro: Ciutadella/Villa Olímpica (L 4)

The area north of ▸Barceloneta, in what was then an abandoned industrial park near the beach, was redesigned as the Vila Olímpica (Olympic village) for the 1992 Summer Olympics.

Olympic harbour A new local recreational area was created, and the Olympic harbour and marina have been popular with locals and visitors ever since. Those who'd rather not walk there can conveniently take one of the golondrinas (▸MARCO POLO tip, p.238) or a trimaran over from the harbour. Alternatively you can explore the harbour area and coastal strip by rented bicycle.

The harbour district is dominated by the twin high-rise buildings of the Hotels Arts Barcelona – one of the best and most exclusive hotels in the city – and the international Mapfre Corporation. Both are exactly the same height, and at 153.5m/504ft they are among the tallest buildings in Spain.

Marina Village Between the towers and the beach extends the spacious Marina Village. The shopping centre specialises in high-end clothing, shoes, and accessories.

El peix d'or The stretch of beach in front of the hotel is dominated by a gigantic 50m/164ft fish sculpture, whose bronze mesh changes depending on

Nightlife in Port Olímpic

the light, sometimes sparkling and sometimes more subdued. »El peix d'or«, the »goldfish«, is a work of American arcitect Frank O. Gehry.

The rectangular harbour basin is bordered on the landward side by the Passeig Marítim del Port Olímpic and closed off in in the north by the Moll de Carles I. The area is dominated by great **seafood restaurants**, and though they may appear somewhat dull from the outside, their terraces offer a lovely view over the harbour.

To the south of the towers are the Casino von Barcelona and the town beach of Platja de Barceloneta with many popular bars and restaurants that remain open until the small hours. In a northerly direction is the Nova Icària beach. In towards the city, along Avinguda Nova Icària, you will reach the former Olympic Village. After the Games the athletes' accommodation was converted into residential flats and the district has become a popular part of town.

Platja Nova Icària

★★ Rambles

✴ F/G 6–8

Location: Between Barri Gòtic and Raval
Metro: Catalunya (L 1; auch FGC), Drassanes, Liceu,
Catalunya (L 3)

The Rambles (Castilian: Ramblas) are a 1.2km (0.75mi) long open-air Eldorado for street artists, florists, pickpockets and tourists. Barcelona's famous pedestrian boulevard extends from Plaça de Catalunya to the Columbus Monument.

Bustling Boulevard

The boulevard is filled with life at any time of day, with a colourful current of people rolling along as if on a river bed – a comparison that is not that far off, considering the meaning of the word »rambla« (sandy ground) has always led to the unconfirmed assumption that a river once ran along here. What is certain is that in former times a sandy track ran along this area outside the city walls. By the end of the 18th century it had been converted into a road that ran through the old city centre and, as it was longer than any other street at the time, it received a plural name and was divided into individual sections. Noblemen and the wealthy bourgeoisie settled into luxurious townhouses along the Rambles throughout the 19th century, and the road took on the character of a grand boulevard with its trees, benches, and artistic wrought-iron structures. When the bourgeoisie began to prefer other residential areas as a result of the city's expansion around 1900, an increasing number of seamen and residents of the seedy Barri Xinès district (today's Raval) moved onto the Rambles.

Even today, the boulevard is divided: while the upper part embodies the Catalan characteristic of »seny« or common sense, the lower part reflects the second Catalan trait of »rauxa« or passion. Visitors should walk the **core of the Rambles**, between the harbour and Plaça de Catalunya, at least once. It cuts between the **Barri Gòtic** on the northeast side and **El Raval** district to the southwest. Pedestrians crowd along the sycamore-lined central walkway, while long lines of cars honk their horns pushing along the narrow roads either side. The Rambles are a gigantic stage where the whole spectrum of the city's daily life can be experienced. Determined business people rush through the crowds with their briefcases while pensioners sit on one

Barcelona's famous pedestrian boulevard is always busy

of the benches reading their newspaper in peace. Elegantly dressed hotel guests step out of fancy limousines while housewives with their hands full of shopping from the Boqueria market pretend not to notice the heavily made-up prostitutes. Merchants plug their goods, lottery dealers loudly predict the next big win, and tourists stroll through the sea of flowers at the flower market or stop at one of the many book and newspaper stands. In between, buskers, painters, gamblers, mime artists and beggars court the attention of passers-by, while pickpockets attempt to go about their daily business without being noticed. The waiters, on the other hand, notice everything and balance their trays through the pushing and shoving of people and cars with amazing skill and dexterity.

Rambla del Mar

Looking at the Rambles from the Columbus Monument, one first notices the newly created Rambla del Mar (▶Port). It forms a connection between the Columbus Monument and Moll d'Espanya with its diverse offerings of recreation and entertainment. .

Rambla de Santa Monica
Near the Columbus Monument begins the Rambla de Santa Monica, heading towards the northwest. A marine commandant's office is located directly to the left of the entrance; a few steps further on (corner of Portal de Santa Madrona) is the **Centre d'Art Santa Monica** with ambitious temporary art exhibitions, and the parish church of the same name. Behind the Rambla – somewhat set back from the street front – is the wax museum (▶Museu de Cera).

Rambla dels Caputxins
Next left from Rambla dels Caputxins is Carrer Nou de la Rambla with its Palau Güell, while on the right-hand side a passageway opens up to ▶Plaça Reial. A few steps later, on the same side of the street, Carrer Ferran Jaume I, the quickest way to the Barri Gòtic, comes into view. Again on the left-hand side, is the Gran Teatre del Liceu. The Rambla dels Caputxins ends at Plaça de la Boqueria. From here, Carrer del Cardenal Casanyas leads north to the Santa Maria del Pi church.

Rambla dels Flores
On the northwest side of Plaça de la Boqueria starts Rambla de Sant Josep. It is commonly called Rambla dels Flores (rambla of flowers) because of the colourful **flower market** that takes place here every morning. The market hall on the left-hand side is well worth seeing (▶Bouqueria).

Palau de la Virreina
Next comes the Palau de la Virreina (Vicereine's Palace), which was built from 1772–77 as a residence for Manuel d'Amat i de Junyent, former Viceroy of Peru, and named after his wife, the Vicereine, who lived here after his death until 1791. The façade of the building features neoclassical elements, while the interior is late Baroque. Today, the palace serves as an exhibition space, mainly for Catalan artists.

Església de Betlem
At the crossroads of the Rambla dels Estudis and Carrer del Carme stands the Església de Betlem with its Baroque façade. The former Jesuit church was built from 1681–1732. Ignatius Loyola, founder of the Jesuit order, Francesco Borgia, third general of the order, and the birth of Jesus Christ are depicted in the entrance. The rich Baroque furnishings of the church interior were completely destroyed in a fire in 1936 and its new design of non-decorative neoclassical forms is of little artistic importance.

Palau Moja
Opposite the side façade of the Església de Betlem, just off the Rambles, stands the Palau Moja, Palau Moja, a palace dating back to the Baroque period.

Rambla dels Estudis
The Rambla dels Estudis, starting at the entrance to Carrer del Carme, is the setting for the bird and ornamental fish market that takes place every morning. Together with Rambla Canaletes it connects to Plaça de Catalunya.

The northwestern continuation of the Rambles, at the other side of Plaça de Catalunya, is Rambla de Catalunya, which extends through Eixample to the Avinguda de la Diagonal. Like its neighbour, ▶Passeig de Gràcia, running parallel to the north, this section of the Rambles is an elegant street with classy shops and beautiful street cafés. Unlike the adjacent grand boulevard and the Rambles to the southeast, the wide walkways of Rambla de Catalunya are not too crowded.

Rambla de Catalunya

Raval

✦ F 7

Location: between Rambles and Paral·lel
Metro: Liceu (L 3)

In the Raval district the in-scene and poverty, art and crime, as well as people from all over the world, come together.

Until the 1990s El Raval was a centre of prostitution, drug dealing and petty crime. The so-called Barri Xinès, the Chinese district, in the lower, seaward part, was particularly notorious. Much has changed over the intervening years, although all the above vices still exist here in some measure. El Raval is a district in the midst of change. Entire streets have been pulled down to make way for new housing. The extensive redevelopment has changed El Raval into a place with two distinct sides: northern Raval has been turned into a **trendy neighbourhood** with exclusive restaurants, modern galleries, and often elegant apartments; here too, the MACBA and CCCB arts centres (▶Museu of Contemporary Art) lure an international and affluent crowd into the old streets. The southern part of the district, meanwhile, is still very much for the »common people«. A large number of immigrants, primarily from the Indian subcontinent, Latin America and northern Africa, have opened up shops here. The prostitutes who keep watch for potential customers in the narrow alleys are still there, but attract no more attention than a veiled Muslim woman or a student from Northern Europe peddling his/her bike though the alleyways.

A district transformed

!   *Shops in Raval*   **Insider Tip**

MARCO ⊕ POLO TIP

There is so much to discover in the colourful district of Raval. Quirky shops like **fantastik** (Joaquim Costa 62), with items from alien cultures which appear so strange and yet are really everyday objects. **ras** is a combination of art gallery, design shop and design bookshop (Doctor Dou 10). Wondrous aromas emerge from the adjacent establishment (Doctor Dou 12). **Barcelona Reykjavik** is an organic bakery where the bakers can be seen at work. Specialty Spanish and Catalan cheeses have been sold at **Mentegueries Puig** (Xuclà 21) since 1943.

Traditional alley in Raval

In the heart of El Raval, behind the covered market (▶Boqueria), stands the old **Hospital de la Santa Creu** (Hospital of the Holy Cross), a large building complex arranged around a cloister. It was founded in 1401 but took more than 200 years to complete, which explains why the individual buildings have different styles. From Carrer del Hospital the building is entered via a 16th-century wing, with a chapel on the right-hand side. In the middle of the cloister there is a Baroque cross with twisted shaft and behind it a large archway with a beautiful staircase. Towards the end of the 19th century, it became obvious that there were not enough rooms at the old hospital. As a result, architect Lluís Domènech i Montaner was commissioned to build a new, more modern building in ▶Eixample, the ▶Hospital de la Santa Creu i de Sant Pau.

The **Biblioteca de Catalunya**, founded in 1914, is located in a section of the former Hospital de la Santa Creu. It currently contains about one million volumes as well as a special department for the works of Miguel Cervantes de Saavedra, author of Don Quixote. The reading room is only open to library members. Coming from Carrer del Carme, the entrance is accessible through a gate on the right-hand side. Notice the large, coloured painted tiles (1681), which depict scenes from the life of St Paul. The inner courtyard with two-storey arcades and a statue of St Paul from the 17th century, and the stairway, are also decorated with colourful tiles.

Sant Pau del Camp

The church of Sant Pau del Camp (St Paul in the Field) on Carrer de Sant Pau was built on a piece of land that was then located outside the city (hence: »in the field«). Today it stands on the boundary between the Old City and the new developments built at the foot of ▶Montjuïc in the 19th century. Sant Pau del Camp is a Romanesque structure dating from 1117, built on a Greek cross plan (cross-dome church). Notable is the beautiful main portal with marble capitals dating from the Visigoth period. Adjoining the simple interior with its dome is the Gothic chapter house, from where you can step out into the cloister.

Ribera

☀ G 7

Location: north of Via Laietana
Metro: Jaume I (L 4)

Ribera is the city's new in-district. More and more bars, tapas bars, boutiques and delis are opening up in the streets around Passeig del Born. Not to be missed are the Gothic church of Santa Maria del Mar and the Museu Picasso.

Im the Middle Ages, the centre of Barcelona comprised what is today known as the Gothic Quarter (Barri Gòtic), including the northeastern districts of Sant Pere, Santa Catarina, La Ribera and Born, which were not yet separated by the broad Via Laietana. It was only at the beginning of the 20th century that, like in Paris and Madrid, a swathe was cut through the Old City and its urban sprawl. This artificial divide resulted in the medieval districts developing differently: the **Casc Antic**, as the conglomerate of districts beyond the Laietana is officially called, was given a reprieve before it was discovered for tourism and as a chic in-district. | **Trendy area**

It was predominantly artisans who settled around the monastery of Sant Pere de les Puelles, which was founded in the early 13th century. In comparison to other areas, Sant Pere is still an intact Old City district, which is clearly evident in the romantic triangular Plaça Sant Pere. The shops and businesses premises along the Carrer Sant Pere més Baix are pleasantly old fashioned. This is, so to speak, the high street of the barri, which is also home to the magnificent ▶Palau de la Música Catalana. | **Sant Pere**

Further down towards the sea comes the district of Santa Caterina. The most spectacular building here is the **Covered Market**. Designed by the architects Enric Miralles and Benedetta Tagliabue (EMBT), it was given an undulating roof that spans the halls like a colourful rolling landscape. | **Santa Caterina**

A few streets further on begins La Ribera, whose narrow streets are home to a number of grand mansions. Indeed the district, which | **La Ribera**

La Ribera was discovered for tourism and as a chic in-district

came into being with the foundation of the monastery of Vilanova del Mar, was for a long time the economic hub of Barcelona. In La Ribera lived craftsmen belonging to the various guilds, such as the silversmiths in Carrer Argentaria, but also sailors and merchants as well as the Bastaixos, freed slaves who unloaded the cargo from the ships. These load carriers also brought the stones down from Montjuïc, with which the Esglesia ▶Santa Maria del Mar was built, from 1329. In his bestselling novel Cathedral of the Sea, Ildefonso Falcones recounts the fictional story of a load carrier in the 14th-century Ribera neighbourhood. The church of Santa Maria del Mar is without doubt one of the (if not the) most beautiful churches in Barcelona. It stands at the centre of what is currently the trendiest area of the Old City. The structural change began in the mid-1990s and was further accelerated through the expansion of the ▶Museu Picasso in 1999. Since then numerous boutiques from fashion and jewellery designers, as well as bars, tapas bars and cafés have installed themselves behind the ancient walls. La Ribera is also the place to go for gourmets in search of delicatessens, wine shops and smart patisseries, and they can even visit a Museu de la Xocolata – a museum of chocolate with attached school for would be chocolatiers. Also worth seeing are the ▶Museu Barbier-Mueller d'Art Pre-Colombi and the old ▶Llotja de Mar stock exchange, as well as the ▶Parc de la Ciutadella that adjoins the district to the north.

** Sagrada Família

✦ H 5

Lage: Plaça Gaudí
Metro: Sagrada Família (L 2, L 5)
❶ April–Sept daily 9am–8pm, Oct–
March 9am–6pm

Admission: €19.30
**www.sagrada
familia.cat**

**The Church of the Sagrada Família, officially called Temple Ex-
piatori de la Sagrada Família (Expiatory Church of the Holy
Family), is the best-known sight in Barcelona and also one of
the world's most unusual-looking churches. Furthermore,
even after more than a century of construction, it still remains
unfinished (▶MARCO POLO Insight p. 254).**

When **Antoni Gaudí** took over the church's construction in 1883,
the plans and initial work on the crypt for a purely neo-Gothic
church had already been completed. Gaudí changed the entire design, although – as with his other structures – no binding overall
concept ever emerged. The plans
were constantly changed and developed while construction was in progress. The artist originally planned, for
example, rectangular towers next to
the façades, but then changed his
mind after the towers had already
partially been built, and gave them a
rounded form. This method of working naturally resulted in construction
making very slow progress. Originally, Gaudí estimated that around 10 to
15 years would be needed and the
funding, which was supposed to
come entirely from donations, set
tight limits. So the »Church of the
Poor« and **the most important
work of Catalonia's most influential architect of modern times**,
largely remained a shell in the 20th
century, which took shape only very
slowly, and God alone knew whether
it would ever even be completed. But
in recent years construction has pro-
gressed very rapidly. This is thanks to
the nearly three million tourists who
visit Barcelona's most famous build-

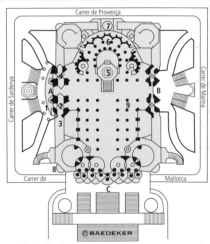

Sagrada Família

A Passion Façade
B Nativity Façade
C Glory Façade

1 Entrance
2 Vestibule
3 Church model

4 Kiosk
5 Altar (with crypt below)
6 Apse
7 Virgin Mary Chapel
8 Gaudí Museum
9 Model workshop

Gaudí's Uncompleted

The architect Antoni Gaudí expected completion of the Sagrada Família to take a very long time! The model on the right-hand side shows a section of the central nave which is still under construction. The estimated completion date varies between 2020 and 2026.

❶ Dome and Towers

It will still take some time before the central dome and its towers will be entirely completed. Jesus Christ is symbolized by the central dome, the Virgin Mary by the two towers, and four more towers represent the Evangelists.

❷ Stone Forest

The weight-bearing columns of the Sagrada Família inside the church are reminiscent of trees, which branch out at certain points.

❸ Manifestation in Stone

In accordance with Gaudí's wish, the interior of the Sagrada Família shall lways be illuminated at night so that the light can shine through the perforated walls: the words of Jesus Christ manifest in stone.

❹ Choir Galleries

Two galleries opposite each other are reserved for choirs.

❺ Gaudí's Hanging Chain Model

A hanging string or chain represents the optimum distribution of stress of an arch or dome – but inverted. Turning the model around results in the arches, vaults and tree structure of the Sagrada Familia.

The western façade, with Christ's Passion. Unlike the richly ornate Christmas façade, this porch with six large, angled columns is made of bone-like pillars symbolising death.

ing site each year, their entrance fees going straight towards the continuation of the project. The desired date for completion is 2026, one hundred years after Gaudí died (having been struck by a tram). Even though much of what has been built since 1926 has been contentious, the (almost) end result is a stupendous building, and one of which the devout architect would surely be proud. Certainly Pope Benedict XVI elevating the Sagrada Família to the rank of a basilica before 7000 believers on November 7, 2010 would have made him very happy.

The Sagrada Família hasn't only inspired admiration. While Salvador Dalí gave the church his highest praise, George Orwell found it simply repulsive – reason enough for every visitor of Barcelona to see this spectacular construction and to form his/her own opinion.

Design The church has a total length of 110m/361ft and a height of 45m/148ft, the unfinished main central tower (including the cross) is planned to reach a height of 170m/558ft, and the surrounding towers 115m/377ft. Presently, there are eight of these towers, their tips faced with ceramic mosaics. The finished façades include the Nativity Façade (Matthew, Judas, Simon, and Barnabas) and the Passion Façade (Jacob, Bartholomew, Thomas and Philipp). The Glory Façade (Andrew, Peter, Paul and Jacob) is yet to be completed. From 1986 there was a concerted effort to finish the nave, and this is now largely completed. Artistically speaking, the Temple de la Sagrada Família is a highly unconventional mixture of existing styles and new creations. The floor plan, the division of the spaces and sweeping lines are mainly in keeping with the Gothic style, as well as the neo-Gothic style that was so widespread in the mid-19th century. Yet these elements have been combined with organic, flowering ornamentation derived from the Art Nouveau period.

Symbols Gaudí worked a great deal with symbols. He considered the church as a whole to be a »sermon in stone«. The powerful Torre del Salvador and the altar were intended as an allegory of Jesus Christ. The planned twelve towers were to embody the Apostles; the three façades, the life of Christ. Gaudí himself was only able to finish the eastern façade depicting the birth of Christ. The **Passion Façade (west façade)** depicting the suffering and death of Christ was completed in 2002, its sobering and angular figures created by Catalan sculptor **José Maria Subirach**. Some critics reject these sculptures as being tasteless and unfitting in comparison to the other, softer decorative forms. Others consider it to be a legitimate, modern continuation of Gaudí's work, which has become a task for several generations. One should pay special attention to the portrait of Christ in Sudarium (shroud), created with the bas-relief technique that makes it appear to be facing whoever is viewing it. The **Nativity Fa-**

çade **(east façade)** can best be seen from the small park at Plaça Gaudí – beyond Carrer Marina. The three archways symbolize faith, love and mercy. They appear to be classic Gothic structures that have melted into softer forms. Countless details reveal themselves on closer inspection: for example, wingless angels with long trumpets (allegedly emulating guards) and a tree of life comprised of green ceramic tiles on which doves hover. In total, the mosaics are said to represent well over thirty different bird species, and almost as many different types of plants. At the moment they are working on the main tower, which is steadily rising over the crossing.

Towers

There are wonderful views from the towers of the Nativity and Passion façades. Both have lifts going up inside them. If you want to have a fearless and exhilarating traverse of the narrow bridges between the towers and descent of the spiral staircase that winds down inside the Nativity Façade, it's best to have a good head for heights. In any case the ascent provides incomparable glimpses of some of the construction details, especially the tops of the towers that are reminiscent of a bishop's mitre, and at the top you will be rewarded with fantastic views over the city.

> **MARCO ⊕ POLO TIP**
>
> ! **The early bird** **Insider Tip**
>
> It is worth making an early start to climb the towers of the Sagrada Família and enjoy the museum at its best. Lengthy queues develop as the day progresses, particularly during the summer months.

The **museum** is situated beneath the nave. The sketches and photo documentation of existing Gaudí works and their historical archetypes are interesting. In special sections you can see for example preliminary plaster casts for the sculptural ornamentation, as well as a large model of the church that was presented in Paris in 1910. The studies of the window and façade design clearly illustrate the principle of »leaning columns«, which Gaudí developed out of Gothic buttresses. Also of interest is **a model of the structure's statics**: Gaudí experimented with hanging models with weights and strings that represented the structure and the anticipated forces that would act upon it.

Antoni Gaudí was laid to rest in the **crypt** in 1926. At the front of the crypt hangs a photographic reproduction of the Passion Façade; to the right (in Catalan) there is the iconography of the individual motifs, and in one of the side rooms to the right, a cross-section model showing the nave and aisles. A multimedia show is also available. Church services are now celebrated in the crypt.

The small **outbuilding** with the undulating roof is an architectural gem. Gaudí had made it his mission to construct a school building using the minimum possible amount of material. Inside you can see a classroom and a desk.

Santa Anna

G 7

Location: Carrer Rivadeneyra
Metro: Catalunya (L 1, L 3)

In a narrow side street just to the east of Plaça de Catalunya is the monastery of Santa Anna, which was founded by the Order of the Holy Sepulchre in the 12th century and dissolved in 1835.

Original Romanesque church

The nave and chapter room (both still intact) were constructed in the 15th century; other sections from this period were torn down in the 19th century. The originally Romanesque church has no outstanding artistic treasures, but it does have its own appeal. It was built based on a cross-shaped floor plan with rectangular choir. The interior of rounded archways, partially changed in the 14th century, is dimly lit through small Romanesque windows. The tabernacle is a replica of the 15th / 16th-century original from, which has been lost. To the left of the entrance, the **All Saints Chapel** (14th century) displays contemporary paintings and a scene depicting the Entombment of Christ from the 15th century. The very charming Gothic cloister is accessible from the church, from where it is possible to reach the chapter house.

✳ Santa Maria del Mar

G 7

Location: Plaça Montcada
Metro: Jaume I (L 4)

The church of Santa Maria del Mar (1329–83) is a straightforward church with two aisles but no transept. It embodies Catalan Gothic architecture in its purest form, the likes of which can hardly be found in other large medieval structures.

Favourite church of the Barcelonians

Next to the cathedral, the church is the **most important place of worship in the city**, and many consider it to be the **most beautiful**. It was built on top of a late Roman necropolis in which St Eulàlia was originally buried. A large rose window is set into the façade above the decorative main portal. The artistically sparse interior with its slender pillars is almost completely empty – the furniture and choir were destroyed in the Civil War – which makes the impact of its silent, open space even more powerful.

The beautiful stained glass windows mainly originate from the 15th to 17th centuries and tall clerestory windows lighten the interior.

Many Barcelonians consider Santa Maria del Mar the city's most beautiful church

Also noteworthy are the stone bosses in the archway above the main altar depicting the Coronation of Mary. A Gothic statue of the Virgin is located on the high altar, behind a model of an old trading ship. A black Madonna stands in the chapel next to the left side door. The entrance to the crypt is located underneath the raised altar space.

The small square to the right of the church, Fossar de les Moreres, is occupied by a memorial that is set into the ground like an amphi-theatre and features a long wall of polished stone and a curved pylon bearing an eternal flame. The memorial is dedicated to Catalan sol-diers killed by Philipp V's troops in 1714 while defending the city.

Memorial

Santa Maria del Pi

G 7

Location: Plaça del Pi
Metro: Liceu (L 3)

On the small Plaça del Pi in the Barri Gòtic stands the Gothic church of Santa Maria del Pi (St Mary of the Pine Tree), the so-called church of the poor.

The church's overall rather austere façade is punctuated by a pointed portal with a Gothic statue of the Virgin and a large rose window. Neither the squat towers flanking the façade nor the main belltower have spires. The sparsely decorated interior is framed by chapels. The clerestory windows above have colourful stained glass dating from the 15th to 18th centuries, though many are copies of the originals, which were destroyed in 1936. The Gothic tomb of Arnau Ferrer, who fell in the siege of Catania (Sicily) in 1394, is located next to the sacristy door. Gold and silversmith work, as well as other sacred art is on display in the church treasury.

Plaça de Sant Josep Oriol The shaded Plaça de Sant Josep Oriol borders the left nave wall of the church, where some lovely shop fronts vie for attention. A memorial to the poet and playwright **Angel Guimerà i Jorge** (1845–1924) stands in the middle of the square underneath a group of trees. An art market is held here on Sunday mornings.

Teatre Nacional de Catalunya

J 6

Location: Plaça de les Arts
Metro: Glòries (L 1)

www.tnc.cat

The new Teatre Nacional de Catalunya (National Theatre of Catalonia) and the Auditorium that was completed at the same time are situated to the south of the Plaça de les Glòries Catalanes.

National Theatre of Catalonia For the construction of this theatre, which was inaugurated in 1997, it's impossible to overlook the fact the architect Ricardo Bofill (▶MARCO POLO Insight, p. 50) was inspired by ancient temples. This fine example of postmodern architecture accommodates three stages inside.

The adjacent Auditorium is the home of the National Symphony Orchestra of Catalonia and the Catalan Music Academy. The building designed by Rafael Moneo also contains the ►Museu de la Música.   **Auditorium**

✶✶ **Tibidabo**

✦ F/G 1

Location: northwest of the city centre
Train (FGC): Avinguda del Tibidabo; continuing with the Tramvia Blau and the funicular
www.tibidabo.cat

Towering to the northwest of the city centre is the 532m/1745ft high Mount Tibidabo, one of the most visited destinations in Greater Barcelona.

Visible from afar: the Sagrat Cor on top of Mount Tibidabo

What's in a name? Tibidabo is the highest summit of the Serra de Collserola range, which rises to the northwest of Barcelona. It got its name from the legend that Christ was tempted here by the devil (»I will give thee...« is »tibi dabo« in Latin).

Getting there Even the trip to Tibidabo is an experience. The underground train (Ferrocarril de la Generalitat) runs from Plaça de Catalunya to the terminal Avinguda del Tibidabo. From here, a transit bus or nostalgic cable car (called **Tramvia Blau** due to its dark blue painted cars) travels uphill to the **funicular** (base station 224m/735ft above sea level), which then runs to Plaça del Tibidabo, the last stop before reaching the Tibidabo summit. The Tramvia Blau only operates during summer. An alternative route to Tibidabo from Plaça de Catalunya could be, for example, taking the tram L1 or L2 to the **Peu del Funicular** station, from where the funicular departs. Starting at the top station of this funicular, a small bus (line 111) travels directly to the Parc d'Atraccions. Another possibility would be to take the **Tibibus** directly from Plaça de Catalunya up to Plaça del Tibidabo.

Enjoyment for all ages?

The biggest crowd puller on Mount Tibidabo is the Parc d'Atraccions, an **old-fashioned amusement park** spread out over multiple levels. Various rides are offered (Ferris wheel, roller-coaster, bumper cars, go-karts), as well as other entertainments, such as a computer arcade and the terrifying House of Horrors. The Parc d'Attraccions has little in common with today's typical themed amusement parks; after all, it is the oldest of its kind in Spain. Yet it provides a happy, exhilarating atmosphere with its old-fashioned charm – and besides, where else can one enjoy such a grand view from a Ferris wheel or carousel as from here! There are several restaurants located on the park grounds. A visit to the park is especially worthwhile for families with children, best suited for a half-day or full-day outing. A full-day outing can easily be combined with the ▶Museu de la Ciència, near the Tramvia Blau base station. In addition to the normal entrance ticket, which is relatively inexpensive as practically all of the individual attractions charge an additional fee, an all-inclusive ticket is also available, which allows use of all the attractions. The opening hours change every year; the park is open daily in August, half of the week during the other summer months, otherwise open mostly on weekends only. The **Museu dels Autómats** is also situated in the park including old slot machines, orchestrions, mechanically-powered dolls, model railways, and other automated devices that are not only fun for children.

At the summit of Tibidabo stands the Sagrat Cor, the **Church of the Sacred Heart**. Designed by architect Enric Sagnier and only completed in 1961, it was built in Gothicized style spreading over several levels and crowned by a clearly visible statue of Christ. A very strongly historicized church interior from around 1900 is located on the ground floor; people dressed in the contemporary clothing of that period feature in the apse mosaic. The basilica is located on the second level, a high neo-Gothic space with an almost circular floor plan. A lift leads to a 542m/1778ft high platform with several towers. From here, one can climb to the tower gallery, which encircles the foot of the statue of Christ. The statue offers fabulous **panoramic views** of Barcelona and the sea, of the ridge to which Tibidabo belongs and of the forest-covered mountains of the hinterland. To the south you can see the ▶Torre de Collserola and to the north the Radio Barcelona and Catalunya Radio transmitters.

Sagrat Cor

A small tourist train runs from the top station of the funicular to the 288m/945ft high Torre de Collserola, which was erected in 1990 as a telecommunications centre for the Olympics. The boldly designed tower of glass and steel was the work of British architect **Sir Norman Foster**. After strict security checks, a lift provides access to the 135m/443ft viewing platform, which is encased in class panels. Information boards giving directions and distances make orientation easy. The panoramic views are terrific, as visibility can extend as far as 70 km/43mi, depending on the weather conditions.
❶ July–Aug Wed–Sun noon–2.15pm and 3.15pm–8pm. In the remaining months, the opening times are sporadic, mostly open on weekends; admission: €5; www.torredecollserola.com

Torre de Collserola

Between the southern foot of Mount Tibidabo and the municipal area of Sant Cugat del Vallès lies the 8,000ha/20,000 acre Parc de Collserola, a nature reserve that is highly valued as a recreational area close to the city.

Parc de Collserola

Universitat

✳ **F 6**

Location: Gran Via de les Corts Catalanes
Metro: Universitat (L 1, L 2)

By the end of the 13th century, Barcelona was offering studies in the liberal arts by Dominican monks; in 1401, the studies of medicine and fine arts were introduced; faculties for theology, law and philosophy followed shortly after.

History However, with Philipp V's cancellation of Catalonia's special privileges, the academy was closed in 1717. Studies did not resume in Barcelona until 1837.

Old University From the southern corner of Plaça de Catalunya, Carrer del Pelai heads westward to Plaça de la Universitat. This is where the Old University building is located, which was erected from 1863–73, in pseudo-Romanesque design; the interior includes two lovely atriums and parts of the University Library.

Zona Universitària The spacious, modern complex of the Zona Universitària extends from the southwestern end of the Avinguda de la Diagonal far into the city's Pedralbes district. This is where all the departments including Natural, Social, and Economic Sciences etc can be found .
The **Palau Reial de Pedralbes** directly by the Zona Universitària lies in a very lovely park with many cedar and basswood trees. Frenchman Jean-Claude Forestier was the landscape artist. One of Count Güell's country houses once stood here, but he made the grounds available for the royal palace. The three-story building in Italian style was handed over to the Spanish royal couple in 1924, though the royal family only resided here on rare occasions. The main floor, with its throne room and large adjacent rooms is now used for representative purposes.

Zona Alta

✳ **B–F 1–4**

Lage: west of the centre
Metro: Maria Cristina, Palau Reial, Zona Universitària (L 3)

At a safe distance from the noise and bustle of the centre lie the exclusive residential area of Pedralbes, rural looking Sarrià and Sant Gervasi. The Zona Alta (upper town) stretches along the seaward facing flanks of the Serra Collserola.

Whoever can afford it doesn't live in the centre, where it's crowded and noisy and the air is polluted, but in the Zona Alta, the upper town. It's only really at all urban, however, in Sant Gervasi, which the higher you go merges with the former village of Sarrià. The poshest area of the Zona Alta is Pedralbes. In the old and new districts resides the moneyed aristocracy of Barcelona. Things get a bit more normal around the university campus, which lies immediately to the east of the Pedralbes district.

Desirable places to live

Particularly worth seeing in the Zona Alta are the ▶Monestir de Pedralbes and the Palau Reial de Pedralbes (▶p.264).

Zoo

✦ **H 8**

Location: Parc de la Ciutadella
Metro: Ciutadella (L 4)
❶ daily from 10am on

Admission: €19.90
www.zoobarcelona.cat

The zoo occupies the eastern section of ▶Parc de la Ciutadella. 502 species and around 7500 animals can be seen in the relatively small space.

The zoo's long-time main attraction and favourite among all visitors was a giant, white gorilla, the only albino of its species. He was named Floquet de Neu (Snowflake), as a loveable understatement of his dimensions, and also became a symbol of Barcelona. When the animal had to be put to sleep in 2003 after a long illness at the age of almost 40, his fans were almost inconsolable.

Zoo founded in 1892

The reptile house is well designed, and the aviary, with its special section for nocturnal birds, is also well done. And not only of interest to children are the large, free standing whale carcass and the famous sculpture of the **Senyoreta del Paraigua** (»Lady with the Umbrella«). The **dolphin shows** at the Aquarama are real crowd pullers. The whole complex is set to be modernized by 2015 and complemented by additional facilities at the Parc del Fòrum.

PRACTICAL INFORMATION

What is the best way to get to Barcelona? How do I say it in Spanish or Catalan? Which means of transportation is best to discover the city?

Arrival · Before the Journey

HOW TO GET THERE

By air   Barcelona's airport is about 13km/8mi south of the city in El Prat de Llobregat. It is serviced by all larger European airlines with regular scheduled flights as well as charter flights. The main airlines from UK airports to Barcelona are EasyJet, British Airways, Iberia, Monarch, Jet2, bmibaby and Ryanair, and the journey takes around 2hr 20min. Airport buses (Aerobus) to the city centre at Plaça Catalunya run from the new Terminal 1 and Terminal 2 (A, B, C) of **Aeroport de Barcelona (BCN)** every 10 minutes daily between 6am and 1am. From Plaça Catalunya Aerbus 1 runs to Terminal 1 and Aerobus 2 to Terminal 2 between 5.30am and 0.30am.

Note
Billable service telephone numbers are marked with an asterisk: *0180…

The journey takes around 40 minutes. Trains depart every 30 minutes from Mon to Fri between 5.40am and 10.40pm from the airport station to Estació Sants, Plaça de Catalunya, Arc de Triomf and Clot-Aragó (duration: 30 min.). Each of these stations provides connections to the city's underground system. Between 10pm and 4.50am the NitBus N17 runs between Terminal 1 and the city centre (via Terminal 2 to Plaça Catalunya). The inexpensive T10 ticket, which is valuid for the Metro, busses and trams, can also be used for this. There are taxi ranks in front of all three airport terminals. The trip takes between 20 and 30 minutes. Many discount airlines fly to Girona or Tarragona-Reus.

The **Aeroport de Girona (GRO)** is 90km/56mi north of Barcelona. Renfe trains travel from there to Barcelona; the trip takes around 90 minutes. The airlines often offer a shuttle service to Barcelona by bus to the north bus terminal, which takes about 70 minutes.

The **Aeroport de Reus (REU)** is 125km/78mi away from Barcelona. The Linea Aeropuerto-Barcelona bus line travels regularly to Estacío Central de Sants, Barcelona's central station. There is also a public bus scheduled in accordance with flights from the airport to Barcelona's Estació Sants station. The travel time for both buses is around 90 minutes.Resu Airport is used almost exclusively by discount airlines and can be closed at times during the winter.

By car   Travelling by car it is advisable to take the French motorway (subject to charges) through the Rhône valley, via Perpignan to the French-Spanish border at Le Perthus/La Jonquera (Motorway A9/A7). The Spanish Mediterranean motorway (A7), also subject to charges, then runs via Figueres and Girona to Barcelona. Those preferring the occasionally idyllic coastal road should use the Cerbère/Portbou border crossing.

AIRPORTS
Barcelona, Girona, Reus
www.aena.es

BUS INFORMATION
National Express
Ensign Court, 4 Vicarage Road
Edgbaston, Birmingham

BS15 3ES
Tel. 08705-808080 (8am-8pm)
www.eurolines.co.uk

RAILWAY INFORMATION SPAIN
RENFE
Tel. 902 32 03 20
www.renfe.com (Spanish/English)

By bus Eurolines operate low cost coach travel from all major UK cities to Barcelona. From London, for example, the journey takes 27-29hrs, changing buses in Lyon. Return fares are around £89-£99 per person.

By train Travelling to Barcelona by train is a very pleasant option and surprisingly affordable. For example, the Eurostar from London to Paris connects with the night-time sleeper from Paris to Barcelona arriving in time for an early breakfast the next day. Facilities on the train hotel include berths with private shower and toilet, as well as a restaurant and bar. Those preferring a daytime travel option can take the Eurostar from London to Lille and travel to Barcelona via the beautiful route to Montpelier and along the Mediterranean coast to Barcelona. Individual return fares range from around £160 to £220, depending on level of comfort on the overnight train. For booking information see www.seat61.com; www.raileurope.co.uk; or www.eurail.com.

INWARD AND OUTWARD TRAVEL REGULATIONS

Personal documents Nationals from the European Union, Australia, Canada, USA and New Zealand just need a valid passport for stays up to 90 days. Children now have to travel on their own passport.

Car documents EU nationals can use their national driving licence in Spain for up to one year. Registration and insurance documents must be carried at all times. If your car does not have an EU number plate it needs a sticker identifying its country of origin.

Pets Those planning to take pets along with them require an official EU veterinary **health certificate**, which has entries showing that the pet has been marked with a microchip as well as a valid anti-rabies inoculation. The inoculation must date back at least 21 days, yet may not be older than twelve months prior to entry.

CUSTOMS REGULATIONS

EU Internal Market The member states of the European Union (EU), including Spain, form a common market in which the transportation of goods for private use is mainly free of customs. Certain maximum limits still apply between EU countries: 800 cigarettes or 400 cigarillos or 200 cigars or 1000g of tobacco, 10l of spirits over 22 vol.-% alcohol content or 20l below 22 vol.-% alcohol content, as well as 90l of wine and 110l of beer.

Non-EU countries For travellers from non-EU countries the following duty-free allowances apply: 250 g of coffee, 100 g of tea, 200 cigarettes or 100 cigarillos or 50 cigars or 250 g of tobacco, 2 l of wine or other drinks below 22 vol.-% alcohol content as well as 1 l of spirits over 22 vol.-% alcohol content. Gifts valued at up to € 430 for air and sea travellers and € 300 for railway and car travellers are also duty free.

Electricity

All electrical appliances run on 220 Volt AC. In large hotels one can usually use most European plugs; otherwise an adapter might become necessary.

Emergencies

USEFUL EMERGENCY NUMBERS
Tel. 112
Doctors, the fire department and police and be reached under this number. Calls in Spanish, English, French and German are taken and forwarded around the clock.

Accident emergency / emergency doctor
Tel. 061

BREAKDOWN SERVICE
RACE
(Real Automóvil Club de España)
Tel. 902 30 05 05
www.race.es

Etiquette and Customs

Clothing When it comes to the choice of clothing, whether male or female, Catalans never leave the house without being impeccably dressed, even on humid summer days. Men wear long trousers; only on very hot days will they compromise to wearing knee-length Bermudas, a short-sleeve shirt or a trendy t-shirt. Tight shorts, tank tops or worn-out sandals are not their cup of tea. Beach clothing in general is unacceptable for the city. Men prefer wearing long sleeves and trousers, while women tend to dress up showing a fair amount of skin, yet always in keeping with the latest trends. That counts particularly for the very fashion-conscious youngsters who will also proudly wear navel piercings or daring tattoos if they happen to be trendy. Any kind of body hair, whether on legs or under armpits is an absolute no-no, especially for women. In churches and monasteries, neither men nor women are allowed to enter wearing shorts or with uncovered shoulders. Those who wish to try out Barcelona's extensive cultural offerings in the evening are advised to bring at least one slightly more elegant outfit, regardless of the season. In other night-time venues like the discos clothing that is very informal may not be liked, but it is tolerated most of the time (▶p. 75).

? MARCO ⊕ POLO INSIGHT

Strictly no smoking in Spain

Since January 2011 there is strictly no smoking in tapas bars, restaurants, cafés, discotheques, casinos as well as public buildings like railway stations and airports. While hotels are allowed to reserve 30% of their rooms for guests who smoke many Spanish hotels do not allow smoking at all.

Restaurants, pubs
At restaurants, customers do not choose their own table, but wait until the waiter assigns a table for them. It is absolutely frowned up to share a table with Spaniards even if one politely asks beforehand. This rule does not apply for counters at tapa bars. Here, one will never be served unless bravely fighting for a seat or standing place and getting the waiter's attention. Do, however, make up your mind before the waiter comes to take the order – business here is fast and rolling. The waiters behind the counters are surprisingly quick; in fact, serving is treated like a form of art.

Bills are always made out to the entire table, and the costs are then distributed among the guests. If a group passes through several bars, then everyone gets a turn.

Greetings
The appropriate way of greeting for women is an embrace and a quick kiss on both cheeks, which also applies to only brief acquaintances. Make sure to avoid close body contact. To Catalans, common phrases of civility among women such as »you look pretty« or friendly invitations such as »we definitely have to meet« or »call me« are a matter of courtesy, and should not always be taken literally. Men give each other a friendly pat on the shoulder, while shaking hands is considered a very formal way of greeting.

Health

Pharmacies Pharmacies (farmàcies) are sign-posted with a green cross against a white background. They are normally open Mon – Fri 9.30am – 2pm and 4.30pm – 8pm as well as Sat 9am – 12.30pm. Some pharmacies remain open at other times, a list of which is available outside every pharmacy and printed in newspapers.

Health insurance Visitors from the United Kingdom have a right to free medical treatment upon falling ill in Spain if they use the services and facilities provided by the Spanish national health service (Seguridad Social). A **European Health Insurance Card (EU EHIC)** allows all EU patients to visit a doctor belonging to the Spanish national health service, but note that dental treatment is often not available under this scheme and your card must be produced prior to all treatment, including at hospital, or you will be billed as a private patient. **Purchasing a private travel insurance policy** is highly recommended as repatriation is not included in national health care services. The cost of treatment must be paid immediately and then reclaimed from your insurance company in your home country.

Information

Casaques Vermelles (Red Jackets) In Summer from June to September, in the Barri Gòtic, on the Ramblas and at Passeig de Gràcia, representatives of the Patronat de Turisme (recognizable by their red jackets with the letter **i**) offer all kinds of tourist information.

TOURIST OFFICES

In the UK
Spanish Tourist Board
PO Box 4009
London W1A 6NB
Tel. (0 20) 74 86 8077
info.londres@tourspain.es

In the US
Tourist Office of Spain – West Coast
8383 Wilshire Blvd., Suite 956, Beverly Hills, CA 90211
Tel. (323) 658 7188, fax (323) 658 1061

losangeles@Tourspain.es
Tourist Office of Spain – North East Coast
666 Fifth Avenue, 35th Floor New York, NY 10103
Tel. (212) 265 8822, fFax (212) 265 8864
oetny@Tourspain.es

In Canada
Tourist Office of Spain in Canada
2 Bloor Street West, 34th floor
Toronto, ON M4W 3E2
Tel. (416) 961 3131, fax (416) 961 1992
toronto@tourspain.es

CONSULAR SERVICES
UK
Consulado General Británico
Avda Diagonal 477 - 13
E–08036 Barcelona
Tel. 933 666 200, fax 933 666 221
barcelonaconsulate@fco.gov.uk

US
US Consulate General
Paseo Reina Elisenda de Montcada, 23
E–08034 Barcelona
Tel. 93 280 22 27, Fax 93 280 61 75
consularbarcel@state.gov

Canadian
Canadian Consulate General
Elisenda de Pinos 10
E–08034 Barcelona
Tel. 93 204 27 00, Fax 29 204 27 01
bcncon@sefes.es

Australia
Australian Consulate General
Plaza Gala Placidia 1-3, 1st floor
E–08006 Barcelona
Tel. 93 490 90 13, Fax 93 411 09 04

Informationen Call Center
Turisme de Barcelona
Tel. 00 34 932 85 38 34

In Barcelona
Most tourist offices in Barcelona also book hotel rooms.
Plaça de Catalunya 17 (underground)

In the old town (Barri Gòtic): Plaça Sant Jaume
Estació de Sants Plaça Països Catalans
La Rambla 115
At the airport: Aeroport de El Prat Terminal 1 and 2
Infopista Montseny Àrea de servei Montseny-Sud, Km 117, Motorway AP-7/E-15
Infomation kiosks:
Plaça Catalunya, Plaça Espanya, Sagrada Família, Colom (Portal de la Pau), Estació del Nord, Barceloneta (Joan de Borbó)

INTERNET
www.spain.info
Website of the Spanish Board of Tourism.

www.barcelonaturisme.com
Homepage for Turisme de Barcelona.
Accommodation, gastronomy, entertainment, transportation

www.bcn.es
Website of the Ajuntament (city hall) of Barcelona with assorted information, including tourism, transportation, gastronomy, shopping, markets

www.bcn-guide.com
Lots of useful information on city tours, museums, restaurants and shopping

www.barcelona-on-line.es
Arranges booking of hotel rooms and apartments.

Language

c before a, o, u like »c« as in coffee
c before e, i like »s«
ç like »s«
g before a, o, u like »g« as in great

For easier pronunciation: Catalan

g before e, i voiced »je« as in orange
ll like »y«as in year
l•l like »l«
ny like »gn« as in new
que, like »c« as in cake
qui; u is always mute, qu like English »c« as in coffee
x voiceless »sh« as in shop

For easier pronunciation: Spanish
c before a, o, u like English »c«as in coffee
c before e, i voiceless th-sound, but harder (e.g. gracias)
ch voiceless »ch« as in chain
g before a, o, u like »g«
g before e, i like Scottish »och«
gue, **gui** / **que**, **qui** here the u is always mute, as the English »g«, »c«
h is always mute
j like the Scottish »och«
ll, like »y« in year
ñ like »gn« as in new
z unvoiced th-sound, but harder

Spanish phrases

At a glance

Yes./No.	Sí./No.
Maybe.	Quizás./Tal vez.
OK!	¡De acuerdo!/¡Está bien!
Please./Thank you.	Por favor./Gracias.
Thank you very much!	Muchas gracias.
You're welcome.	No hay de qué./De nada.
Excuse me!	¡Perdón!
Pardon?	¿Cómo dice/dices?
I don't understand you.	No le/la/te entiendo.
I only speak a little …	Hablo sólo un poco de …
Could you help me?	¿Puede usted ayudarme, por favor?
I would like …	Quiero …/Quisiera …
I (don't) like that.	(No) me gusta.
Do you have …?	¿Tiene usted …?
How much does this cost?	¿Cuánto cuesta?
What time is it?	¿Qué hora es?

Getting acquainted

Good morning	¡Buenos días!

Good day!	¡Buenos días!/¡Buenas tardes!
Good evening!	¡Buenas tardes!/¡Buenas noches!
Hello!	¡Hola! ¿Qué tal?
My name is …	Me llamo …
What is your name, please?	¿Cómo se llama usted, por favor?
How are you?	¿Qué tal está usted?/¿Qué tal?
Fine, thanks. And you?	Bien, gracias. ¿Y usted/tú?
Good bye!	¡Hasta la vista!/¡Adiós!
See you!	¡Adiós!/¡Hasta luego!
See you soon!	¡Hasta pronto!
See you tomorrow!	¡Hasta mañana!

Travelling

left/right	a la izquierda/a la derecha
straight ahead	todo seguido/derecho
close/far	cerca/lejos
How far is it?	¿A qué distancia está?
I would like to rent … .	Quisiera alquilar …
… a car	…un coche.
… a boat	…una barca/un bote/un barco.
Excuse me, where is …?	Perdón, ¿dónde está …
… the railway station	…la estación (de trenes)?
… the bus terminal	…la estación de autobuses/ . . . .
	la terminal?
… the airport	…el aeropuerto?

Breakdown

I had a breakdown.	Tengo una avería.
Would you please send me	¿Pueden ustedes enviarme
a towtruck?	un cochegrúa, por favor?
Is there a garage here?	¿Hay algún taller por aquí cerca?
Where is the next petrol station?	¿Dónde está la estación de servicio/a
	gasolinera más cercana, por favor?
I would like … litres of …	Quisiera … litros de …
… normal petrol.	… gasolina normal.
… super./ …diesel.	… súper./ … diesel.
… unleaded./ …leaded.	… sin plomo./ … con plomo.
Fill it up, please.	Lleno, por favor.

Accident

Help!	¡Ayuda!, ¡Socorro!

Careful!	¡Atención!
Careful!	¡Cuidado!
Please call ... quickly	Llame enseguida ...
... an ambulance.	... una ambulancia.
... the police.	... a la policía.
... the fire department.	... a los bomberos.
Do you have any bandages?	¿Tiene usted botiquín de . . . . urgencia?
It was my (your) fault.	Ha sido por mi (su) culpa.
Please tell me your name and your address.	¿Puede usted darme su nombre y dirección?

Going out

Where is there ...	¿Dónde hay por aquí cerca ...
... a good restaurant?	... un buen restaurante?
... a reasonable restaurant?	... un restaurante no demasiado caro?
Please make a reservation for us for this evening	¿Puede reservarnos para esta noche
for a table for 4 people.	una mesa para cuatro personas?
Cheers!	¡Salud!
The bill, please!	¡La cuenta, por favor!
Did it taste good?	¿Le/Les ha gustado la comida?
The food was excellent.	La comida estaba écelente.

Shopping

Where can I find ... a market?	Por favor, ¿dónde hay ... un mercado?
... a pharmacy	.... una farmacia
... a shopping centre	... un centro comercial

Accommodation

Could you please recommend ... ?	Perdón, señor/señora/señorita. . . . . . . ¿Podría usted recomendarme ...
... a hotel	... un hotel?
... a guesthouse	... una pensión?
I have reserved a room.	He reservado una habitación.
Do you still have ...	¿Tienen ustedes ...?
... a single room?	... una habitación individual?
... a double room?	... una habitación doble?
... with shower/bath?	... con ducha/baño?
... for one night?	... para una noche?
... for one week?	... para una semana?

The popular Bus Turístic runs on three routes

How much does the room cost
... with breakfast?
... with half board?

¿Cuánto cuesta la habitación
... con desayuno?
... media pensión?

Doctor and pharmacy

Can you recommend
a good doctor?
I have ...
... diarrhea.
... a fever.
... a headache.
... a toothache.
... a sore throat.

¿Puede usted indicarme
un buen médico?
Tengo ...
... diarrea.
... fiebre.
... dolor de cabeza.
... dolor de muelas.
... dolor de garganta.

Bank

Where is ...
... a bank?
... a currency exchange?
I would like to change
British pounds into euros.

Por favor, ¿dónde hay por aquí...?
... un banco?
... una oficina/casa de cambio?
Quisiera cambiar ...
libras británicas

Post

How much does ... cost?
... a letter ...
... a postcard ...
to Great Britain/USA?

¿Cuánto cuesta ...
... una carta ...
... una postal ...
para Inglaterra/.................
los Estados Unidos?

| a stamp | sellos |
| a telephone card | tarjetas para el teléfono |

Numbers

0	cero	19	diecinueve
1	un, uno, una	20	veinte
2	dos	21	veintiuno(a)
3	tres	22	veintidós
4	cuatro	30	treinta
5	cinco	40	cuarenta
6	seis	50	cincuenta
7	siete	60	sesenta
8	ocho	70	setenta
9	nueve	80	ochenta
10	diez	90	noventa
11	once	100	cien, ciento
12	doce	200	doscientos, -as
13	trece	1000	mil
14	catorce	2000	dos mil
15	quince	10000	diez mil
16	dieciséis		
17	diecisiete	1/2	medio
18	dieciocho	1/4	un cuatro

Restaurant/Restaurante

desayuno	breakfast
almuerzo	lunch
cena	dinner
camarero	waiter
cubierto	setting
cuchara	spoon
cucharita	teaspoon
cuchillo	knife
lista de comida	menu
plato	plate
tenedor	fork
vaso / taza	glass / cup

Tapas

albóndigas	meatballs
boquerones en vinagre	small herring in a vinegar marinade

caracoles	snails
chipirones	small squid
chorizo	paprika sausage
jamón serrano	dried ham
morcilla	blood sausage
pulpo	squid
tortilla	potato omelette

Entremeses/Starters

aceitunas	olives
anchoas	anchovies
ensalada	salad
jamón	ham
mantequilla	butter
pan	bread
panecillo	bread roll
sardinas	sardines

Sopas/Soups

caldo	meat broth
gazpacho	cold vegetable soup
puchero canario	hearty soup
sopa de pescado	fish soup
sopa de verduras	vegetable soup

Platos de huevos/Egg dishes

huevo	egg
duro	hard-boiled
pasado por agua	soft-boiled
huevos a la flamenca	eggs with beans
huevos fritos	fried eggs
huevos revueltos	scrambled eggs
tortilla	omelette

Pescado/Fish

ahumado	smoked
a la plancha	grilled on a hot griddle
asado	fried
cocido	boiled
frito	baked

anguila	eel
atún	tuna
bacalao	cod
besugo	bream
lenguado	sole
merluza	hake
salmón	salmon
trucha	trout
almeja	river mussel
bogavante	lobster
calamar	squid
camarón	shrimp
cangrejo	crab
gamba	prawn
langosta	rock lobster
ostras	oysters

Carne/Meat

buey	beef
carnero	mutton
cerdo	pork
chuleta	chops
cochinillo, lechón	roast suckling pig
conejo	rabbit
cordero	lamb
ternera	veal
vaca	beef
asado	roast
bistec	beefsteak
carne ahumada	smoked meat
carne estofada	pot roast
carne salada	corned beef
fiambre	cold cuts
jamón	ham
lomo	loin or back
salchichón	hard sausage
tocino	bacon
pato	duck
pollo	chicken

Verduras/Vegetables

aceitunas	olives

cebollas	onions
col de Bruselas	Brussels sprouts
coliflor	cauliflower
espárragos	asparagus
espinacas	spinach
garbanzos	chickpeas
guisantes	peas
habas, judías	beans
lechuga	lettuce
patatas	potatoes
patatas fritas	French fries
pepinos	cucumber
tomates	tomato
zanahorias	carrots

Condimentos/Condiments

vinagre / aceite	vinegar / oil
ajo	garlic
azafrán	saffron
mostaza	mustard
sal/salado / pimienta	salt/salted / pepper

Postres/Sweets

bollo	sweet bread
dulces	sweets
flan	cream caramel
helado	ice cream
mermelada / miel	jam / honey
pastel	cake
queso	cheese
tarta	tart

Frutas/Fruit

cerezas	cherries
chumbos	prickly pears
dátiles	dates
fresas	strawberries
higos	figs
mandarinas	mandarin oranges
manzana / pera	apple / pear
melocotón	peach

George Orwell, *Homage to Catalonia*. (Penguin Modern Classics, 2000) Personal account of the Spanish Civil War (1938) Autobiographical report by George Orwell (1903 – 1950) on his voluntary participation in the Spanish Civil War (1936 – 1939) fighting for the Republican side; with detailed descriptions of the political situation at the time, when the Republic not only fought against Franco, but also the left against the left.

Carlos Ruiz Zafón, *The Angel's Game* (Anchor 2010). A prequel to *Shadow of the Wind* leads the reader into a morbid, eery early 20th century Barcelona. David Martín, a young journalist, is led into the dark heart of Barcelona in a story garnished with all sorts of fantasy elements.

Money

Euro   The **Euro** (€) is the official currency in Spain. Rates change frequently, but for the UK pound it has generally been around €1.28 to £1; for the US dollar it has generally been around €0.79 to US$1.

Banks   **Banks** are normally open Mon – Fri 9am – 2pm and Sat 9am – 12.30pm.

Cash   machines   It is possible to withdraw money from Spanish cash machines (Bancomat) using credit cards and bank cards (in combination with the PIN code).

Post and Communications

POST

Stamps   Stamps are available at post offices and tobacco shops, which can be recognized from a sign showing a yellow tobacco leaf and the letter »T«. A stamp for a postcard or letter to other European countries costs around €0.65.

Letter boxes   Letter boxes in Spain are yellow with a red post horn; boxes for foreign mail are marked »extranjero«.

Opening   hours   Post offices (Correos) are open Mon – Fri 9am – 2pm and Sat 9am – 1pm. Only the main post office in Barcelona and the post of-

COUNTRY CODES
From the UK to Spain
Tel. 00 34

From the US to Spain
Tel. 011 34

From Spain
to th UK: tel. 00 44
to the US: tel. 001
For calls from Spain to the UK, remove
the 0 from the respective area code.

fices at the airport in El Prat de Llobregat are open daily around the clock.

Many public telephone booths work either with coins or phone cards. Instructions are given in several languages. €6 or €12 phone cards are available at the branches of the Telefónica telephone company or at tobacco shops. Also very common are credit card phones.

Telephone booths and cards

Currently there are roaming contracts with all common English providers. Whilst driving, phone calls are only permitted if using hands-free equipment.

Mobile phones

Prices and Discounts

Barcelona is located in one of Spain's economically most flourishing regions, and also counts as **one of the most expensive cities in the country**. Prices in restaurants (except for more simple ones), hotels and museums, as well as at other sights (admission fees) are similar to those in the UK and the US. Only public transport is slightly cheaper.

A **Barcelona Card** can be quite cost-effective (►tip). Passengers on the **Bus Turístic** receive a coupon booklet with various discount offers. The **ArtTicket**, an art pass, includes admission to the following museums and cultural institutions: Centre de Cultura Contemporània de Barcelona (CCCB), Fundació Antoni Tàpies,

MARCO ⊕ POLO TIP

! *Barcelona Card* **Insider Tip**

With the Barcelona Card, available at Barcelona's tourist offices and at El Corte Inglés department stores, public transport may be used free-of-charge and also includes discounts when using other means of transportation, visiting museums, for event or entertainment venues as well as selected shops, restaurants and nightclubs. The Card costs €34 (for 2 days), €44 (for 3 days); €52 (for 4 days) and €68 (for 5 days); for children the cards cost about 50% less, respectively; 10% discount by booking online on bcnshop.barcelona-turisme.com.

What does it cost?

Simple meal:
Tapas from €1.60
Cup of coffee:
€1.50 (café solo)

► Prices for restaurants p. 7
► Prices for hotels p. 7

Fundació Joan Miró, Museu d'Art Contemporani de Barcelona (MACBA), Museu Nacional d'Art de Catalunya (MNAC), Museu Picasso and La Pedrera-Centre Cultural Caixa Catalunya. The ticket, valid for six months, costs €20. The Articket is available at the aforementioned museums and tourist information offices. More information is provided by the website of the Barcelona Tourist Office or at tel. 932 853 834. There is also the **ArqueoTicket** for lovers of archaeology.

Security

During the peak season especially, a higher property crime rate is to be expected. In crowded areas, especially on the Ramblas, in the old town and in metro stations, many a purse has forcefully found a new owner, but the success rate of solving petty crimes is rather low. Stay away from the widespread »gambling« (shell games) on the Ramblas. It is also not recommended to park a car where it is unguarded or to leave any valuables (ID, money) inside. If possible, keep valuables on your person. Just bring small amounts of cash and leave larger sums of money or cheques in the safe at the hotel or campground.

Time

Central European Time (CET) is used between October and the end of March, while CEST (Central European Summer Time) is used from the end of March to the end of October (CET + 1 hour).

Toilets

Toilets are usually called »servicios«, »lavabos« or »aseos«. The ladies' room is »Señoras«, the men's is »Caballeros«, or just the letters »S« and »C«.

Transport

PUBLIC TRANSPORT

Barcelona has a well-developed public transport system. Schedules for metro and bus lines are available at tourist information desks (►information).

Metro

The most important means of transportation in the city is the metro (underground), which connects all of Barcelona's main sights quickly and conveniently, thanks to its dense route system and frequent service of trains. The metro network of the Transports Metropolitans de Barcelona (**TMB**) consists of six lines (lines 1–5 and the outer line 9–11); additional lines are planned. The metro runs from 5am until midnight between Monday and Thursday, on Sundays and holidays; between 5am and 2am on Friday, Saturday and weekdays. More information is provided by the TMB information desks at Plaça Universitat and in Sants Station. On some underground routes the metro is complemented by trains of the Ferrocarrils de la Generalitat de Catalunya (**FGC**; Catalan railway) and the Spanish National Rail service **RENFE**. The main stations are Plaça de Catalunya, Plaça d'Espanya and Sants Central Station.

> **❗ MARCO ⊕ POLO TIP**
>
> *Formula 1*   **Insider Tip**
>
> Every Formula 1 fan knows: 30km/18mi north of Barcelona, in Montmeló, is the Circuit de Catalunya, 4.627km/2.77mi-long racetrack, where every year in May the Spanish Grand Prix (Formula 1 race) is held. A train runs from the Barcelona railway station Sants to Montmeló; the trip takes about 40 minutes.

Buses

Barcelona has a large number of inner-city bus routes. Most **red buses** run between 4am and 10pm. 16 night buses (**nitbus**), most of which run via Plaça de Catalunya, operate late at night and early in the morning (11pm–4am). Other special services include the **Aerobus** (► p. 266) and the **Bus Turístic** (► p. 127).

Tram

Besides the nostalgic Tramvia Blue (► Enjoy Barcelona, Sightseeing), the Barcelona tram system has been extended by **new lines** since the beginning of the 21st century, which operate in the northern and southern parts of the city. The lines T1, T2 and T3 leave from Plaça Francesc Macià, via Av. Diagonal to the suburbs in the southwest; the T4 leaves from the zoo, and runs via the Fòrum 2004 to the neighbouring town of Sant Adrià de Besòs in the north.

Tariff system for public transport A single metro (also FGC and RENFE) and bus ticket is valid for all of Barcelona. Changing requires a new ticket. A day pass **T-Dia** may be used for unlimited rides on metros, buses and the local transit lines of the FGC. There are also tickets for two, three, four or five days, which provide unlimited use on consecutive days. Visitors are recommended to buy a group or multiple-strip ticket, particularly the **T-10** ticket (pronounced »Te-Deu«) as it may be used by several people (one strip per person) and is valid for metros, buses, trams, and the local transit lines of FGC and RENFE. Once validated, the ticket is good for 90 minutes to reach the destination with the aforementioned means of transportation. Metro tickets are sold at the automats and ticket counters at metro stations, in tourist offices and TMB centres. Bus tickets are directly available from the driver. Metro tickets are validated at the turnstiles in the station; bus tickets at the yellow box next to the driver.

Taxis There are some 11,000 black-and-yellow taxis in Barcelona. Simply stand by the side of the road and wave one down. Available taxis are identified by the »lliure‹ or »libre› sign behind the windscreen or the green light on the roof. Supplements are charged for advanced booking over the telephone, large baggage, dogs, for trips to the airport and rides at night. There are several taxi companies, e. g. Radio Taxi 933 03 30 33.

Stations The pompous-looking **Estació de França** was completed in 1930 and was only recently renovated. Located on the north-eastern border of the old town it is Barcelona's nostalgic station as it no longer plays an important role for main-line traffic. The majority of Barcelona's railway traffic is serviced by the modern station **Estació de Sants**, located north-west of Plaça d'Espanya. It is used for international trains coming from France, but also for national long-distance connections to Madrid, Andalusia, Galicia, Valencia etc. The trains to the beaches in the southern part of Catalonia are more of regional importance. The new railway station for long distance trains La Sagrera in northeast Barcelona is supposed to be completed in 2016; the new high-speed trains from Perpignan via Girona will arrive here.

TRAFFIC REGULATIONS

The use of seat belts is mandatory. The maximum speed on motorways is 75mph/120kmh, on country roads 60mph/96kmh, and 30mph/48kmh within city limits. The legal blood alcohol limit is 0.5. It is forbidden to use mobile phones inside the car without a hands free set. Vehicles coming from the right-hand side always have right-of-way; cars on roundabouts, however, have the right-of-way over

Telefèric on Montjuïc, on the left in the background is the Sagrada Familia.

entering traffic. Parking places marked blue are subject to charge; parking in places marked yellow is not permitted.

When to Go

Located in a zone of temperate Mediterranean climate, Barcelona hardly ever experiences extreme temperatures. The air temperature seldom drops below freezing and hardly ever rises beyond 35°C/95°F; daily temperature changes vary between 11°C/51°F and 14°C/57°F. Winds mostly come from southerly directions. Barcelona is an all-year travel destination and – unlike in previous years – is visited by foreign travellers all year round. Most tourists come in mid summer; the recommended time to travel, however, is early spring, early summer and autumn. The heat in mid summer is moderated by ocean winds, though air pollution from cars and industrial fumes can become rather unpleasant in less aerated inner-city areas. Some snow may fall during winter. However, warmer days dominate and allow lunching under an open sky.

Index

List of Maps and Illustrations

Photo Credits

Publisher's Information

1st Edition 2015
Worldwide Distribution: Marco Polo
Travel Publishing Ltd
Pinewood, Chineham Business Park
Crockford Lane, Chineham
Basingstoke, Hampshire RG24 8AL,
United Kingdom.

Photos, illustrations, maps::
135 photos, 21 maps and and illustra-
tions, one large city map
Text:
Achim Bourmer, Lothar Schmidt, with
contributions by Peter Nahm
Editing:
John Sykes, Rainer Eisenschmid
Translation: Margit Sander, Tony
Halliday, Barbara Schmidt-Runkel,
Gareth Davies
Cartography:
Klaus-Peter Lawall, Unterensingen;
MAIRDUMONT Ostfildern (city map)
3D illustrations:
jangled nerves, Stuttgart
Infographics:
Golden Section Graphics GmbH, Berlin
Design:
independent Medien-Design, Munich
Editor-in-chief:
Rainer Eisenschmid, Mairdumont
Ostfildern

Printed in China

Despite all of our authors' thorough
research, errors can creep in. The pub-
lishers do not accept any liability for thi
Whether you want to praise, alert us to
errors or give us a personal tip Please
contact us by email or post:

MARCO POLO Travel Publishing Ltd
Pinewood, Chineham Business Park
Crockford Lane, Chineham
Basingstoke, Hampshire RG24 8AL
United Kingdom
Email: sales@marcopolouk.com

FSC
www.fsc.org
MIX
Paper from
responsible sources
FSC® C011918